Life Woven in Sacred Time

Other Books by Tilden Edwards

Embracing the Call to Spiritual Depth:
Gifts for Contemplative Living

Spiritual Director, Spiritual Companion:
Guide to Tending the Soul

Sabbath Time

Living in the Presence:
Spiritual Exercises to Open Our Awareness of God

Spiritual Friend:
Reclaiming the Gift of Spiritual Direction

All God's Children

Living with Apocalypse:
Spiritual Resources for Social Compassion

Living Simply through the Day:
Spiritual Survival in a Complex Age

Life Woven in Sacred Time

Glimmerings from a Long Life—a Memoir

TILDEN EDWARDS

A Crossroad Book
The Crossroad Publishing Company
New York

The Crossroad Publishing Company
www.CrossroadPublishing.com

© 2022 by Tilden Edwards

Crossroad, Herder & Herder, and the crossed C logo/colophon are registered trademarks of The Crossroad Publishing Company.

All rights reserved. No part of this book may be copied, scanned, reproduced in any way, or stored in a retrieval system, or transmitted, in any form or by any means, electronic, mechanical, photocopying, recording, or otherwise, without the written permission of The Crossroad Publishing Company. For permission, please write to rights@crossroadpublishing.com.

Cover and text design by Tim Holtz

Library of Congress Cataloging-in-Publication Data available from the Library of Congress.

ISBN 9780824596064 (trade paperback)
ISBN 9780824596071 (EPUB)

Books published by The Crossroad Publishing Company may be purchased at special quantity discount rates for classes and institutional use. For information, please e-mail sales@CrossroadPublishing.com.

To all my family, friends, coworkers at Shalem, and teachers who have raised, loved, taught, challenged, delighted, and cared for me over a lifetime—all collaborators with the Gracious One's ever-creative, loving, and mysterious Spirit alive in our midst.

Contents

	Acknowledgments	ix
	Introduction	xi
Chapter 1	Childhood: An Ever-Migrating Life	1
Chapter 2	Adolescence: Growing Confidence	31
Chapter 3	Expanding Horizons: Stanford	57
Chapter 4	Summer European Adventures and Back to Stanford	71
Chapter 5	International Student Seminar and Japan	85
Chapter 6	The Harvard Years: Further Opening and Clarity of Call	107
Chapter 7	The Whirlwind Years at St. Stephen's during a Historic Moment in the Church Worldwide	145
Chapter 8	Ministry beyond St. Stephen's	169
Chapter 9	Deepening Contemplative Awareness	179
Chapter 10	The Birth of a New Spiritual Center	195
Chapter 11	Carol Crumley and the Call to Pilgrimage, Clergy Leadership, and the Shalem Society	221
Chapter 12	Contemplative Outreach Beyond Shalem	227
Chapter 13	The Evolution of My Personal Family Life	249

Chapter 14	Aging in a Tumultuous Time	277
Chapter 15	Radiant Love at the Heart of Life	293
Appendix	The Leadership of the Shalem Institute for Spiritual Formation	299
	Notes	301
	Suggestions for Further Reading	303
	About the Author	304

Acknowledgments

I'm deeply grateful to my dear wife, Mary, and my caring friend Dana Greene for their careful reading of this memoir and for their valuable recommended changes that have led to its greater coherence and clarity; and to Gwendolin Herder, publisher of Crossroad Publishing Company, and Emily Wichland, my copy editor, for all they have done to bring it to fruition.

This book has emerged over three years of reflection and many drafts. In a sense, there is never an end to such a lifetime memoir until my life is ended; there is always more to add, revise, or delete. At some point I simply told myself it's time to stop: this is good enough.

Introduction

We love stories. One may be as short as a surprising experience we've had or heard about that we want to share. Conversations are full of such stories. So are news media, novels, biographies, films, and television. We begin as toddlers with fairy tales, children's books, videos, and family legends.

Why do we love stories? At least one reason is that we're equipped to do so. We have *imaginations* that find stories thrillingly expanding our horizons of life's possibilities. They usually have emotional appeal that draws us inside them. They often connect with our own real and fantasied experience, and with our fears and hopes. Stories include a mysterious evolution that energizes our curiosity as to where the story is leading and what shaped its happenings.

We're also equipped with *memories* that allow us to retain stories and pass them on. If a story touches our lives powerfully, it may influence how we see ourselves and what we want to be and do (or *not* want to be and do).

Our memories are selective, though. We don't remember the same story in the same way. We remember only what held meaning and emotional and sensual power for us. Such selective memory leads us to realize that our memories are not objective, like seeing a video of the memories would be; they are subjective. We each see different patterns in the tapestry of the story, depending on our own unique experience of it. We miss things that happened because they did not brand themselves on our conscious memories. I say *conscious* memories because neuroscientific research has shown that when an electrode penetrates a certain part of the brain, past memories are brought back intact in great detail. However, normal *conscious* memories are very selective.

Indeed, at a given time we are aware of very little of the many past daily happenings of our lives, and we don't even want to remember the boring and painful things. If we really were to remember absolutely everything that we think, feel, and experience moment by moment in a given day, we could fill up a whole book with that one day's interior and exterior happenings. What we remember, then, is equivalent to just a cup of water in the long stream of our life experience, a condensation of our lives into a few special memories.

We love stories about life's happenings, however well we do or don't remember them, because they foster a sense of *intimate connectedness* with life beyond our own. Each of us is a variant of a larger story, an evolving human story, that is part of a family, religious, cultural, and earth story, which in turn is part of a cosmic story. In the cosmic story, we each are a unique living spark that, consciously or unconsciously, is influenced by the whole and in turn influences the whole, an amazing phenomenon that scientists have discovered and mystics in their own way have known.

I am aware of being included in a still larger story. It's the story of a mysterious, intimate yet infinite, wise love that shapes and pervades the whole, a love to which we give many inadequate names. St. Augustine, in his own written story (his *Confessions*), concluded that his life would never be made whole until it was taken up into Another's life. Augustine addressed that life as "beauty, so ancient and so new.... You are in me deeper than I am in me."

The story of that radiant divine love is found in many streams of holy scriptures, as well as in the living, evolving story of creation. I believe it underlies the heart of our own stories, each of which is a unique contributor to that ongoing story. That radiant love is seen to be intimately connected with us in Genesis 1:26, where we're declared to be created in the image of G-d. (The dash affirms the ultimate mystery of God in Jewish tradition, which I will use throughout my memoir as a corrective to our temptation to reduce the mystery to less than it is.) To me, that verse means that each of us is a unique shaping and carrier of divine loving Spirit, however hidden to our consciousness. We're given the capacity to freely identify with and creatively care for and delight in one another and the earth. Together we're shown to be distinctive parts of an interdependent whole, emanating from the radiant Whole One.

But there's a catch: the very nature of divine love in Christianity, and I believe in the mystical heart of other spiritual traditions, is *relational*. In Christian tradition that relationality is expressed in the triune nature of God. Even though I'm part of that great triune love, the very nature of love requires that I freely *choose* it as the heart of my being. Paradoxically, I am *part* of a larger radiant love, and I can choose (or at least allow myself to fall into) living from *inside* it. Yet at the same time I am *apart* from that radiant love, with a personal freedom to choose life *outside* of it. When I live outside, my center easily becomes a fragile, narrow, ultimately separate sense of self, drawing me toward self-protective, fearful, controlling behavior. We are all capable of and strongly drawn to habitually living from this broken-off sense of self, where our consciousness is separated from the gracious Source of life, to whom we nonetheless belong. Such living is alluring and reinforced in our cultures and yet it is finally unsatisfying, as St. Augustine knew. We're invited to choose life in the great, ever inviting divine love over and over again.

This condensed view of our complicated human condition, with all its brokenness, sacredness, and mystery, underlies my life's journey. The great German poet Rainer Maria Rilke touches the depth of the human pilgrimage in a succinct and intuitive way:

> *God speaks to each of us as he makes us,*
> *Then walks with us silently out of the night.*
>
> *These are the words we dimly hear:*
>
> *You, sent out beyond your recall,*
> *go to the limits of your longing.*
> *Embody me.*
>
> *Flare up like flame*
> *And make big shadows I can move in.*
>
> *Let everything happen to you: beauty and terror.*
> *Just keep going. No feeling is final.*

Don't let yourself lose me.

Nearby is the country they call life.
You will know it by its seriousness.

Give me your hand.[1]

What's Ahead

My story, like yours, is a unique collage of willful sin, willing love, confusion, surprise, suffering, joy, finding and losing, holding on and letting go, dullness and awareness, illusion and illumination, and mystery. Included for me also, in my trust at least, is the often hidden, grace-filled Spirit breathing love, hope, and fresh possibilities through me. I write grounded in that trust, shaped in me through a long spiritual and social evolution that you will see eventually brings me to the deep and broad awareness of the Christian contemplative tradition and its connections with the contemplative heart of other major *spiritual* traditions. This awareness led to the founding of the Shalem Institute for Spiritual Formation, which became the communal framework for much of my public life and thought.

I want to share some highlights of my story with you, not because it's better or more dramatic or holier than yours but because it may bring a fuller awakening and color to your own memory and a sense of companionship for your story. It may help you recognize or affirm a larger guiding hand hidden in your own journey. Both of our stories, as I implied earlier, are part of the largest story: the mysterious communal wholeness, the love that is G-d. That infinite, ever-evolving biography lives through us and all that is.

We are creatures of unique beauty and capacity for goodness, animated by the Holy Spirit blended in our spirits. This reality to me is ultimately deeper and truer than the expressions of our willfulness, illusions, and oppression of others, born of our misused freedom, confusion, mental illness, and the influence of other love-denying forces that we name "evil."

Once I've shared my growing-up years, I address either primarily with my public vocational life or primarily with my personal life. I describe my time as a parish priest in the District of Columbia's inner city during the civil rights, anti-poverty, and Vietnam War years, later as the director of a regional social action and education center, and especially my many years as executive director of the Shalem Institute for Spiritual Formation.

I also share the evolution of my personal and family life, some often surprising experiences of contemplative outreach, and finally, a few happenings and spiritual reflections drawn from my older years.

My hope is that you'll find enough of what I write to connect with your own life and complement it in a way that makes this memoir a worthwhile read.

Chapter 1

Childhood
An Ever-Migrating Life

Texas Beginnings

I had a difficult birth into a difficult family situation at a difficult moment in American history.

I finally came out of my mother's womb at 10:20 p.m. on September 21, 1935, after a fifty-two-hour struggle to come into the world. According to my mother, there wasn't room for me to come out on my own, and the inexperienced intern replacing my vacationing ob-gyn finally saw that he would have to cut open my mother and drag me out with forceps. He had to use such force that my head emerged elongated. When Mamo, my father's mother, saw me in that Austin hospital, my mother told me that she was so shocked by my distorted head that she prayed I would die.

But I was meant to live, and my head came back to normal size, leaving just a small scar on the left side of my face from the pressure of the forceps to remind me of my difficult birth. That effortful beginning seemed to set the stage for a lifelong tendency toward effortful striving, a drive to doggedly press my limited mind to birth deeper and broader understanding, and to press my average body extra hard to birth skill and strength.

My mother was only sixteen years old when I was born; my father was nineteen. They had married the year before, under pressure from my mother's old-school parents, holding the view that you should marry the person you're steadily dating as soon as possible. When she unexpectedly became pregnant, she had to drop out of the University of Texas in Austin. My father was just finishing law school there, in the depths of America's Great Depression. For years after graduation he struggled to find a decent job as a lawyer. We moved from town to town in East Texas as he looked for sustainable work. We survived in part on occasional handouts from my mother's parents in Marshall, Texas.

I have a few memories from those earliest years. In the first one, I was about two years old, sitting alone in a chair in the front yard of our house. I was wearing my pajamas, with my wet underpants on top of my head. I felt helpless and humiliated. My mother, being very young and inexperienced, had asked my father's stern grandmother what she should do to get me to stop wetting my pants. She took her advice. (Later in life when my mother had become psychologically sophisticated, she apologized profusely for ever having done that.)

The second memory may relate to the same problem of wetting my pants. I remember going into the bathroom and loudly spanking myself, yelling "Bad! Bad!" to be sure it got my mother's attention. I think I semiconsciously knew that if I punished myself before she did, it would be easier on me. I don't remember her ever actually hitting me or screaming at me, but somehow I got it into my little head that wetting my pants was not to be tolerated—that I was capable of not doing it. My mother said I always was very sensitive to others' feelings and needs. Along with that came a very early superego awareness of right and wrong, as conditioned by my parents and the dominant culture of that time. Children were not to be coddled, and they needed to behave themselves and do the right thing or pay the price.

My third memory is a happier one: tap dancing in kindergarten. I still remember the steps of the little dance we were taught. It was the discovery of rhythm, movement, and skill merging and bringing a sense of embodied joy in the moment. It also was the first experience I remember of being with other children. As an only child, constantly moving to new towns, I lived much of my early childhood without playmates.

My happiest memory of those earliest years was spending the first grade in Houston. I thought we were finally in a place where we would stay. There I developed a close friend my age, Bill Ben, who lived just down the street. I felt a budding self-confidence. That confidence was expressed one day when I was standing on the steps outside my school. I was kidding around with a girl I liked, and I spontaneously leaned over and kissed her. She slapped me, but that didn't take away my sense of happy boldness!

One bad memory from that year was crashing my bike into an oncoming car on the busy street where we lived. I can still hear my mother screaming my name from the steps of our house. Bill Ben's father was working on the roof of his house a block away and saw what happened; he came running to help. Fortunately, the car had swerved just in time so that it didn't run over me, but I smashed into its side. I was shaken up, my bike was ruined, but miraculously I was only scratched up a bit. A wordless feeling of gratitude welled up in me that I had missed going under the moving car by only a matter of a few seconds. I wasn't allowed to ride a bike again until I was in seventh grade.

I lost my growing confidence after we were forced by my father's job situation to move yet again, this time to Livingston. In our short-lived time there, I slept on a couch in the dining room, which compounded my sense of isolation and being alone in a town where I knew no one but my parents. I had my first nightmares there, of menacing ghosts floating around the dark room. I would cower under the covers to escape them.

Another memory of those few months in Livingston was living through a hurricane that left huge streams of water rushing down the street, which left me in both awe and fear. When the wind and rain died down, I convinced my mother to let me go outside and walk in those gushing rivulets, where I felt the aliveness and power of the water.

At one time in those months, on the front porch of our house, I sassed my father and he slapped my face. It was the only time I ever remember him striking me, but I felt then that I deserved it.

I still have a photo of Dad with my mother and me on the nearby beach in Galveston, where I built my first sandcastle and met the mystery of the ocean waves and tides. I came back to Livingston that night with the worst sunburn I would ever have in my life.

The economic hardness of the Great Depression was compounded by the clouds of war. The mass drafting of men into the armed forces led my father into the Coast Guard. He was sent to New Orleans for orientation while my mother and I moved in with my grandparents in Marshall. I spent the first half of the second grade there, struggling to understand the math and other things being taught that were new to me. I knew no one in the class.

My only relationships in those months were with my mother's parents, Nick and Mary Babare, who represented reliable stability of place and care in my growing-up years. My grandad was twelve years old when he came to this country from the island of Hvar in Dalmatia, then part of the Austro-Hungarian empire, now part of Croatia. My grandmother was born in Canada, but her family also was from Dalmatia. For many years they lived in Tacoma, Washington where my mother and her brother were born. My grandad and his brother built a shipyard there, but after a few years he decided to leave Tacoma and strike out into the pioneer days of becoming an independent oil operator, eventually settling in Marshall, Texas.

In Marshall, I loved walking Lindy, my grandparents' collie, and putting my arms around him and feeling his warmth and pulsing energy. One day I discovered a small black-and-white stray dog in the bulldog family living under the garage that added to my joy. I named her Rosie, and I took good care of her. The dogs were my only friends.

I also delighted to spend time in my grandmother's vegetable and flower garden. I can still remember the wonderful fragrance of the tomato leaves when I rubbed them, and the daffodils that seemed to magically appear in the spring. On the other side of the house were two huge pecan trees. After collecting the fallen pecans, I would sit in the kitchen with my grandmother and shell them, eating many along the way. The trees also fascinated me in the wonder that a big tree could grow from a tiny nut.

I don't know how much that experience with pecans affected my eating habits, but I know that ever since I've loved eating nuts of any kind. To this day, almost every dessert I eat, if I have anything to do with it, will have nuts in it. They give a lively crunchiness and special flavor to whatever food accompanies them. If a brownie doesn't have nuts in it, its taste is dead to me, like a saltless potato chip.

Speaking of food, I was strongly conditioned in childhood with an enforced asceticism. Instead of fasting, my cross was carried in having to clean my plate. I was allowed to choose one kind of food that I didn't ever have to eat, and I chose liver (which we rarely had). Otherwise, *everything* had to be eaten, whether I liked it or not.

One time when I was about six, I refused to eat my black-eyed peas, and the next morning at breakfast my mother put that plate of uneaten black-eyed peas, cold, in front of me. I could eat nothing else until I finished them. The amazing thing is that I've *liked* them ever since! In hindsight I'm appreciative of that enforced childhood requirement to eat whatever I was given. It gave me a chance not just to tolerate but to learn to appreciate a wide range of Earth's bounty, along with the human creativity in cooking it. That creativity really is a special gift, offered to others through the stream of recipes in infinite numbers of cookbooks. *Having* to eat to live also provides a certain equality and humility to human life, and a basic kind of community. As a child, gathering around the table with family or others to eat was always something I looked forward to, even when the food was meager and simple.

In Marshall I was endlessly fascinated with the electric train my granddad bought me and placed around the Christmas tree. When it moved, it sounded a whistle that made the train come alive. When I lay in bed for a nap or at night, I could hear the real train whistles from trains passing through Marshall. Those haunting sounds move me to this day. They draw me out of my small thoughts into a wordless, expanded consciousness. In my imagination—trains going to distant places, distant lands—they opened a much larger world that was more than I knew. I suppose the whistling gave me my first vague awareness of a mysterious larger reality drawing me into itself, a reality that was larger than any name I could give it.

Summer thunderstorms also opened me to a larger consciousness. I can still see myself alone in the house, lying on a bed in the afternoon for a nap. The window is open and the scent of a coming rain fills the room. Suddenly a great streak of lightning lights up the sky and a powerful clap of thunder quickly follows. Heavy rain begins to beat on the roof. As that repeats itself for the duration of the storm, I am caught up in wordless awe. At the same time, I feel very cozy, safe, and dry beneath the sturdy roof of the house. Rather than feeling fear, I am lost in wonder at the breakthrough power of the storm.

Though I couldn't word it as such at the time, I felt a kind of cleansing, renewing power in that storm. Biblical experiences see divine power and judgment in such storms. Today I still feel some attention-getting revelation of truth born in a storm's striking power, a call to attention, to something larger than the trivial daily thoughts that can take me over. They call me to a larger consciousness. They can be deadly and tragically destructive, but they also might free us, grace us, for a larger sense of life.

When I was six years old, I touched awesome nature in a different way when my grandparents drove me and my mother to Carlsbad Caverns in New Mexico. The ramp through the huge cave was very crowded. Lights made transparent the bodies of water that suddenly appeared from time to time, and they eerily lit up the incredible stalactites and stalagmites, of which I was in awe. I never noticed my family had disappeared from my sight. Eventually we found one another, to the relief of my panicked mother.

I repeated that visit to Carlsbad Caverns much later in life, and I visited other famous caves as well, including those at Lascaux in France, with their incredible prehistoric human pictographs. Always the caves felt scary in their darkness and hardness yet alluring in their beauty and womb-like shelter from the storms, cold, and heat outside of them. I could see how they became securing homes to animals and humans alike. When I emerge from the darkness of a cave I feel I've moved into a different world of light and life.

In Marshall, my grandad recognized that I had no father with me (and no other grandfather either; my father's father had died in his fifties), so he took me under his wing and taught me what he knew. He brought me out to the golf course that he loved and gave me beginning lessons in how to play. He also gave me my first swimming lessons in the pool at the golf course. I remember the scratchy, itchy wool of the swimsuit (standard in those days), but it was worth wearing it: I had a grandad who cared about me.

Sometimes he took me with him to the oil wells he had drilled or acquired as an independent operator. He let me climb up on the oil tank ladders to measure how much oil had been pumped into them. I can still hear the hollow echo of the big tape measure dropping to the tank's bottom when it was nearly empty.

One of my prized possessions in Marshall was a wind-up portable Victrola record player. I had very few records, but one was worth all the rest: a dramatization of *Tarzan of the Apes*, which I played over and over. Since I was alone a lot, I had a few books I had been given that I prized and repeatedly read, such as Charles and Mary Lamb's *Tales from Shakespeare* that my mother had read as a child. When my mother was home, she would read stories and sing to me after I climbed into bed for the night. Those were intimate, repeatable moments amid all the disruptive moves and solitude of those early years. What is more intimate for a little child than snuggling up with a parent and hearing stories that draw you into a larger world? Then when you can read by yourself, you still have the felt intimacy as you share the lives of the stories' characters.

Air conditioning didn't exist in those days, and in the summer, East Texas is almost as hot and certainly as humid as it gets anywhere in this country. The heavy, hot air seeped into my brain and often left me lethargic and tired, as if I was living in a sauna. I and everyone around me seemed to move in slow motion. Mildew sprang up in humid, closed spaces and contributed to my respiratory problems all through childhood. The one relief I remember were the few times we went to the icehouse in downtown Marshall and bought homemade ice cream. Refrigerators were just coming in; some people still had "ice boxes," cooled by huge blocks of ice delivered by the ice man.

When my mother was with me in Marshall, I had to sleep on a couch in the dining room as I had done in Livingston. In the summer, the crickets were chirping so loudly that I felt scared, alone, and overwhelmed, although I don't think I ever told anyone. I knew there just wasn't anywhere else to sleep.

Life with My Paternal Grandmother

In those early years I also visited my paternal grandmother, Margaret (I called her Mamo), in East Texas. Her husband, my grandfather, was the first Tilden Hampton Edwards. He died when my father was sixteen years old. At the time, he was manager of a hotel in Paris, Texas, where my father was born. His father, Augustus Edwards, born in Kentucky, drew the names Tilden and Hampton from two politicians of the time—the 1870s and '80s—who he admired, especially Samuel J. Tilden, who won the popular vote for president in 1876 but lost the electoral college vote.

Mamo lived with her sister, Laura, and their mother, my great-grandmother Katy Gerbers, who grew up in Germany, and her husband, Charles Flanders, who was a railroad conductor from Cincinnati. When he retired early, he and his family ran a general store and boardinghouse in the small town of Waskom, Texas. That's where my mother went to high school and met my father.

I have a strong memory of spending some time one summer on a family farm near Cooper, Texas. It had a water pump instead of running water, an outhouse (with newspapers for toilet paper), chickens, and a cotton crop ready to pick. I remember watching my great-grandmother Katy out the kitchen window catching a chicken and ringing its neck, then bringing it into the kitchen to pluck the feathers and cook it for dinner. Milk was fresh from the cow. I helped churn the butter, pump the water, and swat the swarms of flies on the front porch.

Aunt Laura was a very strong, never-married lady. She offered me tough love. For my sixth birthday she gave me a pair of roller skates. When I first skated with them while Aunt Laura watched, I remember falling and skinning my knee. My eyes were welling up with tears until I heard her yell at me: "Don't you cry, Little Tilden (my dad was Big

Tilden); you get back up on those skates and keep going." That helped me immediately screw up my determination to forget crying and just skate—a lesson that toughness was the norm for surviving in this life.

I rode on the tractor with Aunt Laura when she was plowing a field, then she put me to work picking cotton alongside a little African American girl my age, who I liked a lot. Aunt Laura teased me about it. I had no conscious sense of enforced racial separation and discrimination in those early years, although most of the African Americans I saw were certainly in inferior jobs and lived separately from whites. No one I knew in those Texas years ever talked about racial segregation and injustice, except my father. I saw a very warm, caring relationship between my Marshall grandparents and their African American maid, Willa Mae, but in hindsight I realize there was a line that could not be crossed. Enforced white superiority was taken for granted.

If I had remained in East Texas, I would have come to realize that I was in a very conservative part of Texas, an extension of the Deep South that it adjoined. My father, as a struggling young lawyer in those Depression years, was a justice-seeking liberal. In later life I learned that he took on the legal defense of an African American small businessman who tried to join the Chamber of Commerce in an East Texas town. The man not only was refused but for such insolence he was threatened with being tarred and feathered if he remained in town. In the end he fled, in fear for his life.

Dad also defended a group of oil refinery workers who were trying to unionize and had been locked out of their refinery. I was proud of him for his defense of those workers and that businessman. His courage and dedication helped bolster my own sense of wanting to care for those suffering injustices, including racial and labor injustice. I would join that battle more directly in later years. In hindsight I'm aware of what an overprivileged position I was in growing up—a white male with well-educated parents. My underprivilegedness, to the extent you could call it that, came in being a frequent outsider growing up, always having to start from scratch in finding friends as we kept moving around; by having no siblings as companions who could be outsiders with me as we moved from place to place; and by being raised fatherless after age seven by a single mother who was mostly away at school or work.

In the middle of the second grade, my mother and I moved yet again, this time to New Orleans to be with my dad where the Coast Guard first sent him. Very soon after we arrived there, he was suddenly transferred to the Coast Guard Academy in New London, Connecticut. My mother and I stayed in New Orleans for the rest of the second grade, living in a boardinghouse. We were poor then, and my mother took a job in a chicken factory to help support us. I remember nothing from those months except feeling very alone both in a school, where I knew no one, and in a boardinghouse where there were only adults. We all ate together around the boardinghouse table. The symbolic image of myself in that time is a memory blip of standing in the school playground during recess, wanting to be part of the fun but knowing no one and not being invited to join. I felt like an outsider, someone who didn't belong there.

New York City

In the summer of 1942, we moved to New York City, where my father now was stationed and could live with us after finishing his "ninety-day wonder" wartime Coast Guard officer's training course in New London. Needless to say, New York was an even bigger jolt than all the other moves put together. My mother managed to find us a fourth-floor apartment at 25 East 10th Street in Greenwich Village, despite the terrible shortage of affordable housing there at that time. In hindsight, we were doubly lucky because the neighborhood was indeed a kind of village made up mostly of small shops, brownstone townhouses, and relatively low-rise apartment buildings wedged between lower-Manhattan and Midtown skyscrapers. It was a manageable-sized area that I could familiarize myself with and where I could eventually feel at home. Whenever I've returned to New York in later life, I've always headed to the Village to conjure up memories of my life there.

Childhood: An Ever-Migrating Life

I began the third grade at St. Joseph's Roman Catholic School on Christopher Street, about a fifteen-minute fast walk from our apartment. That walk included passing through Washington Square Park at the bottom of Fifth Avenue, the only park I would ever know.

My family on both sides were mostly Catholics. When I was a baby, I was baptized by a priest at the Catholic chapel near the University of Texas in Austin, and I went to Mass on Sundays with my family. In New York I moved into the full pre–Second Vatican Council immersion in Catholic teaching and culture. The Sisters of Charity ran the school. Despite the school's strictness, I have basically good memories of my three years there in the third through fifth grades. I felt a part of a "way of life," which had the answers and religious practices for everything important needed in life and a huge community of Catholic people with whom to share it all, especially including the huge number of Irish and Italian families there at the time.

Each day, at some point, Sister Edwina would tell us to stand up in the classroom and form a line on one side. The line moved forward as each person who arrived in the front of the class recited what we were all supposed to have memorized from the *Baltimore Catechism*: "Who is God? God is the Supreme Being, infinitely perfect, who made all things and keeps them in existence." Catholicism was so strong in New York City, and so confident of itself in those days, that it anchored my constantly disrupted life in a larger, stable, ultimately benign, unshakable cultural and religious reality. Why we are here, who made and watches over us, and how we are to live was made indisputably clear. I never once remember questioning, or hearing anyone else question, anything we were taught.

Once in a while, a priest from nearby St. Joseph's Church would address the classroom. We would all immediately stand at attention and stop whatever we were doing as he entered the room. That priest (and other priests in the parish) would be in the confessional listening to our juvenile sins. I can still feel myself kneeling in the dark confessional, hearing the priest slide open the little door to listen to me as he sat sideways, not able to see who I was. I immediately crossed myself and said,

"Bless me, Father, for I have sinned." I don't remember being disturbed by confession. The list of sins we were taught was an objective list of mostly trivial things. The ending was equally rote, being given a penance of so many Our Fathers and Hail Marys to say as I knelt in a pew afterward.

Besides monthly confessions, the devotional practices included prayers in class, children's Mass on Sundays where we sat together by class with our teacher, frequent Monday novenas, Rosary prayers, prayer cards with pictures of saints given to us, grace before and after meals, no meat on Fridays (plus Wednesdays in Lent), and crossing myself whenever an ambulance passed by. Some classmates had little home altars that I envied. I was in the boys' choir, wearing a red cassock, white surplice, and big red bow, singing our parts in the Mass in Latin. I felt at home in church, knowing that I fully belonged somewhere and that I knew what to do and what was going on. At the same time, I was mesmerized by a sense of awe touched with fear. Something mysterious and precious was happening at the altar that was beyond my comprehension and questioning. I just needed to trust the priests' and the sisters' witness and guidance.

The long religious habits worn by the sisters with long rosaries hanging at the side were a witness in themselves, showing that they believed in G-d and G-d's calling so deeply that they would wear clothes that expressed their total sacrificial and willing commitment. They also carried a sense of authority. I can remember times when a sister would walk by my desk, her huge black habit flowing and her long rosary beads clinking against one another, and I felt her absolute authority. I don't remember if it ever happened to me, but when a student acted up in class, they would be called up front, told to hold their palms up, and the sister would sharply beat their palms with a ruler. Everyone in the class could feel its sting.

G-d as presented in school during those years was personal—really in your face. He (and he was unquestioningly a "He") was the divine giver of an unquestionable way of life and the judge of goodness and badness. Mary, Jesus, and the saints were ever at hand, available in our prayer to care for our human needs and to judge and forgive our behavior. The Roman Catholic Church was the infallible channel of spiritual truth. The rest of the Christian and religious world was invisible to me. I don't remember being inside a non-Catholic church, synagogue, or worship house of other faith traditions, or having any friends who were non-Catholic. It wasn't as though non-Catholics were put down; it's just that the Catholic world seemed so immense and inclusive of religious truth and practice in New York City that there simply was no need to pay attention to anything else.

On the fellow-student side, I had entered a much tougher, more aggressive culture than I had known in the South. I don't remember anyone else being new in my third-grade class. I entered with my Texas accent, my weird first name, and a vulnerability that was tempting to exploit. It only happened a few times, but I vividly remember running away at lunchtime, chased by a bunch of boys in my class. I hadn't done anything to them; I was just an outsider, a soft target for collective attack. Fortunately I was a fast runner, but where to run to? The only place that came to me was to run into the parish church a few blocks away. Being good pre–Second Vatican Council Catholics, the chasers were awed and inhibited in church, but one of them sat in the pew behind me and reached out to hit my back as I was kneeling. They soon tired of that restricted atmosphere, though, and walked away.

Once, on a weekend, I was walking near the school when just one of those chasers appeared alone and walked by me holding a sack of empty returnable bottles that he was bringing to the store. He said something insulting to me, and since he was just one person instead of a gang, I was emboldened to hit him. It made him drop the sack, and I heard one of the bottles break. I walked away in triumph. I don't remember him ever bothering me again.

I made some close friends in my class. I was finally in one place long enough to do that in a sustainable way. One new friend lived in my apartment building: Sigrid ("Sugar") Muller was the daughter of our building's superintendent. She had a sad-looking English bulldog named Happy. Among many other things we did together was visit Mr. Painter and his two dogs in the resident hotel building next to our apartment house. He was a publisher of pulp fiction. I remember once walking with him to his bank, and he let me see the $5,000 bill he was going to deposit, which really wowed an eight-year-old who had never seen such big money.

Another friend was Charles Fuhrman, whose father was the super of an apartment house a few blocks away. I remember him showing me the peaked, tasseled metal helmet and white cape of a Prussian soldier from an earlier generation of his family.

A third close friend was David Redpath, who was the smartest kid in our class (later he became a vice president of Pan American Airways). We would meet and play together in Washington Square Park or play with his metal erector set in his apartment.

Once David, Charles, and I were walking together down Bleecker Street in the Village. It was a tough area that we otherwise avoided, but it was in a store there that we could buy caps for our cap guns during the war. I was proudly wearing my leather holster with a cap gun in it. We passed an alley where a bunch of older kids were playing. One of them stopped me and said, "Give me your gun; you can keep the holster." My two friends kept walking ahead as though they didn't know me. If you were streetwise in New York in those days, you sensed when a gang was near, and especially if you were younger, you learned to disappear. I quietly gave the gun to him, then caught up with my friends, with watery eyes at my loss, sad that they didn't stick by me but understanding why they didn't.

The other time I remember getting robbed was in Washington Square Park on a snowy weekend. I was wearing my leather aviator's helmet with goggles. An older kid who was sledding there asked me to let him borrow it. I didn't want to do it because I suspected I would never get it back, but he was intimidating to me. Sugar was with me and yelled at him to leave me alone; he gave her a bloody lip, grabbed my helmet, and never gave it back. But I was sheepishly proud of Sugar's defense of me, and guilty that I hadn't stood up to him more strongly, even though he was older.

My first entrepreneurial adventure was a surprise. One summer I took the green cardboard roof of the playhouse in our living room and brought it outside. I set it up on a first-floor apartment window ledge that was just high enough to let me turn the roof into a table. I set my little tin bank on top of it. I can't remember what moved me to do that—I guess I was playing "store," but I wasn't really selling anything.

A kind-looking old lady walked by and asked me what I was selling. "Nothing," I said. She smiled, slipped a quarter into my tin bank anyway, and walked off.

Suddenly it occurred to me that maybe I *could* sell something. So I went back to my apartment and brought down a bunch of used comic books I had saved and put up a "For Sale, 10 Cents" sign. Superhero comic books were the rage for youth in those days, and they were my only treasure. Amazingly enough, some people came by and bought them, including a bellman from the residential hotel next door, who said one of the resident's was looking for a particular comic book that I had.

By the end of the summer I had collected ten dollars in sales, a big amount for a poor boy in those days. I can't remember what I did with the money. I think just having been able to sell things that people wanted was my biggest reward.

We indeed were poor then, living off part of my father's small wartime military salary. I remember my mother keeping a written record of expenses right down to ten cents for shoelaces. My occasional special treat would be to go to the local drugstore counter with enough money for a milkshake. I appreciated it the more because I knew how seldom we could afford it. Only very rarely did we ever go anywhere for entertainment that cost anything.

I was a latchkey child. My mother was a student at New York University majoring in psychology, and I usually came home after school to an empty apartment. I did my homework, played with my toy soldiers and Tinkertoy, and then at 5:00 p.m. I would turn on the radio in the bedroom, lie down in bed, and listen in awe for an hour to serial dramas such as *The Green Hornet, Superman, The Lone Ranger,* and *Captain Midnight*. I sent in a Wheaties box top to get a *Captain Midnight* decoder ring. During the program they would read off the numbers that I would enter on the ring, which would spell out a secret message. I have no memory of the messages but a clear memory of how much I loved getting them.

I read every issue of the Classics Illustrated comic books series, which dumbed down classical literary figures to something a nine-year-old could understand. I also looked forward to the latest issues of superhero comics. Recently, my ten-year-old grandson, Marcus, sat next to me with a big book describing different superheroes. As he turned each page, he asked me if I knew that superhero. There were probably a hundred superheroes described and pictured. I was astounded at how much the list had expanded since my youth. (Missing from the lineup was Plastic Man, who could stretch his arms around corners for many yards to capture fleeing villains!)

Meals in our kitchen were simple and cheap: dry cereal with milk for breakfast; peanut butter and jelly sandwiches that I took for school lunch, maybe with an apple; and for dinner, macaroni and cheese out of a box, or ground beef with a canned vegetable and maybe potato or rice. Grace before eating was the standard Catholic version. I didn't complain about the food we ate because I really didn't know any alternative.

During the war we had regular blackouts at night. A siren would sound and everyone had to turn off all their lights. I can remember looking out our fourth-floor apartment window and seeing a volunteer neighborhood warden yelling up to people who still had their lights on. I don't remember being afraid of an actual attack but rather my eerie feeling when I looked out the window and saw total black stillness outside, as though the neighborhood had been abandoned or everyone had gone to bed at the same time. Patriotism seemed universal, with drives to collect metal, paper, and other things needed for the war effort, and jokes and gestures shared among us children that made fun of Hitler.

In the winter of 1943, my father was ordered to leave for the Pacific war theater. He had been issued a lightweight white officer's uniform to wear for what was supposed to be a tropical Pacific assignment. At the last minute, his orders were changed and in the middle of winter he was sent with his lightweight clothing to freezing Great Britain. He was a port officer in Glasgow and later, I think, Southampton. Near the end of the war, as a mere first lieutenant, he and another young officer were assigned to attain the surrender of a large German ship loaded with armed troops anchored in the port of Bremen. They were quaking in their boots at such an assignment, wondering if the captain would offer to surrender or resist and capture or kill them. The ship's captain eventually came down to them and surrendered as an independent entity from the German state, in order to receive better conditions of treatment. My dad had many other stories from his two years there, about hard living conditions in Britain and the chaos of war.

I missed my dad terribly while he was gone. He used to climb under the covers with me when I went to bed and in the dark create incredible yarns about the pirate Captain Kidd. I could feel his warmth next to me; his caring and stories meant a lot. I can remember that he came home from work very tired every day, but I have no memory of being with him except at bedtime. Of course, at this time, mothers raised children and fathers mostly watched or did other things. But not having him around left a big hole, and there was no other man around to substitute for him. I wanted him to come back so badly. I loved to read the occasional letters he sent us; I still have some of them.

It was extra devastating, then, when my mother sat me down one day and told me that he was never coming back to us. During his time in Glasgow, my dad developed a relationship with a Scottish Jewish woman and asked my mother for a proxy overseas divorce so he could marry her and convert to Judaism. This came as a complete shock to my mother. She was deeply hurt and furious. Through several years of psychotherapy that she had undergone in New York (very rare in those days), she had strengthened her own sense of self-worth and was able to keep her integrity and live with dignity after the divorce. But I couldn't accept it. For years I yearned for them to come back together.

My Mother, Marie

In the New York years, my mother applied the latest psychological understanding of how to raise a child from her psychology courses at NYU. That included no oppressive demands and much careful verbal guidance of me toward consenting internally to do the right thing. She was loving and supportive, and she tried to be a good mother while being a good student at the same time.

She also was a companion, for lack of a better word. She was only sixteen years older than me. When I was eight, she was just twenty-four. I remember her telling me once that she really didn't know how to raise a child, never having done it before and having no close friends around who had. She wanted the best for me, but she wasn't sure how to foster it. I took that conversation unconsciously as a need for me to partially raise myself, as she was still raising herself. In that sense we were friends on equal footing, coping with life together. Such a relationship was made easier by my being a "good boy" who she trusted to make good judgments, which I think was partly due to her successful psychology-grounded way of conditioning our relationship, reinforced by my being an only child, which made me more susceptible to adult authority and modeling.

I had ambivalent feelings about being a "companion" to her. I felt too young for that. I just wanted a confident, caring mother. But there would always be that companion dimension of our relationship until I was grown, including her wanting to know what I thought of some of the men she seriously dated over the years after the divorce. That always was a hard question, because though I wanted her to be happy, I really wanted only my real father in the house.

Life went on after my father's proxy divorce overseas, and despite his absence, much of it was good. Annie Dillard, in her *An American Childhood*, well said that the joy of children is a kind of gratitude, the gratitude of a child "who wakes to her own energy and the brisk challenge of the world."

Enjoying City Life and Other Adventures in New York City

I did well in school. I loved my friends. I roller-skated in Washington Square Park, learned to ice skate on the rink at Rockefeller Center, played stoopball off the steps of row houses, and on a few special occasions went to the zoo in Central Park and to Jones Beach. That's as far as many New

York children, especially the financially poor, ever traveled. Many never had seen a live chicken until Macy's had a special exhibit of them.

I had some experience of nature and small-town life before moving to New York, but I nonetheless was awed one fall weekend when we traveled to the home of a friend of my parents in a tree-lined suburb in Connecticut. I helped rake leaves into a pile in their big backyard, then someone lit a match and set it on fire. I had never seen or smelled leaves burning. It felt like a different world than the urban Manhattan I had come to call home. Despite its strangeness, there was something alluring about that scene. I felt a dim sense of what "home" would mean there, with a separate house, an intact family and dog, and a yard with big trees on a quiet, safe street.

Manhattan, though, still felt like my home. On Sunday mornings I loved to stop by the great arch in Washington Square Park on the way to church and look up Fifth Avenue in awe: it was virtually empty and silent, as though people and cars had just evaporated overnight—such a contrast to the boisterous sounds and sights of other days of the week.

I did a little hellraising with some classmates sometimes by racing down the Sixth Avenue subway stairs and back up the other side, screaming as loud as we could. That quickly stopped for me, though, after I was singled out by a subway guard who grabbed my arm and held me down, yelling that he'd have the police arrest me if he ever caught me doing that again. Terrified, I never went down those stairs after that.

Sugar and I sometimes mischievously hid in the bushes after dark next to the sidewalk in front of our apartment building and suddenly beamed our flashlights onto people as they passed. We also ran up and down the fire-escape steps of the Albert Hotel next door, and found steps in other buildings, as part of searching out potential escape routes if we were ever being chased by anyone. When walking down a street alone, I would always cross to the other side, or turn around and go down a different street, if I saw two or more older boys walking toward me.

When I was nine, I developed a mysterious ailment that kept me out of school for a month. I couldn't open my jaw fully. I spent time in two hospitals. In the first one, there was a wounded soldier recovering in the bed next to me. He flirted with the nurse, who he called "Carrottop." Doctors couldn't figure out what was wrong with me and sent me to the Children's Hospital. There I vividly remember a huge room full of many iron-railed cribs. I felt humiliated being put in one of them at my age, but I silently accepted it. I also remember an intern trying to get a needle in my thin-veined arm; after many failed jabs and more bleeding, an experienced nurse mercifully took over and with one jab finally got the needle into the vein. Eventually they gave up on medications and simply lanced the big blood clot that had developed behind my throat.

When I finally went back to school, my mother gave me a box of chocolates to share with the class, in gratitude for all the cards my classmates had sent me. I stood in front of the class and was tongue-tied—I couldn't say anything to them. Sister Corona Rosaire, my fifth-grade teacher, mercifully just took the box and passed it around. She took the last piece and ate it herself, obviously relishing the taste. That shocked me a little, given the ascetical stereotype I had of the pre–Second Vatican Council sisters' lives—I thought they weren't supposed to indulge in anything tasty. She was a strict teacher but somehow she let me do bizarre things in that class after I returned from the hospital. I remember finishing my classwork before others in the class one day and going up and sitting on top of the wastebasket beside her desk. She just ignored me (the class did too). I soon gave up on trying to get a self-centered rise out of the class after that.

Just a few years ago, I was in surprising email contact with Rina De Paoli, a girl in that class who had come across one of my published books. I remember her as a nice, pigtailed beauty on whom I had a fifth grader's crush. She told me that she had kept up with Sister Corona Rosaire until she died in her nineties. She also sent me an eighth-grade graduation photo of that class, three years after I had left the school. I was shocked at how vulnerable and cowed everyone looked, including the boys who seemed so tough when I was there

On Victory in Europe Day in 1945, there was a huge celebration in Times Square. Our neighbor Mr. Painter invited Sugar and me to go with him to the spontaneous huge gathering there, and my mother gave me permission, as long as we were back by 9:00 p.m. We didn't get back, though, until after 10:00. My grandparents were visiting from Texas, and I can still hear my grandfather yelling at me for the first time ever when I came in, calling me a "spoiled brat" for scaring them by being so late. Even though Mr. Painter was responsible, I cringed with guilt and didn't sleep easily that night—but it was a once-in-a-lifetime special celebration in Times Square that made it worth bearing the guilt.

When my father returned to New York from Britain at the end of the war, for a few days before leaving for Houston (where his new wife, Naomi, and baby Pamela would soon join him), he came to see me. He gave me a Scottish Guard's cap and a British helmet with a bullet hole through it. Both gifts were awesome, although the helmet was a little scary. I still have the cap. When he came to pick me up from school the next day, my classmates were awed by his lieutenant commander officer's uniform (his final rank at the end of the war). That moment gave me a little more status with the boys who had chased me.

Dad had never been confirmed as a Catholic and somehow the school arranged for us to be confirmed together apart from my class, at St. Patrick's Cathedral. I had already received First Communion, dressed in a white suit and tie, with my class the year before. Since I didn't have a Christian first name, I had to choose one at my Confirmation. I chose John because I liked the sound of it. It also gave me a real first name to supplement the three names on my birth certificate that were derived from three last names: Tilden Hampton Edwards. I never used that Confirmation name, though.

At the Confirmation ceremony with my Dad, what was most memorable was the ritual slap on my cheek the bishop gave me as I knelt before him, meant to be a reminder of the sacrifice and commitment needed in Christian life.

Saying goodbye to Dad at the end of his brief visit to New York was hard. He struggled to find a decent job in Houston. After several years he was chosen for a very good one that he kept for the rest of his career: he became a federal administrative judge for maritime legal cases. He was assigned to the port of San Francisco. I did not meet any of my siblings or my stepmother, Naomi, until we all ended up living in the San Francisco Bay Area when I turned twelve years old. In the earlier years between then and the divorce I had no contact with Dad, apart from his rare letters.

My mother continued to date in New York, but my childish dream was that she would eventually get back together with my dad. I didn't want anyone else to take his place. As it turned out, no one ever did. Despite her constant dating over the years, she never found the right man, one she really trusted and loved, though she came very close a few times. She never really gave up the search. I remember her telling me when she was seventy years old that she lied about her age when she joined a gym so she would be seen as younger in the eyes of a nice man she might meet there!

Illinois and Oregon: Brief Stays

"Wake up, little Tilden. Breakfast is ready." My Aunt Faye's voice woke me from a sweaty summer sleep on the screen porch. I was in the house of my Aunt Faye and Uncle Nick, in the small town of Centralia, Illinois. It was July 1945. My mother had sent me from New York to live with her brother and sister-in-law for the summer. They had no children, so as usual I was the only child in the house.

Since air conditioning still didn't exist in homes, it was always swelteringly hot. But there were two paradises of cool air conditioning that existed in town: Walgreens and the movie theater. I wanted to go there as often as I could. Even those islands of relief were soon cut off due to a polio outbreak that confined all children to their homes. It became such a boring summer after (keep in mind, there was no TV yet and nothing much worth listening to on radio for a ten-year-old) that I have no other memory from that time whatsoever.

Toward the end of the summer I assumed I would be going back to New York. I was shocked to hear that my mother had packed up everything from the apartment and was going to drive to Illinois and pick me up—we were going to live with my Great-Aunt Lucretia in Portland,

Oregon. I was deeply dejected. After establishing wonderful relationships with my friends in New York and feeling at home in the city after years of disruptive moves, here we were on the road again, to a place I had never been and where I knew no one. I was just about to turn eleven years old. My resistance was useless—it was a done deal I just had to accept.

When we finally arrived at Aunt Lucretia's row house in an old Portland neighborhood, we were greeted by her and her housemate, Ralph Colonna. Ralph was the pharmacist at the drugstore next door. Aunt Lucretia's husband had died some years before. She owned a few houses in the neighborhood and lived off her rental income. Her brother, the patriarch of a large family of seven siblings, was my grandfather in Texas. My mother, having grown up in Tacoma, Washington, knew all of them and their families in the Pacific Northwest to a lesser or greater extent. I expect my grandfather persuaded his sister Lucretia to take in my mother and me and take care of us so we wouldn't be left without family support in New York.

Two good things about the house helped overcome my reluctance to start life anew there. The first was that I had a room of my own—for the first time ever. The second was that there was a piano in the living room. Ralph played it and composed simple songs. I found a beginner's piano book that helped me teach myself a few basics, which blossomed into a lifetime of stroking the keys that brought sounds of consolation and inspiration to me. In a way, the piano became my closest friend in a year ahead when I would not have a close human friend my age.

I entered the sixth grade in the neighborhood school where, as when I moved to New York, most everyone had been together in school and friendships for many years. Playing softball in gym class was symbolic of my social outsider status. The coach asked two boys to choose who they wanted to be on their team. I was the last one chosen, both because no one knew me and I had never before played softball or any other team sport. There was no gym or playing field at St. Joseph's School in New York. The closest thing to a sport was a stoopball pickup game somewhere after school, with whoever else might be around. My exercise in New York mostly came from long walks to and from school.

The one game that I was good at in Portland was dodgeball. I don't think many of the kids really cared whether they were hit by the ball, but I did. I did everything I could to dodge the ball and hang in there until only me and a couple others were left. That determined energy would be the hallmark of my sports life in years to come.

I did okay in school otherwise, including getting enrolled in a media class where we visited the *Oregonian* newspaper office and played roles in a school radio program. Occasionally after school there was a neighborhood pickup softball game near our house or a game of hide-and-seek, in which I was allowed to join as the tolerated outsider. But my non-school time was mostly at home with my family and the piano, with occasional visits with other family members I didn't know.

Ralph Colonna was heavy into opera, and one time a famous Italian opera singer visiting Portland showed up at our house unexpectedly for dinner with some friends. We all had to pretend we had eaten already because there wasn't enough food for the guests. My aunt served a huge plate of spaghetti and pulled out the big block of hard cheese she always kept under the sink to grate onto spaghetti. Afterward, the singer regaled us with song. It was the first operatic voice I had ever heard—a close-up, overwhelming experience of beauty and volume.

My mother, still trying to finish college, enrolled at Reed College, which was well known for its heady seriousness. She dated a man who at one point invited her to a formal dance. I can still see her beaming as she descended the staircase wearing a black formal evening gown, with all of us admiring her. I don't know that she ever went to a formal dance in her life again.

Come Christmastime we drove up to Tacoma for an annual extended Babare-family gathering, a kind of gathering I had never experienced before. We stayed at the home of another of Grandad's four siblings, Aunt Mary Love. She and her husband had invited the whole family and neighbors to a Christmas Day pancake brunch. I think about thirty-five people of all ages showed up over a two-hour period. In the afternoon I played Monopoly with some cousins my age, one of whom, Mary Lu, became a lifelong friend.

The next day, the family migrated to Day Island, just outside Tacoma, to the home of my grandfather's brother George and his wife, Mary. Planted in my mind still is an image of about forty people of all ages standing at the water's edge with someone taking photos of us. I had a wonderful sense of belonging. There was a unique place for me in this crowd, as there was for everyone else. I never again experienced such a sense of "big family" belonging, except when I returned to Tacoma for my grandparents' fiftieth wedding anniversary.

As my year in Portland evolved, my experience of extended family evolved. Cousins my age appeared for a day, and we visited older generations—my sense of family community sunk in. Once, some of us spent a few days at Seaside, a beach community not far from Portland, staying in a bed and breakfast. I renewed my awe and love of the sea during those days. I had never experienced a low tide that receded two miles out to sea, a special feature of that beach. In those low-tide, ocean-free sands, you could see hundreds of bubbles appearing from clams under the sand's surface. I had my first experience of "clamming"—digging up clams, putting them in a bucket, and eating them for dinner.

Moving Yet Again—On to California

Well, here we go again. I found out that at the end of the school year, my mother and I would move to San Jose and stay with my grandparents, who had just moved there from Texas to retire. They had a small two-bedroom house on the edge of town. The street dead-ended into a peach orchard. The house had a detached screened-in porch in the backyard. That was to be my bedroom. At night it was a little like being back in Marshall, where I had slept on the dining room couch, with masses of crickets blaring away outside. Here, such insects were compounded by spiders, roaches, and other creepy-crawly things. I felt alone and a little scared every night.

The aloneness spread to many of my days as well. It was the loneliest year I've ever known. There were no children my age in the neighborhood. I was just turning twelve years old and entering the seventh grade in a junior high school several miles away. I knew no one. I was interviewed by a student reporter for the school newsletter because I was a new student. She asked me who my friends were in school. Embarrassed to say I didn't have any, I blurted out "Forest." I didn't really know him, except as someone I played paddle tennis with after school sometimes. He told me once that the gym coach had mentioned my name in his gym class, holding me up as a model of someone who tried really hard to play basketball well (I had never played it before that year), even though I was just an average player. He was right. All my life I tried hard to do well in school and sports, to make up for my "averageness" (at least as I saw myself) and to have something to be proud of. Not having a community of friends or any other opportunity to belong beyond my three-member family there, I gave my all to do well and be accepted in school.

The one other place I had opportunity to do well and to express myself was with the piano. My grandparents bought one for me, and they paid for piano lessons from Ms. Cox, which continued weekly for the next three years. As in Portland, piano music was not just something to learn but a place for relationship, for musical friendship through the composers' intimate melodies and rhythms. I poured my unexpressed feelings into it and it gave me inspiration and contentment. The price of all the tedious early work of learning and practicing technical scales was worth it. Beyond the scales, I could move into popular and classical music.

The psychic effect of my aloneness led me to an unusual habit of kneeling down in the house occasionally and imaging a radiant Jesus kindly looking at me. I was doing that in the kitchen once when my grandmother walked in. She was the most religious person in my family. Instead of being concerned about finding me doing that, she immediately respected it. I was very embarrassed that she had found me and very grateful that she sympathetically let me be.

I don't know whether that experience was Christ's compassionate presence drawing me to companionship or just a desperate psychological compensation for my aloneness. I don't recall my continuing it after that year. (Many decades later, I will return to face-to-face contact with an image of Christ when I discover praying with classical icons.) I still went to church with my grandparents on Sundays. (My mother rejected the Catholic Church after her divorce, angry at the excommunication that automatically came with divorce in the years preceding the Second Vatican Council.) I remember no other religious connection then, apart from grace at meals and maybe a brief prayer before falling sleeping in my isolated screened-porch bedroom.

Life as a Boy Scout

Later that year, my mother and grandparents showed their worry about my aloneness when they told me they had discovered a Boy Scout troop that met every week at the Willow Glen Methodist Church near my school, and they encouraged me to join it. I knew nothing about Boy Scouts, and I agreed with some trepidation to go to a meeting the next week. As it turned out, it was the best thing that happened to me that year. Mr. Fine, the scoutmaster of Troop 25 (a baker by trade), had developed a large, dedicated troop of boys ranging in age from twelve to seventeen. The troop held up the Boy Scout code of healthy, responsible, disciplined communal values, and it offered opportunities for practical learning and service that positively contributed to my sense of identity, purpose, skillfulness, and connection with nature. I finally felt a place of accepted and constructive belonging beyond family that was to endure for years.

I still have my merit badge sash from that time. As I look at the symbols representing each badge now, I don't recognize what skills many of them stand for. Those I do recognize are for first aid, public speaking, music, public health, semaphore signaling, cooking, scholarship, and I think home repairs.

I had never been camping before. I don't even remember ever hiking in the woods. Now on camping trips at least once or twice a year I would begin to befriend nature, to recognize its many harmless and harmful creatures, trees and plants by day, and its stars by night. I would learn how to collaboratively set up and ditch a pup tent, start a fire, cook food over the fire, and learn to look forward to gathering around the fire at night to hear the leader tell stories.

My most intimate memory of nature came at the end of a long hike up to Tuolumne Meadows, an elevation of seven thousand feet, in Yosemite National Park. The troop spent the night in sleeping bags carried in our backpacks, with no tent equipment. When I crawled into my sleeping bag and looked up at the cloudless sky, I saw the most awesome sight I had ever seen: a vast black sky filled with the seemingly infinite cloud of stars in the Milky Way. They were so bright that they lit up the meadow. Shooting stars suddenly appeared that made the sky seem alive. I was overwhelmed and speechless. I felt so small amid such grandeur. I sensed a great living mystery that transcended all thought.

A more ominous confrontation with nature occurred several days later. We were taken in our truck to Mirror Lake in Yosemite Valley, not far from our campsite. In the middle of the lake, a fair distance from land, was a big rock jutting out of the water. A few troop members swam out to it with Norman Sommers, the assistant scoutmaster. I saw them climb up on the rock and lie down, sunbathing. It looked inviting. Although my grandad had given me several very elementary swimming lessons long before, I can't remember ever seriously trying to swim after that. As all swimmers know, your body remembers what it once learned about swimming, even after long gaps between swims. In my mind I remembered a basic arm-over-arm (freestyle) way of swimming and kicking, but I didn't know how to properly breathe along with those strokes.

I plunged in and gave it my all. I was completely out of breath when I finally touched the rock, feeling I had just barely managed to make it. I expected there would be a place to gain a foothold. Instead, the lake seemed bottomless at that point. I slipped under water, leaped up, and yelled "Help!" with what felt like my last breath. Norman saw I was in trouble. He jumped in and hauled me to the other side of the rock where I could get a foothold and climb up. I lay down next to the other scouts and my breathing slowly came back to normal. I felt humiliated that I hadn't made it on my own and at the same time very grateful to Norman for saving my life.

Once again, as at my uncertain birth, I was meant to live. Once again, I was saved through another person. That's a lesson in needed dependency. My effort, no matter how great, isn't enough to get me through life. I need the efforts and concern of many others (as they need mine). In this case, my grandad had given me beginning swimming help (which he had learned from someone else) that empowered me to swim out to that rock. But that wasn't enough. I needed Norman, a trained swimmer, to get me safely onto that rock.

We don't have to look far to see how much we need one another's gifts and caring to live and the mystery of hidden grace that brings these resources to fruition among us.

Chapter 2

Adolescence
Growing Confidence

After my first year in San Jose, we moved to a house at the other end of town, where there was room for me to sleep inside the house. The move meant that I would be changing schools yet again, to Herbert Hoover Junior High School, where I knew no one. The one happy continuity was my weekly meetings with Troop 25, which continued to give me a healthy "boy community" as I entered adolescence. I also began sharing those values by helping lead the den meetings of a Cub Scout pack for elementary school boys.

Life had five basic dimensions now: school, family, scouting, socializing, and music. I could add church, but that was only on Sundays with my grandparents and was somehow isolated from everything else, although I do remember a long argument with a school friend, Jerry Mutz, where I defended the church and religion. I was supported by another friend, Babs Lester, who told me she was going to be a missionary. I also worked in the school cafeteria as a service project, but somehow that didn't qualify as a memorable dimension of my life.

I gradually found a place in my new school. After two years as an outsider, I came to be an insider again; I belonged. I was interested in all my class subjects, and good teachers helped that positive feeling. I began a lifelong intrinsic interest in learning, rather than just approaching subjects with an expedient attitude of "I have to listen in class and do my homework to get along, but I'd rather be doing something else." I liked excelling in my classes, incentivized by feeling on equal ground with other students as we used the same curriculum we had in my last school. They were ahead of me in knowing one another, but in class we were all facing something new that put us at the same starting gate.

Learning the Manual Arts

Shop classes taught by Mr. Fingado gave me a lot of anxiety. All boys were required to take three of his classes: wood, metal, and electric shop. He was a gentle teacher, with a missing finger from an encounter with an electric saw. But nothing he did could overcome my mental and physical sense of poverty in those classes. I can still see the piece of wood clamped in my vice to create a breadboard. As I planed the top of it, I suddenly saw a piece of the board splintering off at one corner. The intended breadboard was basically ruined (or you might say permanently wounded). My only consolation was glimpsing another student's board sinking in the middle as he hopelessly tried to plane an even top. At least I wasn't the only klutz in the class.

Miraculously, I managed to finish the next assignment in that class fairly well: making a wooden broomstick holder and painting it. I kept looking at it in disbelief that nothing had gone wrong. I carried it home with great pride. My grandad, who was a master carpenter and once a shipbuilder, must have thought that he had at least 1 percent of shared genes with me.

In metal shop, I always seemed at risk of slicing off a finger, but I managed to do the minimum to pass. Fortunately Mr. Fingado was extremely lenient in grading us. Electricity shop was a great mystery. What electric currents were and did seemed magical. I managed to build a simple radio wiring set, but I never fully understood why it worked.

Another "manual arts" class was much easier for me: typing. Our typewriter keys in the class had no letters or numbers on them. We had to memorize what they were, and always begin typing with our fingers over the same keys so that we could learn to use all ten fingers and type rapidly. I was proud to receive a "forty words a minute" pin at the end of the class. It turned out to be the most practically valuable class I've ever had. I'm typing this right now with all ten fingers hitting keys and without looking.

In higher math later in my schooling, I had the same sense of mystery as I did in electric shop: even when I could figure how to do algebraic equations, I never understood *why* they worked. As math became more complex in later years, it took the place of those dreaded shop classes. They both called upon an impoverished side of my brain. The anxiety of my self-doubt in those classes made my performance worse. Plane geometry was the one math class that felt concrete: circles, triangles, and so on—shapes that you could *see* even though you needed algebra to understand it.

I happily joined the choir, but at age fourteen that didn't last long. I still remember Mr. Rathbun, the choir director, taking me aside one day and telling me that my voice was changing and there was no place in the choir for unpredictable voices.

Learning the Language of Music

Music, like math, is a different language, learned and appreciated in a different part of the brain. As I mentioned earlier, I had a serious piano teacher outside of school with whom I learned the language of music little by little over the next two years. The music of each composer she introduced me to taught me more about the possibilities of music to birth joy, strength, tenderness, sorrow, rapture, and rhythm. A quality of full, wordless, felt "presence" was cultivated in me.

Playing the piano was an especially great consolation and inspiration for me in my circumstances. I was living as an only child, with an absent father and an often-absent mother trying to finish college and dating men on the side. I loved my grandparents, but they were so different from me. My friends lived too far away from our house to be with very much. That was my context for going through the strange, new feelings of early adolescence. Sharing the companionship of great composers as I stroked their uplifting notes on the piano keys was a daily time of integrated presence, a steadying tiller on a rocking boat.

The music of great composers drew me to them beyond the piano. I wanted to hear their language in person, spoken by virtuoso instrumentalists and singers who knew how to draw out their music's intimate beauty and strength. When concerts were offered at the San Jose Municipal

Auditorium on weekends, I would take a bus there whenever I could to hear well-known pianists (Arthur Rubenstein, for example), symphonies, or light operas (San Jose wasn't capable of mounting grand opera). When I couldn't do that, I would listen to recorded music. At school I played the piano in the school orchestra, pretty pathetically as I recall. It was intimidating to try to keep up the rhythm with all those other instruments. Actually, I think the whole orchestra was pretty pathetic! Most of us were new to our instruments.

My Awkward First Love

One day at school, Felice Miles, a student in my grade, performed a piano concert. I can still see her long, wavy hair and soft eyes and feel her calm composure as her fingers beautifully expressed some classical composition I can't remember. But her name and face I will never forget. I was smitten. I just sat and looked at her with a wonderful sense of intimacy, as though I was touching her face and sensing her fragrance, even though I was ten feet away.

I was awed by her presence. When I talked to her, I felt a shy awkwardness. I was so lacking in self-confidence with the opposite sex that I couldn't bring myself to be with her for more than a few minutes. When I knew her birthday was coming soon, I bought her a fake-jeweled pen at a stationary store and wrapped it up as a present, but I couldn't bring myself to go to her house and deliver it. Astounding as it may seem to anyone not a young adolescent, I convinced my mother to bring it over to her on her birthday and tell her I couldn't do it myself because I had to do something with my grandad that day. Now how stupid is that for an excuse? But what other excuse wouldn't be just as stupid? She sent me a thank-you anyway.

We danced together occasionally at the "Hoover Hangout," which was a junior high dance on Friday nights at the local Methodist Church. All the girls would line up on one side of the room and all the boys on the other, nervously talking with one another and waiting to choose or be chosen. I don't think Felice and I were ever together for more than a few minutes. I never gave her a chance to reject me, and I never gave myself the chance to really get to know her and maybe lose my idolization of her. I was to move away again at the end of that ninth-grade school year, and I would never see her again. To this day she still comes before my eyes as a quiet, beautiful, unapproachable goddess.

No other girl in junior high school overwhelmed me like that. One day my classmate Shirley Taormina stopped me in the hall and confided in me that Arlene Spitzer had a crush on me. "Although I don't know why," she crudely added. I was touched that a girl had fallen for unconfident me, so I later found a time to talk with her. I remember once we held hands walking around the block, but nothing really stirred in me and any potential special relationship quickly evaporated.

Other Relationships

Early in my first year at Hoover Junior High I met Jack Boyce. He had a stutter, a big smile, and a big bike. We played untutored tennis together after school. I remember the first time I visited his family house. It was so small that the only space left for him to sleep was in the attic, which you needed a ladder to climb up into. It was unbelievably hot there in the summer. I felt sorry for him, but he seemed very accepting of the situation. I remember biking around with him. Yes, biking: I finally was allowed to have a bike after my crash into a car in first grade. I also remember going to his house after dark and looking through his nifty reflecting telescope. I saw Saturn with its rings, Mars, and a bright star. It was the first time I had ever looked through a "real" telescope. There was something magical and intimate about seeing faraway planets through it.

I was allowed to bike around alone after school and on weekends. In those days, San Jose was a basically safe town, and I explored areas far from home. My long-challenged desire for belonging showed itself in my sense of pride in living in San Jose. It had such a cross section of Americans that national companies would poll people there about their choices for food, clothes, and other retail goods. The population was about eighty thousand. Now, being in the center of Silicon Valley, its population has rocketed to over a million people. Surrounding the city in my time there was a countryside that burst into bloom in the spring. Just about every kind of fruit orchard filled the air with sweet fragrance and filled the eyes with beauty. All the orchards eventually were sacrificed to developers responding to the need for housing as the population grew.

My mother, away at college most of the time, was rarely around, so I interacted mostly with my grandparents. Being a young adolescent, I began to feel a certain distance and withdrawal from them. This withdrawal was compounded by their lack of much formal education—both left school as I recall after the fifth grade—although my grandad was a math whiz and a smart businessman, and my grandmother was a master cook and gardener.

Once, when my grandmother asked me to mow the lawn, I exploded in shaking anger, not wanting to do it then. I raced the lawn mower over the grass as fast as I could, with my grandmother sadly looking on. When we went out to dinner together, I would often bring a book and read it while we were waiting to be served. I felt I had nothing to say to them, and they rarely talked even to each other. They were tolerant, though, and probably bewildered of my new adolescence. I don't remember being a brat very often, but inside I often felt alienated and judgmental toward my family. These feelings left me judging myself as not a good person worthy of others' respect. G-d seemed pretty dead in my consciousness then, although I still dully went to church with my grandparents. Thank G-d adolescence doesn't last forever!

We got along best when we went to baseball games or bowled together, and when grandad took me to play golf with him. Sports have a way of transcending even adolescent funk.

One More Year in San Jose

In the fall of my last year in San Jose, when I had turned fourteen years old, I was offered my first paid job: flagging cars into parking spaces on the dusty, eucalyptus tree–lined spaces around Stanford University's stadium on Saturdays during football season. I was proud to know that I was worth being paid to do something, however little it was.

In school I was increasingly confident in my classwork and in relating to fellow students. I had the audacity to run for "chief justice" in the annual school elections (which, as I remember, was a pompous name for the small, powerless task of presiding over a student committee that examined students whose behavior violated school rules). Three others vied with me for the position in an election that was preceded by a full student assembly during which each candidate gave a speech about why they should be elected. I remember standing in the stage wings listening to the pitch of the candidate who spoke just before me. When I went out on stage after her, I froze in the face of the whole student body looking at me and the glare of the stage lights; I completely lost what I had memorized to say. Instead, I basically just became an echo of the previous candidate, literally mimicking some of the words I remember her saying. I left the stage humiliated; my speech guaranteed my defeat. Somehow, though, I didn't dwell on the defeat and went on with my life.

I continued my piano lessons through the year and practiced daily. My teacher began to give me more difficult classical music to learn, and I began to buy Broadway show music and some popular songs, a habit that continued for years. I told my teacher that I would be moving away that summer. She told me that she felt she had taught me all she could and that she had planned to turn me over to a higher-level teacher and ask him to arrange for me to give a public recital. I was flattered, but at the same time I breathed a sigh of relief. I was terrible at memorizing music, which was required for a recital. I didn't want to end up as I had in my "chief justice" speech, where I drew a humiliating blank in front of the audience.

At the end of that academic year in the ninth grade, we had an outdoor graduation ceremony in the municipal rose garden, which I passed every day on my way to school. Besides receiving my diploma, I was surprised to receive the American Legion Award that characterized me as much more than I knew I really was, with lofty words on it such as "high qualities of honor, courage, scholarship, leadership, service, companionship, and character." I was sure I didn't live up to these qualities, but what they told me was that my teachers and fellow students now thought of me as an "insider" who, like most everyone else in the class, had contributed something to the school community. Yet again, come fall, I would have to start all over as a perfect stranger to everyone in another city.

During that last year in San Jose, my mother finally earned her bachelor's and master's degrees in psychology at Stanford. She moved to Los Angeles that winter to enroll in a PhD program at UCLA and to scout around for a place for us to live near a good public high school for the coming year. I was left with my grandparents to finish the ninth grade.

Crossing the Country for the National Jamboree of the Boy Scouts

That last summer in San Jose I took part in the first National Jamboree of Boy Scouts since before World War II, which took place in Valley Forge, Pennsylvania. My scoutmaster volunteered to bring to the Jamboree anyone in Troop 25 who wanted to come. My eyes widened at the prospect of such an adventure, and my family supported my excited request to go.

After weeks of preparation, about a dozen Troop 25 Scouts, along with other area Scouts, all decked out in full Scout uniform and loaded down with sleeping bags and other equipment, met at the San Jose train station. We boarded a special Jamboree-bound train, which would be our home for six days, sitting and sleeping in a chair car. Along the way to Valley Forge, we had stops at the Grand Canyon and in Washington, DC, with tours at each stop.

After leaving the Grand Canyon and crossing into Oklahoma, we found ourselves in a heat wave reaching 106 degrees during the day, which led the air conditioning on the train to break down and never come back on. The heat in the steel train cars was stifling and humid. We stripped off most of our clothes, mopped ourselves with towels soaked in water, drank whatever liquid was available to drink, and listlessly sat around yearning for the heaven of cool air, all day and night. The train gradually left the Deep South behind and the air slowly cooled down to a tolerable temperature.

The weeklong Jamboree itself was amazing. Nearly fifty thousand Scouts arrived by train, bus, and plane, including some from twenty foreign countries. We had a designated area where we set up camp and pitched our pup tents. My friend Mel Sommers was my tent mate. We exchanged little things from our region of the country with other Scouts we met. (I had some redwood tree bark to exchange, which in hindsight was a pitiable choice.) We had mass gatherings to hear President Harry S. Truman and General Dwight D. Eisenhower speak to us and to see a dramatic reenactment of George Washington and his troops triumphing in the battle of Valley Forge. On Sunday, we divided into different religious groups for services. Each regional and international country group created special "gateway" entrances to their area with images of their region's topography and culture.

When we boarded our train after that week, I felt like I had entered another world that I would never see again but that would live in me forever.

Our first stop on the return trip was an overnight stay and tour in New York City. I had written Sugar, my close friend from my three years living there, to meet me in Grand Central Station the hour before we left. She did. I was overjoyed to see her after four years, during which we had continued to write to each other. I felt a little awkward standing together, with no available place around us to sit for an hour. I was wearing my Scout uniform with short pants and long socks. She looked so grown up. Who was she now? Who was I? We talked about old times, what had happened to our friends, and how life was going for us (on a very shallow level). Here was someone with whom I had been so close, yet the years of growing up apart from each other had left us as virtual strangers, even as we still cared for each other. The hour quickly passed; we hugged each other, then I ran to catch my train. I never saw her again.

After leaving New York City, I continued to be glad for my friendship with Mel Sommers, who was someone with whom I could completely be myself throughout the trip. Our Jamboree train took us to Rochester, where we toured the Kodak plant, then up to the awesome roar and size of Niagara Falls. We continued to Detroit and toured the Ford Motor plant. We then went to Chicago and visited museums and the zoo, and we saw a major league baseball game. When we arrived at Glacier National Park, we joined an Indian ceremonial powwow and then rode in a bus for many miles on the Sun Highway through the heart of the park. Our last stop was in Seattle, where we had a land and boat tour of that beautiful area. Finally, after three weeks away, we arrived home in San Jose. My mind was filled with so many memories of that jam-packed time that I felt like a veteran of a unique, massive set of experiences that I just couldn't adequately convey to those who weren't with us, as much as I tried.

New Life in Hollywood and a Long-Term Good Friend

In late August I packed my belongings, said a sad and grateful goodbye to my grandparents, and took the train to Los Angeles to join my mother. She had found a small apartment on North Cherokee Street, just a few blocks from Hollywood High School, in the lower-priced flatlands beneath the Hollywood Hills. Rich children lived in the hills; their children met with the flatlands children in the halls of Hollywood High. With seventeen hundred students, class and ethnic lines were blurred. Most film studios had moved away from Hollywood by then, but some actors and directors still lived there, and the film world's residue still showed itself in the school emblem, "The Sheiks," adopted from a famous old Hollywood film. It also showed up sometimes in the used books I had in class. One had Lana Turner's name in it. I also discovered that Carol Burnett went to Hollywood High when I was there.

The four-building campus was arranged more like a small college campus than a normal one-building high school. On the first day of school, I walked the six blocks from home to get there, dressed as casually and nondistinctive as I could so I would fit in. When I found my tenth-grade English class, I remember sitting at the back, on the right side, where I wouldn't be conspicuous. Sitting next to me on my left was a short, studious-looking guy wearing glasses. Before the class started, we introduced ourselves. His name was Charles Krahmalkov. He soon became my best friend. I remember meeting his parents in their small apartment in the flatlands, not far from where I lived. His father was a character actor who, judging from their small apartment and what I was told about the gaps between his acting jobs, was making just enough money to survive. Charlie's very loving mother had a permanent tremor in one arm.

Charlie and his family were Jewish, as were many of the students at the school, although not nearly as many as at nearby Fairfax High, where at least 80 percent of the students were Jewish and the school virtually closed down on Jewish holidays. I felt a special connection with Judaism because of my father's conversion when he married his Jewish second wife, Naomi. Their three children, my siblings, were being raised in the Jewish tradition.

Charlie was very scholarly and had a loose friendship with a handful of other bright, rather nerdy boys in our high school class. They occasionally invited me to join them at the home of Eugene Epstein, whose father owned the huge Pickwick Bookshop on Hollywood Boulevard. What would such nerds like to do when they gathered together? Well, this group played charades and drank Coke. I managed to be an equal with them in charades. However, most of them were heavy into math and science, which I wasn't. I took as few such courses as I could get away with and still get into a good college. Charlie once told me that they looked down on me accordingly. One of them later became an astrophysicist, and I think most of the others ended up in equally scientific positions.

Fortunately for my ego, Charlie was a little more upbeat about my academic capacity (at least outside science and math). At the end of the school year, he signed my copy of the annual school yearbook: "To my brilliant colleague and associate professor of A10 English," which was obvious hyperbole but typical of his formal style and respect for me that would mark our lifelong relationship. I never considered myself his intellectual equal, though. Eventually he became a professor of ancient Near Eastern languages at the University of Michigan at Ann Arbor, where he would remain for the rest of his career.

When the first boys foods class was offered at Hollywood High, Charlie, along with Bob Nussbaum, another one of the nerdy student circle, decided to take it. I wish I had also, although I would have hoped for a better outcome. When the two of them had a team assignment to bake a chocolate cake, they forgot to add any kind of leavening. When they opened the oven and took out the cake, the teacher came by and saw a collapsed, flat glob. She exclaimed, "That's an F cake if I've ever seen one!" It was a humbling experience for what were likely two straight A students.

Actually, I did a fair amount of cooking at home. My mother was busy: her PhD classes at UCLA; the First Congregational Church's young adult group; dating; and eventually the University of Southern California's mental health center, where she worked. I was left at home many times to make my own dinner. My mother's cooking, I'm afraid, wasn't much better than mine, so I wasn't missing much. I didn't resent having to cook and eat alone so often. As with everything in my life so far, it was just something I accepted—something that needed to be done.

Becoming a Serious Tennis Player

A different part of my high school years was the world of sports. I took tennis lessons at the Los Angeles Tennis Club (for which you didn't have to be a member). I made it on to the school tennis team. I practiced almost daily at a public court near our apartment, mostly with my new friend Harry Ohls, who was also on the school team and whose father was a tennis pro.

In my second year, just before the school tennis season began, I went tobogganing with some friends in the nearby San Bernardino mountains. Three of us rode in one long toboggan down the very steep chute. I sat in the back, with my legs held in the lap of the person in front of me. At the bottom of the chute, when we were going at top speed, we hit an ice bump that led the person holding my legs to let one of them go as he reached out to save his jacket in his lap from falling off the toboggan. My right leg fell outside of it, twisted backward, for the rest of the long run down.

That led to a full leg cast for a torn cartilage and a broken knee bone, and to walking on crutches for at least a month. I remember the threat I felt all the many times I had to go up and down the school staircases to get to my classes. A full leg cast meant that my right leg couldn't bend at all. Especially when I went downstairs, every step down was preceded by bending my waist so my crutches could touch the next step below, and then hopping down with my left leg to the next step, hoping that my plastered right leg could tilt down to the step and not tilt me forward beyond my crutches, which would lead to an uncontrollable fall on hard marble stairs. Anyone bumping into me on the crowded stairs could also create that disaster. I was fortunate that neither ever happened. The doctor thought I would have a permanent limp, but when the plaster cast was sawed off, I was very grateful to discover that I could walk normally.

The next year I returned to the tennis team, and for two straight years we won the Los Angeles public high school tennis championship. I wasn't proud of my playing, though. I could play well in practice, but in competition I cramped up far too often. I felt the pressure to win for the team too strongly, so I couldn't relax and play my best. When I proudly wore my letterman sweater to school, with two crossed tennis racquets in the middle of a big red *H*, I secretly felt I didn't deserve it for my cramped playing. I felt the sweater at best showed my *potential* to be a good player if only I could play in school competitions as well as I could in practice. It also expressed my sheer love of the game.

Sports Editor of the High School News

In my junior year, I took Mr. Thorpe's journalism class. I secretly hoped that I might be made assistant editor of the school newspaper in my senior year. I knew that my friend and classmate Marty Hind would be better as editor and I would be as good as anyone else in the class as assistant editor. Well, I didn't get the position. Mr. Thorpe instead gave me the job of sports editor. That meant writing all the articles about school teams for the weekly newspaper. I was crestfallen, but I took it on.

Among other things, being sports editor required me to go to all the football games and take notes about who did what when. One night game was especially hard to follow. I took some friends with me in my mother's car to Canoga Park High School to cheer on the team and give me some company. We arrived in a fog so thick that it blurred the field. I had to run back and forth along the sidelines for the whole game, pen and paper in hand, trying to see the numbers on the jerseys of players who were moving the ball down the field and scoring. My raucous car mates made it worthwhile, though. I was a little worried about what my mother would say if she saw the remains of the lipstick hearts on the passenger side-view mirror spontaneously drawn by Felicity Bach, a classmate whose bold freedom I attributed to the liberating conditioning I imagined she had from her famous British psychologist father.

I dutifully did what I had to do as sports editor that year, but I never really enjoyed it. I wanted to cover so many other events happening at the school, but that was not to be. I compensated a bit with a different kind of journalism with my old New York classmate David Redpath, with whom I had kept in contact. He had created a monthly pamphlet that he sold for ten cents, with articles about all kinds of things. I volunteered to be his "Hollywood reporter," writing articles on what life was like in Hollywood and the larger Los Angeles world. That entrepreneurial adventure lasted for about a year.

My required physical science class was taught by Mr. Burleigh, who I will never forget. He was a naval captain in World War II, which had ended just five years earlier. He brought his sense of military authority and order with him. Every time we had a test, he would have us sit according to what grade we had gotten on the test. He would announce everyone's grade. Once, I didn't hear what grade he gave me, so I went up to his desk to wait for him to come back from talking to a student at the door. I needed to get to my next class and he was still at the door when I noticed his grade book was open on the desk. I decided to look for my grade so I could leave. He saw me do that and furiously strode back to the desk, berating me for looking at the grade book. For doing that, he said he would change the A he had given me to a B. There was a separate grade category called "deportment," which is where I should have been penalized for such an infringement, but he chose punishing my grade instead.

Culturally, these were the quiet '50s. You didn't challenge teachers, and in any case, I was too shocked and too much in a hurry to get to my next class to say anything. As it turned out, that lowered grade ended up lowering my grade for the whole course, which was doubly painful because I wanted to go to Stanford and every grade counted toward or away from that realization.

An amazing follow-up note: Forty-five years after that, my wife, Mary, and I moved into a house in Bethesda, Maryland. Our neighbor across the street was David Burleigh, and he was from California. I quickly discovered that he was Mr. Burleigh's son and was two years ahead of me at Hollywood High! David had been a career navy officer like his dad, and I saw his father in him. When I told him what his father had done in that class, he said he readily understood how his father could have done that. We ended up being good neighbors, as long as we didn't talk politics.

A very different teacher than Mr. Burleigh was my physiology teacher, Ms. Vollmer. She sat us in pairs at double desks so we could help each other. Her class was in the building close to the busy intersection of Sunset Boulevard and Highland Avenue. Whenever a hook-and-ladder fire truck zoomed by outside, sirens blaring, she would stop whatever she was doing, run to the window, and pull up the blinds, screaming in delight and jumping up and down. Along with such ecstatic outbursts, she was a great teacher.

An Embarrassment as a Debater

My most embarrassing moment in the classroom was during an inter-school extemporaneous speech contest, where the only audience in the classroom was the judge and my friend Charlie, who was an accomplished debater and speaker. Charlie was there basically to support me. The judge had given me a subject; the rules allowed me only a few minutes to prepare my response.

I can't remember the subject, but I vividly remember what happened in the middle of my speech. Charlie suddenly burst out laughing, and I knew I hadn't said anything funny. I was completely perplexed. I knew his laughing wouldn't help me with the judge. I managed to keep talking until my time was up. Afterward, in the hallway, I asked him what possessed him to start laughing. He told me that he suddenly realized what the word was that I had used repeatedly but that he didn't understand. The word was *chaos*. I knew what it meant, but I don't think I had ever heard anyone speak it. I pronounced it phonetically: "CHA-os," not the correct "KAY-os." I think he thought I was using some esoteric Chinese word, and when he suddenly realized what the word was, he couldn't help but to burst out with a good laugh.

I was properly humiliated, but he apologized, and I forgave him. (I should have thanked him for saving me from continuing to badly mispronounce that word!) Needless to say, I didn't help our team win that contest. I have no memory of other contests, but I somehow managed to get elected to the school chapter of the National Forensic League.

Continuing Musical Appreciation

I continued a daily habit of piano playing that fed a different part of my psyche. Once, Charlie brought over his violin to my apartment and at one point we exchanged instruments and managed to eke out a crude version of the melody to Beethoven's *Ode to Joy*. In junior high school, where I played piano with the school orchestra, we exchanged instruments occasionally and I screeched out notes on a cello. Charlie built on that primitive stringed-instrument knowledge and helped me translate it to the violin, as I helped him with the piano notes. What we played was really bad, but it kept us humble and laughing.

I found a new piano teacher and played new musical compositions with her (including a little Dave Brubeck jazz), but after a few months other things began to take priority and I stopped, never to be taught piano again (although I kept playing from time to time). I was taught about the history and types of classical music in a wonderful music appreciation course in high school. It wasn't just lectures; it involved listening to recordings of the greatest composers and schools of classical music from the sixteenth to twentieth centuries.

Some popular music moved me, though. From my earliest adolescent piano-playing days, I joined most of the world in collecting certain love songs. They touch a different, tender place in me than most classics. I was especially moved by love songs that were part of a larger story in Broadway musicals, such as "One Hand, One Heart" in *West Side Story*, which still moves me close to tears when I hear it even today. Such songs just melt me into a spongy-hearted romantic.

Gregorian chant in church was a very different kind of music that drew me to a quality of presence that's hard to describe. It has a mysterious, intimate (but not romantic), haunting quality that quieted my mind and opened my heart in awe.

Each night in high school I went to sleep not with music but with poetry. At 10:00 p.m. I tuned into *A Thing of Beauty Is a Joy Forever*, a radio program where poems were read back to back, together lasting for fifteen minutes. It was a wonderful way to drift off to sleep.

My religious life still clung to a Catholic identity. I passed the Blessed Sacrament parish church every day on the way to school. I went to Mass alone on Sundays (my mother going to a Congregational church instead). Sometimes I stopped by during the week just to appreciate the awesome silence and the mystery-carrying sanctuary candle inside its red-glassed holder that symbolized the living Presence. In school I attended the Catholic Newman Club. I was in an "organized religion" holding pattern, but as time went on, Catholicism increasingly faded from my life.

Developing a Strong Conscience

I suppose my Roman Catholic formation helped to explain how strong my conscience was related to the importance of recognizing good from evil. My mother's influence was another contributor, not so much in what she said but in the way she freely yet responsibly seemed to live and in the freedom she gave me to make my own decisions and basically live my own life.

That wasn't hard for her to do because she came to see how I would come around to responsible decisions on my own, as I did when we were in New York. It's easy to trust someone who interiorly really *wants* to be a good person. That's not to say that I didn't semiconsciously realize that there was a certain self-interest in that too, since being responsibly "good" is rewarded by teachers, friends, family, and most everyone else I engaged in life.

I was happy to have moved beyond those rebellious early adolescent times of a few years ago in San Jose, along with dislike of myself in feeling so alienated and judgmental.

Crossing Strong Gender and Cultural Lines

Gender separation was much more real in those days. Outside of classes, I was with boys much more than with girls. At lunch and on the grounds after lunch, girls sat mostly with girls (some in all-girl social clubs) and boys with boys. I practiced tennis almost every day after school with boys, and I was a member of the all-male tennis team. Only girls took home economics classes, and the precedent-breaking boys' foods class, of course, was all boys. Gym classes were strictly separated. Only boys took the required semester of United States Army ROTC. I had male friends over to my apartment and vice versa. Sex was an alive subject, but I don't think nearly so dominant as today. A relative prudishness existed in much of the social culture compared to more recent decades.

Yet over my senior high school years I managed to cross the gender line and get to know well several girls, some of whom I dated. Charlie and I sometimes double-dated, always with the same girls: he with Paula Levin, and me with Jackie Hathaway. In time, Jackie became my steady girlfriend. She was beautiful, artistic, and very reflective about life. I still have a photo of us at the senior prom together. We continued to communicate by mail after I left for college, but in time our relationship gently faded away.

Summertime Life

In the summer between my sophomore and junior years, I briefly worked behind the counter at the local Sears, explaining to customers how to fill out the "Easy Payment Plan" form and then taking their money. That job lasted two days! I was given almost no training for the job. It included mathematical calculations, which I barely comprehended, and even that comprehension blanked out in the face of a customer staring me in the face and asking questions. At the end of the second day I was told not to come back. That was humiliating, but on the other hand, it was certainly a relief.

I found another job pumping gas at a service station on Sunset Boulevard. I had a kind manager, but he had to set me straight when he saw me reading *Thirty Days to a More Powerful Vocabulary* when there were no customers. I needed to look like I was working even when there was no work to do.

I had one disaster in that job: An old man drove up and asked for me to put a quart of oil into his engine. I found the proper quart can that his car needed and plunged a metal funnel into it that allowed the oil to pour out. I turned it upside down in the oil pipe of his engine and left it there. Suddenly I noticed that not much of the oil was going into the pipe; it was spilling out all over his engine. I hadn't pushed the metal funnel completely down into the lid of the can. The man was furious. I felt helpless; the damage was already done. I was lucky that the manager was away at the time and that the man decided to just drive away in a huff. I felt guilty about it and made sure that never happened again.

The station was just a few blocks from Hollywood and Vine, a hub of movie-related activity. Beautiful would-be starlets frequently took to the surrounding streets hoping to be seen by film directors, producers, or influential actors. Ours was one of those streets, and when the manager shouted "Ninety-nine," that was the signal for all employee eyes to look up and see some beauty walking by in high heels and scanty dress. I had many an eyeful that summer! Sometimes I felt sorry for them, knowing how few would ever fulfill their Hollywood dreams.

The next summer I found a job selling programs at the Hollywood Bowl, the famous outdoor theater for symphonic music and other artistic performances. (It was also the place where Hollywood High held its graduation ceremony.) I got a different kind of eyeful in that job, seeing the range of music lovers who showed up at every performance. The rows near the stage were for the rich, and sometimes the famous. It was always a privilege to work those rows because I could depend on some of the rich to tip beyond the price of the program. I also got to hear some good live music that brought me back to those San Jose days when I traveled alone to the civic auditorium for concerts.

Later that summer I took the train alone to Centralia, Illinois, to spend a few weeks again with my Uncle Nick and Aunt Faye. I needed to change trains in St. Louis to get to Centralia, and I had an hour's layover before the second train arrived. I still have a vivid memory of going to the platform and seeing my train slowly *leaving* the terminal, not *arriving*—I had the arrival and leaving times mixed up! I knew the train would pass through the East St. Louis station next, so I hopped into a taxi and implored the driver to drive me there as fast as possible. I arrived just in time to see the train slow down, but it wouldn't stop. I ran alongside it and yelled to a conductor hanging out of one train car to stop and let me board. He didn't respond, and the train slowly kept going, but too fast for me to jump on with my suitcase. I helplessly watched it disappear. I called my uncle and explained what had happened and that I couldn't get another train for four hours. I felt frustrated and mortified. I attribute my nightmares of missing a train or plane for years to come in part to that little traumatic experience.

Centralia might as well have been in East Texas in terms of summer heat and humidity. When I was there a few years before, you'll recall that the only escape was going to air-conditioned Walgreens or the movie theater. Air conditioning now was just beginning to come into homes, but the only room in the house that had it was my aunt and uncle's office. I slept on a couch in the living room, heavy with unrelenting heat day and night, and I slipped into their office for a few minutes of respite whenever I could.

My uncle kept a kennel of hound dogs for hunting. I had never hunted or held a gun in my life. One day he took me into the woods, showed me how to hold his hunting rifle, lined up some glass bottles on a fallen log, and told me to aim the gun at them and shoot. I felt glad the bottles I hit weren't birds or animals.

Uncle Nick followed in his father's footsteps and became an independent oil operator. I accompanied him when he went out to measure how much oil was in the tanks of his wells, as I had done with my granddad in Marshall many years earlier. Some of the wells were in the middle of cornfields; occasionally my uncle would pull some corn cobs off a stalk and that night we would eat the freshest, sweetest corn I've ever tasted.

Apart from these drives to the wells, though, it could be a boring time, especially since there were no young people to pal around with in the neighborhood. Even though the heat was as high as 106 degrees, I would go to the nearby public tennis court almost every day and endlessly practice serving tennis balls on an empty court. I could almost see and certainly feel the humid heat rising from the asphalt court. No one else was crazy enough to be there; it was a sign of my desperation to do something active and out of the house. Inside the house I played a lot of canasta with my aunt. I also watched the Republican National Convention on TV while I was there—my first extended exposure to the rituals of national party politics.

I was drawn in awe many times as I watched the sun mercifully set on those hot days. I had a little camera and took many pictures of them. They brought me as close to a sense of a mysterious larger reality as I would come during that summer.

I recently discovered a diary I had kept on that visit. For the train trip to Centralia, it spends three pages waxing romantically over a beautiful sunset that I saw out the window of the train as the train was passing through Arizona. When the sun had set and I lamented that no stars had appeared to herald the "night life of the sky," my diary declared, "At last! A star has appeared. It is quickly followed by another bright, twinkling gleam—then another—and another! Yes, night has truly come—the signal for life to rest before continuing its weary toil—to sleep beneath the universe which has unveiled itself in all its stellar glory to this humble Earth." I was reminded of my awe described earlier when I slept in the open beneath the Milky Way in that seven-thousand-feet-high meadow in Yosemite National Park.

When a softball game was scheduled in the cooler evening darkness in Centralia, I would go with my uncle to the local softball field where he played on an amateur team. I backed up the shortstop and fielded the balls that got away from him. Occasionally I was allowed to hit a pitch and run around the bases.

Sports are valuable special arenas for people to be involved in the joy, skills, ordering rules, and team community that transcends racial and class lines engendered by each sport. They also can have a vital spiritual dimension. Some years ago, I wrote an article that presents sports as a potential arena of spiritual purpose and contemplative practice.

The climax of that visit to Centralia was a weeklong fishing trip to the Lake of the Woods on the Minnesota-Canadian border. The only times I had ever fished before that trip were with my uncle on a small lake near Centralia. My aunt and uncle had a Nash sedan where the back seats folded down—very advanced for that time—and very needed on this trip. We couldn't find a motel and had to pull off the road and sleep in the car. At one point, my uncle let me drive, even though I had little experience driving; I think Aunt Faye was petrified. It didn't last long. We came to a sharp curve in the road after a few minutes and I was going too fast to make the turn well. We ran off the road onto the gravel shoulder, with brakes screeching. That was the last time I would touch the wheel with them.

When we arrived at the lake, we moved into a rented cabin. The most memorable day there came when my uncle rented a boat and paid a Chippewa Native American guide to go out fishing with us for the day. At lunchtime we stopped at a little island; our guide made a fire on the beach and fried some of the fish we had caught. That was the freshest fish I have ever eaten.

At one point, we portaged our boat across a forested area to fish on another lake. There we were, heavy boat held up over our heads on the trail and swarms of mosquitoes attacking us like an invading army from the sky. With our arms carrying the boat, we could do nothing to defend ourselves except move as fast as we could. We finally reached the other lake, quickly pushed offshore, and paddled until the mosquitoes gave up the chase. Many of them had already feasted on our blood.

It was worth it, though. When we put out our fishing lines, after a while my pole suddenly bent in half and the line was spinning out of the reel at unstoppable speed. Then there was a pause. The fish stopped briefly to rest as I slowly rewound the line, then a huge northern pike surfaced close to the boat. When we managed to get it into the boat, our scale said that it weighed ten pounds. It was the largest fish I had ever caught—and ever would catch. I felt a little guilty because my uncle, an avid and experienced fisherman, never caught one nearly as large on that trip, but I was amazed and quietly proud.

I was always happy to see that whatever we caught, we ate, froze for the future, or gave away to someone who needed them, rather than throwing them away. I could never really appreciate fishing and hunting as "sports," disconnected from need.

The End of High School

In the spring of my senior year, I was accepted at Stanford, where my mother attended and my son would much later receive a master's degree from the School of Education. In those days it wasn't nearly as big a deal to pay for a private university as it is today. My first year's tuition was $1,400, although that was still high enough to exclude many students.

When the Hollywood High senior class yearbook came out and I asked various people to sign mine, I had a wonderful feeling in having been in a school long enough to have made enduring personal friends and a sense of appreciation from others (as I had felt at the end of junior high school in San Jose), as reflected in people's written comments in my book.

It was sad, even a bit traumatic, to be leaving not only the school but my home there to go off yet again to a new place where I knew no one.

That summer of 1953, as a kind of last hurrah with my mother before leaving home for college, she splurged and the two of us went on a three-week whirlwind tour of Europe. We flew to New York and crossed the Atlantic on the USS *United States*'s maiden voyage to Great Britain. I found out that Milton Eisenhower, president of Princeton at the time and brother of Dwight, was aboard. I had the chutzpah to arrange a meeting with him to talk about what he thought was important to care about in my education (or some trumped-up subject like that). He politely met with me, but I can't remember a word he said. He later wrote me a note wishing me well. The other person I remember meeting on the ship was a Catholic priest. I told him I was Catholic but that I had stopped going to church and had a lot of questions about religion. He looked sad and said he would pray for me. In hindsight I expect that was just a routine response for him, but at the time it moved me—a sign that he cared about my spiritual life. He was the first person I remember talking with about my lost faith in those years.

The days flew by in Europe. I empathized with the old movie *If It's Tuesday, This Must Be Belgium*. I had brought a 3D camera and took endless pictures with it. One highlight for me was watching a kindergarten class in Copenhagen, where the kids seemed so happy and the teachers so wisely imaginative in drawing the children through the routines and teachings of the day. Another highlight was taking a funicular train through tunnels to the Jungfraujoch, Europe's highest train station, at the top of a huge snow-covered mountain in Switzerland. At the top was an ice palace and, when the clouds parted enough to see it, a view of the green valley far below. I felt the grandeur and beauty of the earth as never before.

We returned home by plane from Copenhagen, which in 1953 was a very different experience than such a flight would be today. It was a noisy four-propeller plane that made refueling stops in Greenland and Winnipeg in the Canadian province of Manitoba. Even though it was a large passenger plane for its time, it was small by today's standards. By the end of the long twenty-four-hour flight, all of us passengers had become an informal, exhausted extended family.

Once home, I realized what a privilege it was to take such a trip. Overseas travel in those days was much rarer than it is today, given the greater speed and range of opportunities for travel now.

Chapter 3

Expanding Horizons
Stanford

It's early September 1953. I see the sandstone buildings of the Stanford campus looming ahead of my mother's car. We stop at Encina Hall, where all first-year men must live. I say goodbye to my mother and carry my luggage up to my assigned room, anxious to know who my roommates will be. The rooms were made for two people, but housing was short at the time and three students were squashed into each room.

Soon after I moved in, my first roommate, Don Bennett, showed up at the door. The first thing he said to me was, "Are you a Mormon?" If I had said yes, he said he would have turned around and walked out. He was a Presbyterian from Salt Lake City and had been proselytized by Mormons all his life. He couldn't take any more of it. We got along fine that year, even though we didn't have much in common.

My other roommate, Bob Antle, arrived soon after Don. He was from Watsonville, California, a farming community about two hours south of Stanford. He had been on his high school football team and wanted to try out for the Stanford team. Short and strong, he played tackle. About all I can remember of him was his returning exhausted from long football practices. Sadly he didn't make the team, which wasn't surprising given that the Stanford team was a national football powerhouse. I had almost nothing in common with him, and we rarely talked. He was from a different world, and I think he was a little contemptuous of me. My sport was tennis, which was a fluffy sport to a football player like him (even though it's very physically demanding).

I had my own comeuppance with sports. I was arrogant enough to attend tryouts for the freshman tennis team. When I arrived at the courts,

I saw coaches watching incredibly good players. I gave up on the spot. Stanford normally has one of the best tennis teams in the country. I was not in their league.

My athletics in college sometimes meant playing noncompetitive handball or tennis, often with just the "partner" of a backboard. I also took two courses in the athletics department. One was a class in fencing. I had never held a foil in my life and knew nothing about the sport. In a way, I felt like I was reactivating my toddlerhood thrill of sword fighting with a stick, or later in childhood watching the three musketeers duke it out with swords in the movie. Wearing protective masks and vests, fencing is usually harmless, especially dueling with the light, bendable foil (as we did in the class) rather than with sabers or épée. The sport is full of rules, forms of self-protection, and thrusting maneuvers I needed to learn while being ever *en garde*: alert and in dueling position.

I remember the first time I put on a fencing mask and protective vest and picked up a foil. I didn't know which hand to use. I was always ambidextrous, but that didn't mean I could easily alternate use of my hands for everything I did. Over time, each hand was trained to be the dominant hand in doing something. For example, I batted left-handed but threw a ball right-handed; I held a pen with my right hand, but I used a fork with my left hand. Since I had never used my hands for fencing, I had to decide which hand felt most right to hold the foil. I had a terrible time deciding. Both hands felt right—I felt like just holding the foil with both hands. Eventually I decided on my right hand and stuck with it.

My other athletics class was an advanced swimming and life-saving course. It ended with a test in the pool that had to be passed to receive a life-saving certificate. The instructor was a big, heavy guy. The task was to dive in and swim out to him using a special racing stroke where you kept your head out of the water so you could always see the person. When you got up to him, he would drop under the water and you had to go under and put your arm around him in the proper way and swim to the edge of the pool with him in tow.

I was second in line to take the test. I saw the first student swim out, go under the water, and successfully carry the instructor to the edge of the pool. I felt confident I could do that too. When the instructor had gone back to the middle of the pool to pretend drowning, I dove in, swam out, and surface-dived under the water to put my arm around him. This time, though, he had decided to play a panicked drowning person, and he fought me off. I ran out of breath trying to put my arm around his heavy, struggling body; I began struggling in the water myself. I couldn't subdue him and carry him back. It was humiliating, with the whole class watching. Needless to say, I didn't get the certificate. I was grateful for the class, though; I learned a lot.

Only one academic class in the first year was memorable: Western Civilization, which was required of everyone for a full year. Today I expect such a required course would be controversial in many colleges, in its neglect of non-Western civilizations, but at the time it was considered progressive, since so many colleges emphasized American history. It offered more than enough for me at the time—there is a lot to learn about Western civilization, and I had never been exposed in high school to anything beyond elementary American history. I did well enough to be one of the students selected out of the large first-quarter class (Stanford has a three-quarter rather than two-semester system) to be invited to spend the last two quarters in the living room of the young professor's home for an informal, seminar-like environment with students who were really interested in the subject. Instead of taking tests, we wrote papers.

I spent a lot of time at my desk and in the library that first year (actually every year). I was a relatively slow reader. When I tried to skim a book, I often couldn't keep it up, because I would find myself interested in what I was reading and I would slow down. I intended to go on to graduate school and that meant I needed to bear down in my course work and get decent grades. That motivation also pressed me to *force* myself to study, many times when I didn't want to, because I was facing deadlines for papers and tests. My mind would revolt often, and I would have to repeat reading paragraphs because I just couldn't pay attention for long periods. That resolve to hang in with the reading and writing papers could be painful and obsessive. I was willing to pay that price for the sake of mastering the subject matter as well as I could. Writing course papers was easier than straight reading and being tested on it, because papers involved some creativity on my part.

Spring of my first year brought fraternity and eating club "rush" time. Sororities were banned due to a suicide in 1941 and other problems, but women could choose to live in ex-sorority houses by lottery. The seven men's eating clubs had come into being in 1901, preceding fraternities. In my time, they became an alternative to heavily drinking, blackballing (the power of just one person's negative vote to keep out a candidate for membership), hazing, and racial discrimination in fraternities. You still had to be voted into an eating club, but only a majority could keep you out. The clubs made a point of asserting the individual freedom of each member, together with affirming the social values of a racially mixed membership and of supporting one another's academic seriousness. A dormitory next door, Toyon Hall, was reserved for their members, although they didn't have to live in it.

Each club had its own dining/meeting room and kitchen, its own cook (who sometimes was a member in need of the salary), and its own social activities, including such things as building floats for college parades, intraclub athletic events, conversations with invited faculty members, and collectively serenading women at their dorms who had just been "pinned" to a member (i.e., a declared steady relationship with someone). Most of the social life involved informal relationships with other members over meals and meetings in the dining room.

If you didn't get into or want to get into a fraternity or eating club, you could become an "independent," for whom there also was a special dormitory. The good news for this third option was that those students were not discriminated against by the eating club or fraternity members. It was a socially valid and dignified choice respected by most others, certainly by me.

Even though I spent so much time studying, I liked socializing with other people—girls on dates and men in my freshmen dorm and both in classes. I knew, though, that I didn't like what I understood fraternity life to be, and I didn't know much about eating clubs or anyone in them. I was surprised, then, to receive an invitation to visit El Capitan, recommended, I found out later, by the upper-class resident living on my floor of Encina Hall.

When I visited El Capitan, I liked the range of people I met, including five Asians from Hawaii, an African American from New York (African Americans were rare at Stanford then), some brilliant geeks (all club grade point averages were higher than the school average), some extraverted and funny socializers, and people majoring in many different fields. I came to like the prospect of having a steady place for socializing with a broad range of people (although only men) and yet with personal freedom to have a social life outside the club. I was voted in.

Over my years in El Capitan, I had a special relationship with Ralph Moore, the one member I continued to have long contact with after graduation. He was a faithful liberal Christian with a caring but laid-back personality. He didn't push his faith. It was a time in my life when I was a seeker, not a finder, so I found him a good person with whom to explore my religious questions. He ended up going to Union Seminary in New York City.

Sometime during that first year at Stanford, I became active in a fraternity: Alpha Phi Omega, a service fraternity for people who had been in the Boy Scouts and wanted to continue together the Scouting "service" emphasis. I felt a little uneasy about joining, since I thought many other students might see that as a little regressive. I think Scouting was a lot more "done" in those days than now, though, and the fraternity attracted a lot of members. The pledge class the year I became president had forty-five students in it.

Among our many service projects was acting as a volunteer tour guide for visitors to Stanford. That was my favorite job. I was proud of my school, and I loved to show it off to visitors. (I think that feeling stemmed from a sense of being an insider, a feeling of "belonging," so important following my earlier migrating life.) I, wearing my Stanford jacket, would meet visitors under the main arch at the university entrance and walk them around to different sites of interest, wanting to impress them with its beauty and special places, such as the university chapel right in the middle of the original campus.

The school buildings are concentrated in the middle of the huge seven-thousand-acre campus. Those acres wind up from the flats of Palo Alto into the foothills beyond, just a half hour's drive to the Pacific Ocean. The weather in Palo Alto is as good as it gets anywhere year-round, unless you like snow. Little rain, bright blue skies, warm and dry days, cool evenings. Some early mornings are shrouded in fog, but even that I found refreshing. When the fog lifted by midmorning and the sun suddenly showed itself, the contrast was striking.

My school pride also showed itself at football games. I went to all of them, as I recall, always wearing a white shirt needed to be in the cheering section. Under the seats in that section hung square reflecting sheets of cardboard, which we held up to spell out different words and images at halftime. One game I remember was against UCLA, which some of my high school friends who were students at UCLA came up to see. UCLA won the game seventy-two to nothing! It was the worst defeat in Stanford's history. My friends really rubbed it in afterward.

The Stanford halftime marching band was famous for its spontaneous antics, improvisations, and dress, which defied all the conformist norms of many school bands.

In my second year of college, I had to decide on a major. At first I thought I would choose psychology, but I finally decided on anthropology. Unlike the other behavioral sciences, anthropology deals with everything in a culture, not just a slice of it. It felt inclusive, seeing various aspects of culture in relation to one another, showing how each aspect of a culture influences and mirrors other dimensions of that culture. All world cultures were fair game for study, especially nonliterate ones.

Anthropology as a major field of study was just "growing up" in those days. Stanford had recently made it an independent department, separate from sociology. A well-known New Zealand anthropologist, Felix

Keesing, a specialist in Maori culture, had been hired to head the newly independent department. I gave those courses my all, out of intrinsic interest and after deciding that I wanted to get a PhD in the field and make it my vocation. I had a sense that anthropology brings us closest to understanding human communal reality in its enormous variety and interdependence.

Anthropology also included the study of past cultures and their remains—that is archaeology. The most unique course I had at Stanford was an archaeology class that involved going to a recently discovered Native American burial site in the mudflats of San Francisco Bay. It hadn't been "dug" yet—it was our task to begin the dig. With twine we laid out square sectors of the site, and each student was responsible for carefully digging with a trowel in their sector. Eventually we began to uncover human remains and some artifacts that were buried with them. Bert Gerow, our professor, helped us decipher and speculate on some qualities of the centuries-old culture, based on our findings.

In hindsight I feel guilty about that archaeological dig. At that time, there simply wasn't the sensitivity among behavioral scientists to sacred sites, those buried there, and their living Native American descendants. I don't think we had a moral right to do what we did, at least without consent of their tribal descendants, and to my knowledge we had not sought to find any of them from the local Native American reservations and associations. At the very least we could have been respectfully silent together for a minute in honor of those buried there.

The Korean War was in full swing when I went to college, and like many other students, I chose to join an ROTC program when I arrived. I chose naval ROTC (NROTC) as an avenue to participate in the war if drafted, rather than being told how to participate by a draft board. My father's experience as a naval officer during World War II influenced my choice. (Actually, he was in the Coast Guard, but that was assimilated into the navy during that war.)

Stanford gave three units of credit for the program each term. We wore cadet uniforms for outside marching drills. The cap they gave me was too tight for my big head, but I wasn't able to get a larger one. We marched with unloaded rifles and learned to obey commands such as "Present arms," "Parade rest," and "About face." We were told to always start marching on the left foot, and we were taught how to halt together. We also learned to aim and fire revolvers at the shooting range. In classes we learned such things as how to mathematically figure out the aim of a ship's guns so that it accounted for the movement and tilting of the ship. Before graduating we needed to have had math through trigonometry. I needed two courses to get to that point, which I took at Los Angeles City College over two summers. I knew advanced math would be challenging for me and I didn't want my likely low grade to be on my Stanford record. I worked hard in those courses, and I usually understood what was taught, but I just couldn't retain it. What I learned would just quickly dissolve. Even with tutorial help, I couldn't do better than a C+, but at least I passed.

Life in Naval Officers Training Corp

During the second year of NROTC, we were taken on an overnight training cruise in a US Navy destroyer escort, docked at the naval station in San Francisco Bay. That was a stomach-churning adventure. The ship was narrow and light compared to larger naval ships, so waves easily tilted us forward and back and side to side. Once outside San Francisco Bay, the near-in Pacific waters were very rough. We bunked in a crowded dormitory of the ship that night, not knowing whether we would fall out of our cots. The one time my photo ever appeared in the Stanford student newspaper was the week after we returned, where two or three others and I were photographed onboard, talking together (probably bolstering one another's courage to hold on and hold out). That little voyage did not endear me to the thought of possibly spending weeks or months on such a ship in the future.

What really terminated my time with the navy, though, was a moral crisis in the fall of my third year. I took a course on social ethics from a religion and philosophy professor, and I concluded that I basically was a pacifist. I wrote a paper on that subject for the course. In an NROTC classroom that fall, we were shown a film of Japanese fighter planes being shot down by naval ships during World War II. Classmates shouted anti-Japanese slogans and cheered every time a plane went down. I just couldn't take part in that cheering, especially now that the war was ended and we were at peace with Japan.

That was the final blow for me. I went to the office of the NROTC commander, a navy lieutenant. I explained to him my newfound pacifism and my desire to drop out of NROTC after two years. I expected a hostile response. Instead, he shocked me by empathizing with my request. He said if he had to do it over again, he might well do what I was doing. Unfortunately, if I had come to him just two weeks earlier, he could have backdated my withdrawal, but he couldn't now, and he had to write me up in the record in a reprimanded way for my leaving the program.

So that was that. I felt my integrity affirmed in my newly declared pacifism. Actually, the only thing I ever really felt good about in the NROTC program was marching well! Having left the program, my draft status changed to the exemptions given undergraduates. Once I graduated, though, I would be subject to the Korean War draft.

Further Life at Stanford

Only five other courses stay in my memory from college days. One was a course by a renowned historian of Chinese culture, where the professor was a student's dream. He cared about his students, he was penetrating and clear about Chinese culture, and he had the special gift of always being able to end his lecture just as the class-ending bell rang. The worst course I remember was an Introduction to Sociology class by a tenured professor who was so disrespectful of students that all his lectures consisted of his simply reading from his own published sociology book, which already was required reading. Class attendance quickly dropped. I soldiered on, despite my boredom, hoping he might eventually say something that wasn't in the book. He never did.

The third course was what today might be called "science for dummies." It was a yearlong course that included introductions to chemistry, physics, and geology, meant to be a gift to non-science majors in a school that had very many, very smart science majors. One of those three, chemistry, was almost my downfall. I had a partner in the chemistry lab, and we had an assignment to do something that I simply did not understand. For the first and only time in my academic career, I cheated. I copied what he wrote and handed it in. I hoped that my lab partner hadn't noticed my copying. If he did, he didn't do what the school honor code said he should do if he saw someone cheating—that is, start tapping his pencil for all to hear. I never saw anyone cheat nor heard any pencil tapping. Most students at Stanford were smart and well motivated; they didn't need to cheat. There was a tradition of trust that included the professor leaving the room during any test given. I valued getting a decent grade on my record enough to violate that trust. *Mea culpa!* When it came to the physics and geology sections of that course, I somehow understood them well enough and was never tempted to cheat. I loved the concreteness of the geology section, except for the field trip we took to identify rocks amid a hayfield to which I was allergic—I spent the whole time sneezing.

The fourth special course was an introduction to Shakespeare. The teacher, one of the few women on the faculty (keep in mind this was the pre-feminist '50s), was considered a fantastic educator but incredibly tough. I didn't trust that I would be up to her standards, where very good students could still end up with a C, so I audited the course rather than take it for credit. She was brilliant and indeed demanding, requiring complete attention to her in class. Once she saw a student whisper to another student; she immediately gave a penetrating glance to the student and firmly said, "You, OUT!" She retired in my senior year, after decades of teaching. A special appreciation ceremony for her nearly filled the school auditorium. After saying a few things, she made a deep Shakespearian bow and walked off the stage with great dignity.

The last course I especially remember—modern literature—was in the final quarter of my senior year. I had saved taking it until the end, because

I didn't have confidence I could do well in a course I knew so little about (just as I saved statistics for that quarter), and I knew my final quarter grades wouldn't be on my transcript that would help determine getting into a good graduate anthropology program. I really loved the course. It mostly involved reading famous novelists of the last 150 years or so. I came to see what a rich and imaginative depiction of human life, feelings, values, and behavior showed themselves in good novels (and poetry also). It felt so different from the more impersonally abstract, analytical way the behavioral sciences approached knowledge. The complexity of emotions and intuitive insight had a special place in the literature we read, and I really appreciated that.

The course grade was largely determined by a paper we had to write comparing any two novelists we had read in the course. I chose to compare J. D. Salinger's modern *Catcher in the Rye* with Johann Wolfgang von Goethe's *The Sorrows of Young Werther* (published in 1774). I had no confidence in the quality of what I had written and thought I would get a C or at best a B- on my paper. I was dumbfounded to receive an A+! I immediately regretted that I had let my obsession with taking only courses that would help me get into a graduate anthropology program deny me the good literature courses I could have taken earlier. I especially regretted that I had not recognized the value of the literary mind and heart sooner.

My dating life in college played the field. I came to really like one girl. I fantasized about going steady with her, and just before asking her, she told me that she was dropping out of college and becoming engaged to someone in her hometown who I had never heard her mention. I took another girl I liked to some event off campus, where someone collapsed unconscious on the floor. I immediately put my Boy Scout training to work: I laid the person out on their back, put their legs up on a turned-over chair to help bring blood to their brain, and other things I can't remember now. My date was so impressed that she later fell into my arms with gusto!

I took one girl to dances often because she was so light-footed and radiant on the dance floor. I remember once when the outdoor dance floor was almost clear of people late in the evening, with the stars and moon shining brightly overhead. The orchestra was playing waltz music. I led her in some wild, sweeping waltz steps that swirled us around the whole floor—a wonderful feeling of mutual flowing presence.

I had had a few ballroom dancing lessons in the past, but I was never able to swing dance. I somehow "thought" too much while trying to do it, and any dancer knows that good dancing needs you to let go of thought and let the rhythm and body carry you. I tended to think too much in all my dancing, but somehow I had freed from my self-conscious thinking and just exuberantly let go in that waltzing beneath the stars.

During the spring vacation of my second year, I went camping in Death Valley National Park in southeastern California with Ed Reel, a fellow member of El Capitan from Texas. Death Valley has the lowest elevation in the country (just an hour or so away is Mount McKinley, which has the highest elevation). It's incredibly hot in the summer, but in the spring it's still tolerable. We drove there in my car, which had risky retread tires on it. When we reached the park, we veered off to a gravelly, dry creek bed and drove in it for a few miles. When we came back out onto a highway and gained speed, we felt the car tilt and I quickly slowed down, just before a sinking tire would have exploded. After changing the tire, we drove miles and miles through a desolate landscape, looking for a place where we could lay out our sleeping bags for the night. Eventually we found some large, flat rocks on which to camp. Fortunately we had sandwiches and fruit with us, since there was almost nowhere in that huge park to buy anything, certainly not in the area where we stopped.

When we crawled into our sleeping bags, with a little anxiety about desert scorpions and rattlesnakes in the area, I was reminded once again of that time I slept in Tuolumne Meadows in Yosemite. The sky was awesomely alive with shining stars and planets in the total darkness of the park. I had a sense of incredible vulnerability in my little unsheltered sleeping bag amid the overwhelming grandeur of the sky, reinforced by the still blackness of the desert surrounding us. I felt we were at the mercy of mysterious, unseen forces that allowed our fragile, exposed bodies to live undisturbed through the night. When daybreak came, I was grateful they had let us be.

    The one other experience I remember from that trip was a long drive we took across Death Valley into Nevada. The topography still was desert, but we were in old mining territory. We went onto a dirt side road and discovered an abandoned ghost town, complete with fallen-down buildings, cooking pots, and other signs of former human life. Nearby was a mining shaft and small fragments of a beautiful blue ore that had been mined there. It felt as if we had made a rare discovery, since there were no signs that any living human being had been there recently, and we never ran into any other car or human settlement on the road. Our imaginations took off, reconstructing what life must have been like there. We took a few small samples of the ore with us.

Chapter 4

Summer European Adventures and Back to Stanford

Lausanne

I had the opportunity of spend the following summer of 1955 mostly in Switzerland in the *Cours de Vacances* (Vacation Course) at the University of Lausanne. Lausanne is a city in the French-speaking part of Switzerland. I studied French throughout senior high school and my first year of college, but I never really learned conversational French. I wanted to be able to have a second language that I could speak as well as read. I had come to believe that you really need to live in a country that speaks the language in order to speak it well.

Lausanne is built on a hill sloping up from Lake Geneva, with the Swiss Alps soaring up on the other side of the lake. I had trusted that I would find a pension—a boardinghouse for students who, like me, would be attending the *Cours de Vacances*—when I arrived. After spending the first night in a hotel, I spent the next day scouring the city for pensions. The one that really drew me was run by Madame Junod, the wife of a university history professor. Unfortunately it was fully booked. The next morning I called and pleaded with her for a room. After a pause, she said she would do me a favor. Her home was full up, but she said the owner of the house across the street had a room available where I could stay, but I would have all my meals in the Junod house.

I took her up on it immediately, checked out of the hotel, and wound my way up Avenue Victor Ruffy to number 22, the pension's address. That and the house across the street would be my home for most of the summer. The Junods had two teenage children, Philippe and Danielle, who along with their parents ate meals with us and the other boarders around a huge dining room table. At my first meal there that night, and over the course of the summer, I was surrounded by students from different European countries—Sweden, Norway, Germany, the Netherlands, Great Britain, Italy, Greek Cyprus—plus several Americans besides myself.

We were all there for the *Cours de Vacances* and to practice conversational French at the pension, which was strictly enforced by Madame Junod. If you spoke a word of any language but French, she would shake her piggy bank on the table and yell, "*Vingt centimes, monsieur* (or *mademoiselle*)!"—that was the twenty-cent penalty. Meals were a serious business. We had to be dressed properly at the table, including coat and tie for men.

In my room across the street, often I was awakened in the morning by the housekeeper, Madame Jeanne Favre. She opened my door in the morning and with a beautiful smile on her face loudly sang to me in French: "*Bonjour, Monsieur Tilden; comment allez-vous ce matin?*" (How are you this morning?) I say "singing" because Swiss French is very lilting; words rise and fall almost as though they're being sung—at least that's the way she spoke it. She knew no English, so I had to speak in French while still half-asleep.

Every weekday morning I spent at the university began by listening to lectures (in French) on French culture, followed by a French conversation class. My best conversation of the summer, though, was in the pension with Professor Junod. We were alone, and he began a long talk about Swiss history. I never could understand someone speaking in French to me nearly as well as I could make myself understood speaking in French to someone else. In this conversation with Professor Junod I was shocked that I could understand just about everything he said during that sustained conversation.

On some evenings, a group of us, sometimes including Madame Junod, might go to a French movie in town, which was always a French lesson in itself. On some weekends, a few of us would take the train to nearby towns to get a feel of the many historical churches, castles, and other sites that dotted French-speaking Switzerland (which locally is called *Suisse Roman*).

One Saturday, a group of us, including three professors, took a 7:30 a.m. train to Zermatt in German-speaking Switzerland. A sudden rock landslide covered the tracks before we arrived, and we were forced to walk the last four miles to Zermatt, a small resort town. There we boarded a cable car train that took us up into the Alps to the famous Matterhorn. Rain and fog blocked our view much of the way, but at one point the clouds broke, the sun emerged, and we suddenly saw the awesomeness of the great mountain in all its glory, as well as the bright green valley far below us. After our descent, we encountered another landslide that led to yet another long walk to the train station, a long wait in the dark for a train back to Lausanne, and a bus to the pension from there. I climbed the stairs to my room, fell on my bed, and was out like a light after a very long and amazing day.

I often found myself in sustained English conversations with other students that put me in touch with a lot of European views about education, politics, social values, and religion. Virtually all the European students seemed fluent in English, so French was their third (or fourth) language. The Americans were put to shame, as I think all of us were struggling with French as our second and only other language.

Copenhagen and Germany

One of the students with whom I developed a close relationship was Henning von Wienskowski. He was from Northeim, West Germany, close to the border of still-divided East and West Germany. Henning invited me to spend a few days with him and his family in Northheim during a long break in the *Cours de Vacances*, and then travel to Berlin together, where he taught school. I happily agreed. I bought a German dictionary and grammar book and spent enough time with them in the weeks before the break to gain a beginning grasp of the sentence structure and basic vocabulary. English is partly derived from early Germanic Anglo-Saxon roots, so it was always amazing to find so many familiar German words.

I had already planned to attend an international anthropological conference in Copenhagen at the beginning of the break, and I would go to Germany from there. I was invited to the conference by Robert Spencer, chair of the anthropology department at the University of Minnesota, who was a friend of my mother's. Between lectures I spent a lot of time at meals with him and other anthropologists he knew. One time I asked them how anthropologists personally felt about religion. They said the famous anthropologist E. E. Evans-Pritchard was a practicing Roman Catholic, but they thought that agnosticism was more or less modal among them.

One day a Russian ethnologist asked me to read his English translation of a lecture he was going to give and to correct any grammatical and spelling errors I found, which I gladly did. Papers could only be given in English, German, Spanish, or French. I also helped two French-speaking Belgian professors understand some of the English lectures. As a student, it was nice to feel I could make a little contribution. Many of the papers I found tedious, but all the conversations I had on the side made those days worthwhile. One day I found tickets for a performance of José Greco and his Spanish dancers, which was a welcome change from all the lectures.

When the conference ended, I flew to Hamburg, which like the rest of West Germany was undergoing massive rebuilding projects to recover from the heavy bombings by the Allies during World War II. From there I caught a train to Northeim and was met by Henning, who drove me to his home. I gave his family a bottle of French liqueur as a gift, for which they were particularly grateful—it was very expensive in Northeim and they hadn't had any since before the war.

An East German girl was there, with permission to briefly visit her relatives on the east side of the border. With Henning's translation help, over Rhine wine and pretzels, I had a long talk with her about Communism and the Western democratic system. She wasn't used to such controversial political talk in her sheltered Communist schooling. Henning said I helped open her mind a little to the weaknesses of Communism compared to Western democracies.

Henning's father drove me and Henning in his Volkswagen about ten miles to a mountain that held the largest spring in Europe, continuing then to a large reservoir, passing through many towns and villages. We saw many women and men working in the fields, some riding on bull-driven hay wagons. We finally stopped at the East German border. Barbed wire was strung across the road and stretched out endlessly on both sides. Behind the wire was a cleared area where East German police patrolled, ready to stop attempted escapes into West Germany. It was jolting to feel that behind that fence were millions of people involuntarily trapped in a huge geographical prison. It would be many years before the fence would come down.

The next morning, Henning and I left by train to Hanover. There we boarded a very crowded train to Berlin, a city that was divided into British, American, French, and Russian sectors, surrounded by Communist East German territory. East Germany allowed only two trains a day to come to Berlin from Hanover. At the East German border, we stopped. An East German policeman came aboard, along with a Russian guard. Each of us was required to pay the equivalent of twenty-five dollars for the right of passage to Berlin (a lot of money at that time). My passport was thoroughly reviewed.

We arrived in Berlin's new train station, opening into a new city emerging from the hard labor of rebuilding crews that worked in shifts twenty-four hours a day. Berlin was rising fast from its devastating wartime ruins. All the rubble was being piled onto one nearby mountain, to be made into a ski run. The city government and the US Marshall Plan were financing the reconstruction. I will never forget the disciplined, determined energy of Berliners to build a new Germany that I glimpsed in those few days.

The next day we walked to downtown Berlin and took a two-hour bus tour of West and East (Communist-controlled) Berlin. Many bullet-scarred walls were proof of how much street-to-street fighting happened in the final fall of the city to the Allies. Our guide made many anti-Eastern remarks along the route. Henning was disgusted at the appearance of the Eastern zone, which he remembered once was so beautiful.

After the bus tour we visited the very new Free University of Berlin, where a mental health conference was going on over which the famous American anthropologist Margaret Mead presided. We passed American military barracks along the way, and a serene small forest. Later we took a bus to the Radio Free Berlin tower. In a beautiful oval garden there we walked to the eternal flame for peace, justice, and freedom.

Accompanied by a beautiful sunset, we returned to Henning's school. The next day I sat in on a small French class and talked to the students about the American standard of living, culture, and universities. I was surprised that there wasn't much discipline in that classroom, although overall the school was run with many strict rules.

The next day Henning drove me to the Tempelhof Airport to board a plane back to Switzerland. I felt very grateful for the opportunity to absorb a firsthand sense of how that resilient and still divided nation was evolving.

In the second phase of the *Cours de Vacances*, I found the classes slow and boring. During the class I wrote, "In school here, I'm reminded of all the waste of time I felt in certain high school classes. I can better understand now how the motivation and initiative of some high school students is stifled. What a grind it can be!"

During free time, I visited ancient Swiss villages with Roger Watson, who was a Cambridge pre-med student. One day we spent four hours talking about our similar views of religion and what we felt about the meaning of life. We also talked about British socialized medicine and education. He was very critical of his private high school, where students were beaten and courses, such as Latin, were required because of tradition. There were no broad course requirements at Cambridge and Oxford; you took only those that were needed for your chosen field, which was overseen by your tutor. If your tutor was disinterested in your work, you really were left handicapped and less inspired to study.

One Sunday Roger and I attended the Sunday worship service at St. Francois, a very old Swiss Calvinist Protestant church. There were young people there, but in the minority. One minister calmly gave us a basic understanding of the biblical lessons, then another one gave an emotional sermon in French that I couldn't understand. A woman behind us offered her hymnal, which was helpful because we sang six hymns during the service that I found inspiring. That was the only religious service I remember attending in Switzerland. I liked it, but my religious consciousness was still basically in neutral at that point, an attitude reinforced by most of the students around me.

When it finally came time to end my time at the pension, I was reluctant to leave. I had come to know so many students there from around Europe, and Madame Junod had been so kind and involved with us. On my last morning, she saw to it that we ate ham and eggs for breakfast, in my American honor, rather than only the usual croissant. I took a bus to Geneva and then a plane to London, where I would spend my final week in Europe.

London

I took a bus from the London airport to Waterloo terminal and a taxi to the Mascot Hotel, which was old and small, with run-down rooms, but it fit my budget. I felt happy to be there and have a chance to get a feel of that great city. After dinner at the hotel, I took the first of many long walks that week, this one to Piccadilly Circus. It was very crowded, being a central plaza of downtown London. Many Indians and Africans were on the streets. I returned to the hotel exhausted.

The next day I learned was the first day without rain in a month—a good omen for my time there. After breakfast I joined a formal tour of the British Parliament, including the two Houses (which still showed serious war damage) and the Royal Chambers. We heard about many Parliamentary traditions, such as a formal bag in which to put petitions to the government, and the rule that neither the Sovereign (king or queen) nor a member of the House of Lords was allowed into the House of Commons without permission. There was a special chapel for use by the members of Parliament.

The next day I managed to get a ticket for the Suez Canal debates in the Strangers' Gallery. I was amazed at the friendliness and informality of both sides in such a formal country, which contrasted with the rather pompous formal entrance procession of the speaker. There was much laughter on both sides, and much lounging—with feet up on tables. It sounded little removed from a college debate atmosphere, except more relaxed and more fun, despite the seriousness of the issues. Winston Churchill was present both days, but he never spoke, even when he was attacked as "still an empire builder."

Through a contact, I had dinner with a London doctor and his wife. He lamented what he saw as the inefficiency and inadequate funding of Britain's socialized medical system; he was spending a lot of time looking in medical journal ads for doctors in the US and Canada. His wife said she would rather their daughter marry a Canadian woodsman than a pimply London bank clerk. They didn't like the restrictive London environment for raising children, symbolized by the "Keep Off the Grass" signs in its parks. When I returned to the hotel I reflected on how alluring the US and Canada must be for many Europeans at that time, symbolizing greater freedom, space, and a fresh start, especially after a time of destructive war and the austerities involved for everyone during and after it.

The next day, cloudy as usual, I took the train to Cambridge and walked around town for an hour, finding that colleges of the university were spread out all over the city. After much searching I finally found Trinity College, where my Lausanne Greek-Cypriate friend Dennis Severis was a student. The buildings were very old; every seam of their structures felt seeped with tradition. All the students were wearing Oxford gowns, as they had been doing for centuries.

I found Dennis's room, but no one was there. I hadn't been able to contact him ahead of time to tell him I was coming. The door was open, though, and I took the liberty to see what a Cambridge student's digs (two to a room) looked like. Besides separate bed and study rooms, it included a fireplace, a small bar, a couch and lounge chairs, and a fancy bow and arrow hanging on the wall. I could feel the old upper-class origins of the space in these luxuries, along with the special employees available to take care of the rooms and serve the students in other ways. Now Cambridge is a more democratic mix of top students from around the world.

On Sunday I went to my first-ever Anglican Church service. It was on the evangelical rather than Catholic end of that church's tradition. The congregation was a mixture of ages and ethnicities, but it was sparse. The sermon was given by an Indian missionary, who told the story of a frustrated nine-year-old Christian girl in a Hindu school after years in a Christian one. She wanted to read the Bible, but she wasn't allowed to. The story reflected a time when positive interfaith relations were far from the norm.

When it came time for intercessory prayer, a long list of church and sociopolitical situations was included, beginning with prayer for the Queen. I was reminded of the several movies I saw that week, which always began with people standing and singing "God Save the Queen."

When it came time to leave Europe, I boarded my plane home and sank into my seat. The blizzard of people and places that I had encountered in those summer months kept showing up in my mind and heart. I became acutely aware of how much the summer had expanded my appreciation of Europe and its people. Overall it felt like a very privileged time of ever-fresh exploration and new learning, relationships, and experiences, whose impact I couldn't yet fathom. I was homesick and looking forward to getting back to Stanford. At the same time, I was heartsick at leaving behind so many people and places that I would have liked to know more fully.

Back to Stanford and Time with My Fathers Family

All through college I would occasionally spend weekends at my father and stepmother Naomi's house in San Carlos. My half sister, Pamela, was nine years younger than me, and my two half brothers, David and Paul, were each a few years younger than her. We got along well. I had a sense of at least semi-belonging and being welcomed there, although I remember being shocked once by Naomi suddenly asking me, "What do you want from us, Tilden?" I felt some exasperation and non-welcoming in her voice. I don't remember just what I answered, but I know in my heart I mainly wanted to have a sense of easeful family belonging with them. That wasn't always possible. If my father had been drinking too much, dinners would include conflictual comments back and forth with him among family members that made everyone uncomfortable. They weren't addressed to me, but there I was in the midst of a not-very-happy family.

Probably what I wanted most in those visits was time to talk alone and personally with my dad. That would happen after everyone else went to bed. We would sit together in the living room, my dad chain-smoking, and I would pump him with questions about his family and upbringing in Texas (which included leaving home at age sixteen and joining a circus troupe for a while), and about his life during the war in Britain. Sometimes I would ask him questions about his views of things such as pacifism, sex, and politics. Basically I was trying to make up for lost time from all those years growing up without him. He was gentle in his answers, never judging me. I think he carried a lot of unspoken guilt about his leaving me and my mother. Part of me felt I was more like him than I was like my mother, but another part of me held many more of her values and instincts. I remember later writing him in graduate school about how much I still felt I needed him to be a father to me—a mother wasn't enough. I told him how important it was to me for him to keep up an exchange of letters, where I could express my feelings and views about life and he could reply by sharing his feelings and views, which for a while we did.

Apart from our talks when I visited him, I loved to hear him whistle. He had a tremolo that I could never do. He would spontaneously whistle beautiful, haunting melodies that I had never heard anyone else do, with an absorbed, faraway look in his eyes. In later years I heard him at the piano, singing and playing by ear endless popular love songs in his deep, alluring voice. I could see why many women fell for him over the years (with a lot of coaxing from him, no doubt).

At Stanford I found a new friend, John Hill, a psychology major. We both were at a stage of wanting to throw off some of our fear of anger and not using polite language. Neither of us easily swore. One evening I can remember we spontaneously decided to use every curse word we ever knew but didn't say aloud. For a long, wonderful time we just cursed and cursed—with a great new sense of freedom. Keep in mind that in the "quiet '50s" many of us were conditioned by an inhibited dominant culture that kept the harsh and far-out stuff quiet. This was before the explosive times of Vietnam, free love, and drugs. Beer parties, friendship, family, dating, usually harmless pranks, study, jobs, sports, and maybe a little religion seemed enough for many of my college generation.

In my last two years at Stanford, I moved out of the eating club dormitory and into a large private house on campus owned by Ms. Allen. Her deceased husband had been a university professor. She took in about ten students a year. I became "one of her boys." You almost always could find her sitting in her living room chair, which you had to pass coming into the house. Next to her was Pete, her pet parrot, who she would often take out of his cage for lip-to-beak talks and to let him fly around a bit. She had taken in students for many years after her husband died, and she had many stories about them. Some students pressed her to take a vacation somewhere. Her response was to drive her old car a few blocks away and sit under a tree.

The street where she lived dead-ended into a hayfield sloping up a hill. Some mornings the frequent appearance of fog would begin to thin out right at the foot of that field, creating a beautiful scene of glistening, fog-dampened earth and plants suddenly illuminated by bright sunlight. Knowing the fog almost always would lift by midmorning gave me a kind of hopefulness for the day. I still drove to El Capitan for meals about a mile away, in my old Chevy hardtop coupe (bought when I had to live off campus at the beginning of my second year because of dorm overcrowding). Many years later I saw an article about Ms. Allen along with a photo. She had just died (in her nineties). It brought back fond memories. She was a unique and caring fixture at Stanford for decades.

During those last two years I found myself searching for deeper meaning in life than my courses and relationships offered. I had left my Catholicism behind at the end of high school, but the Spirit kept a space in my heart for something else. I found myself attending a Quaker meeting occasionally, as well as a Congregational church whose minister filled some empty place in me when he preached. I also was attracted to a nearby interspiritual and psychological center's seminars (whose name I've forgotten). It was independent of Stanford but included the leadership of a Stanford professor. It was heady stuff, but the discussions about existential realities were more than academic. I'd say it was an oblique precursor to Esalen, the exploratory trans-psychological–spiritual center that appeared some years later.

Transported to My Spiritual Heart

In the middle of my last year, something completely apart from my will and understanding suddenly overcame me and never left. Today I would say that I was transported to the door of my spiritual heart by a hidden gracious Presence. I was given an intuitive sense that a transformational interior change was evolving in me, but I had no idea what that meant. It didn't seem to connect at all with my vocational motivation to apply to four different university PhD programs in anthropology at that time. All I could do was stay open to whatever might show itself.

Acceptance at Harvard University

I was surprised to find that getting into an anthropology PhD program was very different from getting into an undergraduate program. Anthropology at that time was still in its infancy; departments were mostly small, and anthropologists in different schools often knew one another. They seemed to care about my academic record, but they cared even more about who was recommending me. Felix Keesing at Stanford was fairly well known by other anthropologists. His letter of recommendation for me said that "I used all my native abilities" in my course work. Fortunately I think the schools where I was applying did not take that to mean that I had limited abilities but rather that I applied myself fully to my work. (Though the first interpretation may have been correct also! I always carried a certain doubt about my "native" abilities.) I remember Dr. Keesing coming up to me in my chair during a class that included graduate students and encouragingly telling me that I had done better in a test he had recently given us than all but two of the graduate students. In any case, I think he was responsible for getting me accepted into all of those anthropology programs—at Harvard, Yale, Cornell, and the University of California, Berkeley. I chose Harvard, knowing what a wonderful reputation its anthropology department had and being attracted by its location in Cambridge and its centuries of existence.

That successful outcome of acceptances was tarnished by a disastrous interview the previous October with a large interuniversity faculty committee charged with recommending people with high undergraduate academic records for a Marshall Scholarship. This was for two or three years of fully paid graduate study in Great Britain. About forty Americans were chosen each year.

I can't remember exactly the first question asked me by a professor on the committee, but it was something like "What gives you pleasure (or satisfaction) in life?" An insane first answer came to me that I should have suppressed. I quoted Socrates's line about having an itch that you could perpetually scratch. They all laughed. I then quickly tried to give a serious answer, which I can't remember now, but whatever it was, I think my first frivolous answer endured in their minds. A few weeks later I received a letter from the chairman of the committee telling me that not only was I not recommended for that scholarship but that he thought I ought to apply to a "noncompetitive" graduate school (i.e., he felt that I wasn't worthy of any "good" school). I was properly humbled! Insult was added to injury. I just swallowed hard and tried to forget my ridiculous response to a serious question in that interview. Later I felt a little vindicated when "good" graduate schools accepted me.

All my close family came to my Stanford graduation that May. I was on the magna cum laude list, but I knew I never would have been on it if I had to take any more science or math classes, and if I hadn't steadily disciplined myself to work hard in the courses I did take—really extra hard given my difficulty in staying attentive for long periods of reading. Today I might have been seen as having a touch of attention deficit disorder or at least some anxiety disorder. I wasn't the kind of genius that I felt many students around me were, especially in the physical sciences and math (even though I shocked myself by once scoring 140 on an IQ test, taken at a time when I was really relaxed, confident, and probably lucky). I knew I had to do more work than many others to get to where they were in understanding. I paid a price for such tenacious studying in terms of not giving more time to many other good things I could have been doing in those years. But I did what I did, and I'm grateful for all the opportunities I had in college to learn about the world not only academically but also relationally—in the human relationships I formed and the times I spent relating to the mysterious beauty of nature around me with a sense of awe and appreciation.

Chapter 5

International Student Seminar and Workshop in Japan

I spent the heart of the summer after graduation from Stanford in Japan at an international student seminar and workcamp sponsored by the American Friends Service Committee (AFSC). I was drawn to the unique experience that promised to be. An American contingent of about five students were signed up with me.

I flew from San Francisco to Honolulu, getting educated in some current African American realities along the way by my seat mate, an African American Methodist minister. He was on a trip around the world, including the Belgian Congo.

In Honolulu I boarded the USS *President Cleveland*, a large passenger ship headed for Japan. I had a third-class ticket, which meant I was put into a windowless small room with eight bunks for the ten-day duration of the voyage. Most of the third-class passengers were Asian students returning home.

The American AFSC contingent was aboard, and each morning we were given Japanese lessons by a teacher. I had many long talks with some of the students over the course of that voyage. One of them, Akira Ireye, became a longtime friend. He was studying in the United States but his home was in Tokyo. Another was Marilyn Tator. Yet another was Roland Hinderson. He was one of only two Quakers in the group; he had just graduated from Haverford College, founded by Quakers. (I was so impressed with his character and social values that decades later, when my son Jeremy was looking for a college, I remembered Roland and suggested he check out Haverford, which he did. He ended up going there and thriving in every way.)

One of the students aboard the ship was a Chinese engineer who had decided to leave the United States and return voluntarily to Communist China. He wanted to help build the new China begun by the Communist Revolution in 1949. (Keep in mind that this was 1957, so the revolution was still fresh.) I marveled at his idealism, but at the same time I feared that he had a naivete about the Communist system that would disappoint him. Some other Chinese students aboard were returning to China for the same reason.

After a few days, the constant roll of the ship through the waves began to get to me. Passengers in steerage class are more affected by it; you're living on the back end of the ship that has steeper up and down movements in the water than in the middle of the ship, which is reserved for higher-class passengers. The ceaseless rolling seeped into my mind and left me dull, listless, and restless at the same time. There was nothing I wanted to do: stand up, lie down, talk, be quiet, eat, read, exercise. In a way, that left me unattached to everything.

That condition paradoxically may have left me more available for the most important thing that happened to me on that voyage. One evening I found myself standing alone at the railing facing a beautiful sunset over the vast expanse of the sea. Since high school I had been struggling with the question "Does G-d really exist?" Suddenly it struck me that there never could be a sure rational answer to that question; it was finally a matter of trust either way. At that moment I was moved to take a leap of faith and believe that G-d *is*. You could say that I had an intellectual conversion at that moment. I wasn't converted to any particular package of beliefs about G-d, just a fresh availability to the mysterious Giver of life.

This decision also was fed by a growing sense that humans have four gifts that we don't need merely to survive as part of some unguided evolutionary process: (1) an ability to perceive and feel beauty; (2) a capacity for feeling compassionate oneness with other beings; 3) an ability to innately understand certain basic principles of justice and goodness, and to be hurt when these are violated; and (4) an ability to long for and seek a caring Source of life and to be moved by that mysterious Source to live a transcendently meaningful life, however erratically or hiddenly to our consciousness. Altogether, these capacities say to me that we are not on this earth by accident.

I felt there was a connection of that experience with that sudden, enduring sense I had a few months before that some major change was shaping itself in me that was yet to be revealed. Now, in looking at the icon of that sunset, I see that the change had begun. I had crossed a mental divide and chosen to be vulnerable to the divine Mystery. I would never be the same again. Over many years ahead, I came to feel that I wasn't alone in that moment of choice—I was able to choose because I sensed I had been chosen by that loving Mystery to come into this life. I would slowly, slowly move toward a fuller conversion of mind and heart over the years ahead.

Tokyo

On Saturday, June 29, the ship pulled up to the dock in Yokohama on a cloudy, cool day. We were up at 5:00 a.m., still reeling from the typhoon we had encountered the day before that showed us the awesome power of wind and sea and the amazing capacity of the ship not to be torn apart or sunk, as we held on to whatever we could to keep us from tumbling around and our stomachs from heaving. We disembarked and crawled through immigration, customs, and quarantine facilities, until our American contingent was found by Joy and Mojmir Pvolny, who were in charge of the AFSC workcamp program.

We were taken to the Tokyo Friends Center, which really was just a big house. There we were met by Wolf Mendl, the center's director, a very jovial and sharply bright Englishman who once had been the Quaker representative to the United Nations.

After lunch we took a train to downtown Tokyo and walked around to get a feel of the city. It's an overwhelmingly large and energetic place. I experienced the important mutual respect and hierarchical observance shown to one another through bowing (rather than shaking hands). The higher the social station of the person you encountered, the deeper your bow needed to be. In a major department store we entered, women were hired to do nothing but hold a cleaning cloth on the moving railing of an escalator and bow to every customer as they stepped onto it. Apart from the hierarchical side of it, I came to appreciate bowing as a humbling gesture that recognizes the human value of each person.

That evening we went to a long Kabuki performance, a unique Japanese form of theater. Men play all roles—male and female. Actors are elaborately dressed, with heavy face makeup. Their stylized movements take them across the stage. They disappear and reappear in unexpected ways. Even for Japanese, though, it can be hard to understand, since a centuries-old Japanese dialect is spoken. This play was a love tragedy that included extreme expression of emotions, which would be abruptly broken off. The background scenery was spectacular.

That night I had my first experience of an *ofuru*, the steaming hot water bath that Japanese climb into after first washing themselves with soap and rinsing with water outside the bath. In my case, the ofuru was in a big barrel in the backyard of the Quaker center. I marveled at the sequence, since in America we would just climb into a bathtub dirt and all. I recalled that in the eighteenth century, one thing that appalled the Japanese was how dirty (and probably smelly) the European visiting sailors were; they didn't bathe like the Japanese did. Avoidance of germs also showed itself on the trains and streets, where people wore face masks if they had a cold or other communicable disease.

The next morning, Sunday, we joined a Quaker meeting, mostly attended by Japanese. There was an English woman who had come to Japan hoping to find a Japanese ship that would take her and other protestors on a long voyage to Christmas Island in the South Pacific, where the British were planning hydrogen bomb tests.

I spent the hour with a dawning realization that some human faculty in me beyond the intellect was needed to fully appreciate the good, the true, the beautiful, and the One who privileges our awareness of these realities. But I was still too habituated to seeing my mind's reflection on things as the bottom line for "knowing" reality. I had only faint room for that still nameless human faculty to be honored.

In the afternoon I dove into the anthropologist Ruth Benedict's *The Chrysanthemum and the Sword*, commissioned by the American War Department in World War II to help deepen American understanding of Japanese culture. It was thanks to her that the Japanese emperor was left in place as a uniting figurehead in the surrender agreement of 1945.

Travels beyond Tokyo

The next few days were packed with meetings at the International House of Japan and with Japanese college students, as well as visits to the Meiji Shrine and other sites. We also traveled by train and bus to nearby towns. The trips included a visit to a Shinto shrine in Kamakura, with its priests and temple maidens. When we arrived, the shrine was filled with hundreds of schoolchildren who were very curious about us foreigners. "Prayer papers" hung on trees. One handclap was given when praying, along with a bow. A beautiful lotus pond sat in front of the shrine. Another trip took us to Nikko, where we visited a Buddhist temple with a Shinto gate, showing the frequent fusion of the two traditions in Japanese culture.

One trip, to Atami, a lovely oceanfront town, involved an overnight stay in a Japanese inn. The inn loaned us kimonos (women's robes) and *yukatas* (men's robes) for our stay. Two kimono-clad women brought dinner to our rooms, where we sat on the floor to eat while they remained with us, silently kneeling nearby throughout the meal. Afterward we walked outside through a street lined with many souvenirs and ice cream shops to the ocean front, wearing our Japanese dress, with *geta* on our feet provided by the inn. Geta are wooden shoes that make a clopping sound. When you're walking around the town, with lots of other people around you wearing them, it sounds like a bunch of horses clopping down the street.

When we returned to the inn, our bedrolls—futons—had been laid out on the floor, with rock-hard "pillows." As in Japanese homes, there was a very efficient use of space. Bedrolls were put away in a closet during the day so that space is opened for other needs. Doors are paper sliding panels with wood framing. I always felt a wonderful sense of simplicity in the furnishings. Street shoes are left at the front door, whether in a home or an inn, which is both relaxing and a way of keeping indoor spaces clean.

Back to Tokyo

The next day we returned to the Quaker center for a few more days. I loved the Bible readings before breakfast and the silence before each meal. These fed my newly enlarged spiritual appetite, as did other spiritual readings I came across.

Another day, a few of us took a train and taxi to Tokyo University, which some aspiring students take ten years trying to enter. Higher education is highly valued and incredibly competitive in Japan. We met with students in the English-Speaking Union of Japan, exchanging views of student life and aspirations. Some of them expressed great difficulty in finding a vocation where they could live out their idealistic social values.

After the meeting, I had the privilege of meeting for about twenty minutes with Tadao Yanaihara, the president of the university. Meeting him was made possible because of his friendship with Felix Keesing, my anthropology professor at Stanford. He talked about the confusion Japanese people were feeling between old and new cultural values, and how interesting and valuable anthropological field work would be in investigating that tension. He reinforced what I already was beginning to feel: if I became an anthropologist, I would like to specialize in Japanese culture.

On the Way to Kobe College

On July 10, we were taken to Tokyo's Haneda Airport to meet the arriving non-American foreign students, some of whom had been traveling for days. I quickly made friends with a Vietnamese student and an Indian medical student, as well as Simon Gitonga from Kenya, who was finishing a law degree in India.

We spent the night in a YWCA hostel near the town of Kukurizo. The next afternoon we all walked together down a muddy road into the town. We were an amazing-looking group of people from all over the world, walking around together in a very homogeneous culture that saw very few foreigners at that time. People like me looked even more weird: a Westerner wearing a yukata instead of Western clothes. We received many astounded stares. We threw candy to kids near a school, and they then followed us for quite a while. Later we learned that Japanese children had been taught to fear and/or hate foreigners, and how important it was now for them to learn about and have contact with them, as it was for foreigners as well, if we were to move toward peace in the world.

At dinner that night (preceded by a silent grace, as at all meals), we were given our first talk on the AFSC program, giving us a summary of what we would be doing in the days ahead. After breakfast the next morning, we had a fifteen-minute meditation session, followed by some spontaneous singing. The Asians present had an amazing knowledge and appreciation of American folk and popular songs.

After another day of orientation talks, we drove in cars to Nagoya, many hours away. The scenery along the way was beautiful: pine forests, misty mountains, lakes, rivers, farm villages with thatched or tile roofs. I was reminded of so many Japanese scroll paintings that were filled with such scenes, where people and village huts were portrayed as small parts of the larger natural world they inhabited and appreciated.

We stopped for a rice-and-eel lunch. Japanese menus took time to get used to, but little by little I was able to do that—it was that or starve! I even adjusted to the usual breakfast of seaweed soup.

We spent that night at an inn in Nagoya. The next morning, we continued on a difficult five-hour drive to Kyoto, the thousand-plus-year-old city that carries the heart of ancient Japanese cultural tradition, where we spent several days exploring. I walked around with Simon Gitonga, wearing my yukata and the inn's geta. We were quite a black- and white-skinned strange sight to those we passed; I heard many cameras clicking!

International Student Seminar

After Kyoto we drove to the site of our international student seminar: Kobe College, a Christian college for women, with a pretty campus sitting on a wooded hill. There were forty-three students there for our two-week seminar. About half the group were Japanese. The other half, besides the Americans, came from Africa, India, Pakistan, Switzerland, the Philippines, Korea, Hong Kong, Formosa (Taiwan today), Vietnam, Ceylon, Thailand, and Burma. English was the agreed-upon common language.

We all stayed in the college dormitory together. My roommate was Yoshie Kawashime, an international law major from Osaka University. He was very friendly, but my deep voice made me a bit incomprehensible to him (to others as well). In having begun studying Japanese over the last several months, I realized how difficult it must be for the Japanese students (as well as the other students whose native language has no relationship to Indo-European languages) to understand English, which has not only a totally different vocabulary but a very different sentence structure, to say nothing of a different alphabet.

Each day began with a 6:30 a.m. wake-up bell and a 7:00 a.m. breakfast, followed by a half-hour meditation session in the chapel. Days were packed with seminars and panel discussions led mostly by Japanese scholars, and with daily small discussion groups. These were supplemented by many informal individual and small-group conversations about our personal lives and cultures. Sometimes we would learn songs and dances from our different countries. At one point, the Americans taught everyone the Virginia reel.

The overall theme of the American Friends Service Committee seminar was "national interest and international cooperation." The AFSC staff had the hope that students would become more informed and involved in working for peace across cultural, national, and religious traditions. At one point, I was the American speaker for an afternoon forum on whether to give Communist China diplomatic recognition, which I conditionally favored after explaining the American government's positions.

Wolf Mendl, the director of the Tokyo Friend's Center, gave a talk that stuck with me about the value and limitation of approaching problems as a scholar. He said scholars teach us how to think clearly, but we should not simply observe and record life. Rather, we should concentrate on sensitivity—get under the skin of others, even if it hurts. This is more vital, more human, more worth pursuing. He felt we could learn something unique by exposing ourselves to others this way. We should value feelings over intelligence and knowledge if we want to bring peace and goodwill in the world. Sterile is the scholar's life if he lives only as a scholar.

Meeting with Pi-Chao Chen

One of my most vivid memories was a small-group conversation early in the seminar with Pi-Chao Chen from Formosa. I can still see the shocked look on his face when I asked him his opinion about the political situation there. He was not part of the huge mainland Chinese Nationalist Party migration to Formosa that overwhelmed that huge island and made its headquarters there after the Communist conquest of the mainland. He was instead a native Formosan, which has its own culture, heavily suppressed by the Nationalists.

He said that no one had ever asked him for his own political opinion! You were not allowed to express one in the de facto dictatorship of Chiang Kai-shek and his followers. He was near tears with us, expressing his happiness in being able to freely discuss politics for the first time in his life. He wanted real democracy and freedom to reign in Formosa. Because of his views, he was remaining a student in Japan for as long as he could, fearing what would happen to him when he returned home.

That experience was the first time I remember having directly encountered someone who was not able to give an opinion that differed from the party line of those in power. I suddenly realized how many millions of people in tyrannical cultural and political conditions around the world share Pi-Chao's oppression. In a few years I would come to realize more fully how such oppression was right under my nose in my own country, as the civil rights movement began to lift the veil on American apartheid in a massive public way that could not be ignored.

Quaker Meeting and International Night: The Seminar's End

I was on the cleanup and worship committees for the seminar. The latter dealt with the looming Sunday morning service. Two Protestant ministers planned a Protestant service. I said that I would like to be part of a silent type of Quaker meeting as an alternative. A small group of us (including all the Americans) held the alternative worship in the form of a meditative walk and silent sitting time outdoors. Afterward some of us from different religious traditions gave "witness" to our faiths. I had spent two hours the day before preparing to give witness to "nonsectarians in churches."

"International Night" came the next evening, where each nationality prepared skits that reflected something in their cultures. The Americans got together and planned a skit on college dating. I played the smooth wolf. It was a hilarious evening, bringing the transcendent power of humor to our various cultural situations.

Some of the Japanese students were converts to Christianity. Sano San had a typical story that reflected the importance of the Christian welcoming atmosphere. He was warmly welcomed by members of his church and he felt their goodness, which met his need to move beyond his loneliness and find a caring community of mutual belonging.

As the days wore on, I found myself spending free time reading and resting in a pine grove outside the college that overlooked the city of Kobe. I heard the familiar sounds of car horns, trains, and birds. I had come to feel more at home here. There were vital cultural overlaps grounded in our shared human condition.

On our final day in the seminar, we had a full hour of meditation, with opportunity for anyone to spontaneously express whatever they wanted to say to the group about our time together. Farewells for me are always hard, but I managed, as we all did, to let go of one another and move on to the next stage of the summer. Some of us were divided into small groups to travel together to a few famous towns and sites for a week, with the itinerary arranged by the AFSC staff.

Sightseeing after Kobe

My group began by taking the train on a very hot day back to Kyoto for further sightseeing. One discovery that evening was Western classical music tearooms. There were no less than ten of them in Kyoto, plus some jazz tearooms as well. Several of us went to a classical music tearoom, where we saw many Japanese students. Walking around Kyoto was beautiful at night, including not only the silhouettes of the many temples but also the colorfully lit-up restaurants and inns on high pilings along the river, where they have been for centuries. It was a step back in time to a once integral Japanese culture that now is challenged by many new cultural forces.

That afternoon we gathered our belongings and boarded a train to Nara, the ancient capital of Japan. The inn where we were to stay was a long walk from the train station, and the heat and humidity were so great that it felt like we were walking through a huge sauna bath. When we arrived, I jumped into a cold shower to recover.

We had arrived at the inn late, and I felt very sorry for the two women who brought dinner to our room about 10:00 p.m.; they were required to stay with us while we ate. They looked exhausted. I'm pretty sure they had begun the day serving breakfast at least thirteen hours earlier. I wondered if this was typical in Japan, in which case, hotel workers badly needed a labor union! An added factor I expect was that these were women, not men. At that time, women had a decidedly inferior status and much work was expected of them. Of course, in 1957, such inferior status of women was a standard travesty in most of the world and still is in much of it.

The next morning the heat and noise outside woke me at 5:00 a.m. The noise in part was from the clopping of geta in the streets outside. After breakfast, Enomoto-san, our very caring local guide, took us to see some of this old city's famous sights: the huge Daibutsu Buddha statue and a five-story pagoda. Sitting near the pagoda were some school children painting the scenery around them. I was struck by their amazingly mature artistic gifts, especially in depicting nature.

Episode with the Military Police

When we came back to our inn, I decided to take a walk alone down some of the old, narrow streets of Nara, wearing my Japanese yukata, obi (cloth belt), and the inn's loaned geta, joining the clopping crowds. At one point I saw a pair of American military police walking along the street toward me. There were still many American soldiers around in those days. When our paths crossed, the police stopped me and gruffly asked for identification. That unexpected demand birthed an immediate wave of fear in me. Then I remembered that I had decided to put my passport in the long-sleeve pocket of my yukata. I reached in, pulled it out, and gave it to them, hoping that it would show I was a civilian. They looked at it, gave me a disapproving stare, handed the passport back to me, and walked on. American soldiers, it turned out, were not allowed to walk around in Japanese dress. Such civilian tourists were rare at that time, especially in a remote town such as Nara.

I didn't dress as I had to draw attention to myself; I really was a bit embarrassed by the stares given me. My desire was the opposite: to simply try to fit in with the Japanese around me and feel what it was like to be inside the clothes everyone else was wearing. Besides, in the summer heat, such loose-fitting clothing felt cool and comfortable.

Mt. Fuji and a New Work Camp

The next day we boarded a train for Futaminoura, arriving at dusk in this coastal town famous for its amazing sunrises between two huge rocks in the ocean. We were up at 4:00 a.m. the next day and walked to a point where hundreds of people were gathered to watch the slow coloring of the eastern sky and the fiery orange ball of the sun slowly rising. The awed crowd included a substantial number of children with their teachers, another indication of how appreciated nature is in Japanese culture.

After an overnight in Nagoya, we moved on to Lake Kawaguchi, with a magnificent view of Fujiyama (Mount Fuji) rising in magnificent solitude, still snow-covered at the top. After breakfast the next morning, we boarded a bus that climbed up a steep, bumpy road to Mount Fuji's fifth station. When we left the bus, we began the long climb to station 8.1. The sky restlessly kept changing from rain to clouds to fog. I felt the sacredness of the mountain as we encountered pilgrims, each in special dress with a bell and walking stick, climbing with us.

When we arrived at station 8.1 it was 5:00 p.m. We stopped for the night at the pilgrimage inn there. We ate a ham sandwich with rice and some soup (a menu that would be repeated for the next three meals). The inn was basically one huge room, with row after row of futons laid out close to one another. Our group of six, which included two women, settled together in one crowded corner at about 7:00 p.m.

A bell rang at 3:00 a.m. We continued the long walk to the top, a walk filled with the sound of the many pilgrims' tinkling bells. Those bells somehow moved me to an awed somberness. They carried a sense of purpose and meaning in life that transcended and yet pervaded everyday human living.

We made it to the top about 7:00 a.m. The weather was cold, misty, and very windy. I felt as though we had reached beyond our human comfort zone, into a mysterious place where we could not be sustained for long—a kind of frontier of body and soul. I took an extra hour's walk looking for the volcano's crater, but it was too cloudy. I found a Shinto shrine, though, a fitting symbol of the mountain's sacredness. The descent took us about six hours. We had a three-hour wait at the fifth station until the bus finally arrived to bring us back to our inn.

The next day we caught the first of two trains (the second with standing-room only and very hot) that would take us to Yatsumi in Chiba Prefecture, the site of our two-week work camp.

We arrived after dark and took a taxi to a nearby village and the junior high school where we would live. I had eaten almost nothing all day and was starving, but we couldn't eat dinner until after listening to many welcoming speeches by the village master, by the head of the village cooperative society, and by the principal of the school.

After dinner, the men and women separated to help set up a huge mosquito/insect net in different rooms of the school. The men slept in the chemistry room on futons crowded together on the floor under the net. I felt a little awkward with the Japanese students who had joined us, since we hadn't even been introduced to one another yet. I was exhausted when we finally laid down to sleep, but it still was a restless night, given the heat and the sound of a swarm of giant beetles landing on the net above us. I felt very grateful for the net, that and every night.

We were up at 6:30 a.m. After breakfast, our first day of work began at Bethesda House, a home for about thirty physically handicapped women. They helped to support themselves by making purses and other items to sell.

Our job was to clear ground for several new buildings and for two new roads to the house. This meant removing many tree stumps and bamboo groves with the picks and shovels we were given. I came to ruefully respect the incredible toughness and multiplicity of bamboo roots. I chopped and chopped and chopped some more before one would finally give way. It was about the worst thing I could be doing with the case of hemorrhoids I had developed, but I had told no one about them and I didn't want to shame myself by working less diligently than the other students, especially the Japanese, who made up at least half of our group.

The Japanese students' work ethic was incredible. They truly gave their all. I was awed by their complete dedication to the work. Each of them began to take on an individual character as we got to know one another during breaks and mealtimes. The workday ended at 4:30, and despite the hard work, I was feeling a lot more upbeat about the work camp than the day we arrived, when I was so tired and when so many of the students were complete strangers. A sign of our coming together was, after dinner that night, joining in singing some American folk songs that most of the students knew.

The next morning we were up at 6:00 and had a light breakfast of tea and cookies. We left before 7:00 for the fifteen-minute walk to Bethesda House. For the next five hours our picks and shovels dug into the bamboo roots and other obstacles. The work was so difficult and the temperature so hot that we had to rest often. Akira Kuroda worked next to me, and in those break times we came to know each other. He was a philosophy major at the International Christian University and a Baptist. His father was the master of ceremonies in the imperial household (the palace of the emperor of Japan). He was unusually humble and generous, saying he hoped he could work hard despite his lack of experience and small size, and he did work relentlessly hard. In a later conversation with me he explained why he had become a Christian. He mentioned the friendliness and welcoming of Christian churches, as I earlier mentioned another convert had told me. He said that Christian ideas calmed "a nervous element" in him.

After lunch and a little rest break, we returned to our pick-and-shovel work for another three hours. I had never worked so hard physically in my life. Doing so for a worthy cause made me feel I was contributing not just my mind but also my body. I remember reading recently that many people with physically demanding jobs feel that their work is real and worthwhile, and they can't understand how people with desk jobs can conceive that work to be equivalent to physical labor. I felt more closely identified with the millions of such people in the world whose primary work is physical, people who often tend to be looked down on by those who work primarily with their minds without any body participation beyond fingers on a keyboard.

We ended each evening with meditation together, overseen by a meditation committee, of which I had come to be the chairperson—a sign of how important meditation had come to be for me that summer.

One day I had KP duty all day in place of working outside. I was up at 6:00 a.m. I helped cook breakfast, brought it out to the workers, then washed the dishes. A little before lunch I laid down to rest, and somehow in that quiet place many highlights of my life passed before me. Homesick for the past, I enjoyed every passing scene and felt sorry that they were forever gone. I felt closer to my family than ever before. At the same time, I felt grateful for the rare opportunity to be living together now, with all our differences, as one human family.

After breakfast and meditation the next morning, forty schoolchildren and their teachers joined us for work. This was Open House Day for Bethesda House. I was master of ceremonies for a special program that afternoon. Ms. Hayagawa, the physically disabled inspirer and director of the house, shared her thankfulness and love for us. The schoolmaster spoke of his hope that we would set an example for the pupils in our work. The foreign students gave eleven performances that shared something from their cultures. The Americans sang three folk songs and danced the Virginia reel (as we had done in Kobe).

We stopped work at 5:00 p.m. the next day, cleaned up, and made the long walk to the local village of Chosei, where village officials served us curried rice and fruit. The mayor gave a speech emphasizing Japan's desire for peace. A drunken villager walked in afterward and made himself at home. After some dialogue together, we made the long trek back.

On another day, a few of us spent time helping a local farmer in his rice field dig up dirt needed elsewhere on the farm. He first walked us to his house (with his wife walking a few steps behind him—one more sign of women's place in the society, especially on farms at that time). Their house was small and simple, with a special small space for a hanging scroll and for family prayer, as was typical in Japanese homes.

When we returned outside to the rice field, there were long waits between each load of dirt hauled away by the farmer's precious seventeen-year-old horse. Akira was with me, and he shared a lot about Japan's social problems and changes. He had much to say about what the human sciences and art, religion and philosophy, brought together for understanding contemporary cultures. As with most Japanese Christians I've met, he was very devout. Biblical phrases and missionary interpretations fell into our conversation frequently.

Various Quaker Writings

That evening I read *Reality of the Spiritual World*, a Pendle Hill pamphlet by the great Quaker Thomas Kelly. I was moved to write this quotation in my journal:

> I believe there is an extension of our knowledge of God given in inner experience which goes far beyond the limits that the subjective factors of expectation and suggestibility can account for. New and undreamed-of truths open. We become new creatures, new in intellectual molds, new in behavior patterns, new in friendships and conversations and tastes, as the experience of God breaks down the old, inadequate, half-hearted life-molds of religion and of conduct. Scriptures are a social check upon our individual experience, not as a law book, but as a disclosure of kindred souls who have known a like visitation of God.[3]

These thoughts opened a window for me through which I could glimpse what "conversion" can mean, at least in part, and how drawn I was to it, even though my conscious "inner experience" was so small.

Later in the pamphlet I read another quote from Kelly that struck me: "Churches ought to be places where people may know one another in that which is eternal.... This mystical unity, this group togetherness of soul, lies at the heart of the living church." I lamented that at the root of my desire to come to this work camp was that as a group we would share a common search for and finding of "togetherness of soul" at the core level of our sharing. Sadly such a collective desire didn't widely manifest itself. It would be many years later before I would find such a full-blown soul community, as I came to fully embrace contemplative understanding and practice as central to my awareness of the deep Real.

Daily, I had been voraciously reading excerpts from Quaker spiritual writers during the work camp whenever I had a little free time. They fed me as spiritual fathers (and they were still all men at that point, unfortunately). I felt very close to them. Another day's reading that reverberated in me was the view of Howard Brinton about mystical union of the inward Light and the Eternal Christ, who is both in and above history as the way, the truth, and the life. He interpreted this in a broad way that connects with the infinite depths of the soul, which he saw as much the same in all religious traditions. He saw these traditions as united in their desire to overcome self-centeredness by union with a higher, greater life. In all of this an element of profound mystery is maintained.

The Seashore and Boan Festival

At one point in the work camp, after clearing more trees on the road all morning, we took the train to a nearby beach. It was a beautiful afternoon. After swimming in the high waves awhile, we watched fishermen hauling in many fish onto the wide, sandy beach. The scene reminded me that Japan is several islands surrounded by a vast sea, which provides of its abundance the fish and seaweed that helps to sustain human life, and sometimes threatens life when the sea and winds join forces to destructively pummel the mainland. The sea also provides boundaries that have protected the nation from outsiders and created an amazingly homogeneous culture.

When we returned by train to Chosei that evening, we found ourselves in the middle of the annual Boan festival, the return of the ancestors, which included many lanterns and fireworks. I was reminded of the respect and continued place for ancestors that the festival expressed, so beyond what I knew in American culture.

Meetings with Local Leaders

As usual, I was up at 6:00 the next morning for the hardest day of work yet, with Akira as my partner. The harder I worked, somehow the better I felt. The work of the body is so different from the work of the mind. After dinner we played some games together that included the mayor of Chosei and other local leaders of the community. I walked home to our school dormitory very tired but buoyed by a beautiful moonlit evening reflected in the irrigation ponds along the path. No streetlights gave the night sky so much more presence.

Another day after morning work we spent the afternoon with farmers in the area, learning that they are considered to be the top class in the local society. We broke into small groups, and I again had the opportunity of visiting a farmer's home. This one was four hundred years old, yet it had no sign of wear and tear. It was made from pinewood, with no preservative added. The same family had lived in that house throughout its history. The farm had a nursery in addition to its crops that was especially notable for its miniature bonsai trees that were hundreds of years old.

The farmer seemed quite mature and stable. His mother, fitting the traditional pattern, seemed to dominate their domestic life. The farmer's wife did all the work. The grandmother looked after the three children, who were very well behaved. They were traditional Buddhists. When I brashly asked the farmer if they would obey the emperor's command to go to war tomorrow if such came to pass, he answered, "Yes, because of our training." But he indicated the younger generation would not.

On the final Open House Day, the village women and children offered us a three-hour program, including many dances, a recitation of "Washington and the Cherry Tree," and an American and Spanish song they had learned. The children were in grades one to three and showed much talent, composure, and patience. The head of the Board of Education gave us a swashbuckling sword demonstration.

Response to My Talks

Marilyn Tator, one of my American coworkers who was with me throughout my time in Japan, told me toward the end of our two-week camp that the thoughts about religion and culture that I had expressed in gatherings over the weeks were more scholarly and complex than anyone else's. She meant this as a compliment, but it made me sad to think that I must contribute little to others who didn't understand me, especially those whose first language wasn't English. I had to admit that some of the complex things I said I only very dimly understood myself! My thoughts always felt probing and incomplete. I learned from this experience that I must learn to speak more clearly and simply so that others aren't confounded by my searching, abstract words.

Final Days of the Work Camp

The work camp ended on August 20, 1963. We worked on the road for the last time that morning with a sense of satisfaction as we saw how much land we had cleared in those two weeks. That afternoon we spent evaluating our time together.

The next morning we packed and cleaned up our living space in the school. We took the train back to Tokyo, where we explored for our few last days together. One night we ate dinner at a German beer hall. Many American military personnel lived it up there, standing around a piano and accordion, singing German, American, and Japanese songs. Kyoko San, one of our campers, was stunned by the "looseness" of the atmosphere, so different from the decorum of a Japanese restaurant.

The last evening in Tokyo, work-campers gathered at the Friends Center for a farewell dinner and much animated conversation until midnight. We were up early for our drive to Yokohama, where the Americans would return to Honolulu on the USS *Cleveland*. It was very hard leaving these wonderful companions with whom I had spent such an intimate, special few weeks of my life. I vowed to correspond with some of them, which for some years I did.

As I looked back on my two months in Japan during our voyage to Honolulu, I felt I had experienced more there of lasting value than in any equivalent period in my life. One evening, while watching a stunning sunset, I was reminded of my powerful experience with a sunset on the voyage to Tokyo. This time I was aware that my appreciation of its beauty and its filtering of a larger Presence depended on letting go any mental analysis of any kind and just being openly, directly *in* the sunset, letting it be what it was, letting it have whatever effect it had on me, with no distancing thoughts intervening.

I met some new students on the return voyage, mostly from China, the Philippines, India, and Japan. Several were on their way to Stanford University. The famous "power of positive thinking" advocate Norman Vincent Peale was aboard; I heard him deliver two talks.

On the whole, what he said repulsed me, beginning with his expression of cultural chauvinism when he exclaimed, "Can't you just smell the sweetness growing as we approach the United States!" He asserted a basic view of American values that were anti-Roosevelt and uncritically pro-competitive capitalism as a unifying agent that allowed the development of the individual. He came across to me as an apologist for the sufficiency and cure-all capacity of the social and political status quo, as though there was no need for any social criticism or change. Some of his "positive thinking" views I could see would be uplifting to people, but for me, his underlying view of American values left much to be desired.

From Honolulu I flew home to Los Angeles, where I spent a few days with my family and high school friends before leaving for my next adventure: graduate school at Harvard.

Chapter 6

The Harvard Years
Further Opening and Clarity of Call

In early September of 1957, I loaded up my car with everything I could think of that I might need and headed east for the long trip to Cambridge, stopping to sleep at YMCAs along the way. My last night's stop was in New York City. I loved listening to the songs from *West Side Story*, and it was still in its first long run in the midtown theater district of Manhattan. I naively parked my loaded car on the street near the theater and managed to buy a ticket. When I returned, my car had been broken into and cleaned out of anything valuable, including my precious manual typewriter used to type my class papers throughout my college years.

There were no computers in those days. Every class paper was written on a typewriter. I finally replaced my stolen one with an electric typewriter, which had a key that let you "white-out" any mistaken letters. At that time, letters were typed or handwritten. Meanings of words were found in printed dictionaries. Research was conducted in huge printed encyclopedias—no quick Wikipedia help—or at the library. All this meant it took a lot more time to write or research anything than it takes today.

It sounds primitive now, but someone as sophisticated as the author Wendell Berry refused to use a computer when it became available, or even a typewriter. He liked to see the mistakes he had made and ponder them as he handwrote his manuscripts. He liked to slow down his writing. So there are potential losses as well as gains in our capacity for speed now, but personally I'm very happy for the computer. I'm writing this on one, even though it seems to have a mind of its own at times and slows me down trying to figure out why it's suddenly crashed.

Anyway, I was glad I had a chance to see *West Side Story*, even at the price of having my possessions involuntarily simplified. When I finally arrived in Cambridge, it was a new world. I had never been there before. Much of the city itself somehow felt aesthetically unappealing. I realized there was a real "town-gown" divide between the many working-class people living in modest homes around the campus and the faculty, students, and classy buildings at Harvard.

I had a hard time finding the dormitory for students in the Graduate School of Arts and Sciences, where I would be living. When I finally found William James Hall and my little room, I felt it expressed what I later determined was an old upper-class Yankee New England value that I think infused some Harvard decisions: save as much of your money as possible so your children can inherit as much as you did from your parents, and be as parsimonious in your spending as possible. Harvard (at least at that time) seemed to spend its money very carefully. William James Hall was the only dormitory for its arts and sciences graduate students, and it was clear that Harvard had spent as little money as possible to build it. I can't conceive of a more sterile residential building—it had absolutely no frills, not even a public meeting room that I remember. The rooms were tiny. The walls were painted cement blocks. The roll-out window opened directly to your next-door neighbor's roll-out window, and when both were open you might as well not have had a wall between you when you turned on a radio or talked to someone in the room. It was furnished with a basic single bed, small desk, and desk chair. Many college dorms could compare with this, of course, but this was fabulously rich Harvard; it could afford to build a dorm that would provide its graduate students with adequate serious study space, quiet, and maybe a little aesthetic appeal.

I felt another kind of parsimony at Harvard: personal reserve. At Stanford, when you passed someone, you would greet each other even if you didn't know them. At Harvard, even if you had met them, people might pass you by as though they didn't know (or care) about you. It might have been that, most of the time, I was around graduate students who were very absorbed in their studies, probably introverts, and not into "community."

It certainly reflected a different atmosphere from the friendly one shared by not only Stanford but also most of the western United States. In any case, such coldness left me feeling very alone at times.

The day after I arrived I found my way to the Peabody Anthropology Museum where my advisor, Dr. Oliver, had his office. He was a considerate person whom I respected. Instead of telling me to take the formal French exam to demonstrate my grasp of a required foreign language relevant to anthropological literature, he opened a French anthropology book and asked me to read him a paragraph. I stumbled on a word or two as I recall, but I was able to translate the gist of it well enough that he "passed" me on the spot and said I didn't need to take the exam. That was a relief.

I shared with him the courses I wanted to take that first semester, which included a course on Southeast Asian cultures with the first woman anthropology professor at Harvard, Dr. Cora Du Bois. I also wanted to take a course in archaeology that I knew would be required for a PhD. I told him I also wanted to audit Art, Science, and Religion, a course with the famous German theologian Paul Tillich. Dr. Oliver seemed shocked that I wanted to do that. I sensed he was in the modal "agnostic" category of anthropologists that I mentioned earlier, when I was at that international anthropology conference in Copenhagen. I could just hear him saying to himself, "Why in the world would he want to take time to audit that kind of course, so tangential to anthropology?" To me, though, it was an opportunity to continue my religious-spiritual quest that was so strong during the summer in Japan. Oliver swallowed hard and said nothing further.

That course was Spirit-given for me. Tillich had the privileged position at Harvard of being a "university professor," which meant he could teach any course he wanted, related to any subject. Enrollment for this course was open to upper-class undergraduates, who seemed to account for most of the huge class. Tillich helped me realize that I could not escape G-d in some form. He convinced me that G-d for each of us is whatever is our ultimate concern that in effect we worship—we give ultimate "worth" to—in our life. So it wasn't a matter of believing or not believing in G-d but rather recognizing what your ultimate concern is to which you give the highest value and sense of reality. It left me feeling that if this were true, then I really wanted G-d to be as "big" as possible and not some finite idol unworthy of the name.

This realization coincided with my running into an old friend from Hollywood High School in the graduate dining room: Bill Becker. He was a student at the Harvard Divinity School a few blocks away. We had long conversations about my religious quest. That fall he invited me to spend Thanksgiving with his family near Hamilton College in New York State, where his adopted father, Dr. Hartshorne, was a professor of philosophy and religion. As an undergraduate student at Hamilton, Bill had come to be very close to Dr. Hartshorne and his family. Growing up, Bill had a terrible family life, but he saw in this new family how wonderful a family could be, to the extent that he asked the Hartshornes if they would formally adopt him, alongside their own three children, and they had agreed to do so.

My three days spent with them revealed what a sane, caring family they were. I had long conversations with Dr. Hartshorne and Bill. Their reflections on unfamiliar terms such as *grace* and *unconditional love* opened me to foundational dimensions of Christian revelation and life that sunk deep into my vulnerable, ready mind and heart.

When we returned to Harvard, I was moved to investigate the three-year MDiv program (designed primarily for future ministers) at Harvard Divinity School. Was I meant to radically shift my vocation to a religious rather than an anthropological one? This question stayed in the back of my mind as I sat through my anthropology classes. Dr. Du Bois's class on Southeast Asian cultures was interesting. The class was a mix of upper-class undergraduates and a few graduate students. I was surprised one day when she asked me to prepare to give two lectures on the core theories of the well-known Harvard sociologist Talcott Parsons. The theories were very abstract, but I managed to convey them well enough to the class. However, I couldn't help including some views of the psychologist Erich Fromm about the existential human search for truth and well-being that weren't relevant to what I was asked to do. For me, they gave an important background dimension of what it is to be human that I felt moved to share. Dr. Du Bois was sitting in the back of the classroom when I did that, and I had no idea how she would react. I think she was so dumbfounded that I had gone off assignment that she just didn't say anything to me at all afterward.

The paper I wrote for her class was on the Burmese practice of sending ten-year-old boys to live in a monastery for six months to a year. I was amazed that such a practice would exist for an entire culture's formation of children. When my paper was returned, Dr. Du Bois had at first given me a B+ but then had erased the plus, followed by the only comment she had on my paper: "Your style needs improving." When I later saw another first-year anthropology PhD student from that class in my dorm, a nice person who I knew was trying his best, he showed me what she had written at the top of his paper: "This paper is puerile and isn't worthy of a graduate student." She refused to give it any grade. He had a humiliated, depressed look on his face. I really felt sorry for him.

Dr. Du Bois's ruthless comment reminded me of what another Harvard anthropology student had told me about a fellow PhD student in his fifth year in the degree program: his dissertation was rejected and he had to leave without the degree. I began to see that the doctoral program would require me basically to worship at its altar, giving it a tremendous amount of time for years, without reasonable assurance that a degree would be forthcoming. That intuition, together with my boredom in the archaeology class, where we were required to draw a number of pots, among other things, in order to pass the course, began to steer me toward the divinity school.

Deciding on Divinity School

To help me with my decision, I made an appointment with Paul Tillich to explain my dilemma to him in a private meeting. His response basically was "We need Christian anthropologists." That didn't convince me, though. I realized that wasn't what I wanted him to affirm. So I made an appointment with a faculty member at the divinity school, Dr. Hans Hofmann, who was director of a five-year project on religion and mental health. He bridged the behavioral science and religious worlds. He was from Switzerland and said that he had been a patient/student of Carl Jung. He was not very professorial; he was more of an impulsive, free, approachable person, which was a breath of fresh air to me. He was supportive of my making the change. That, together with some reflective prayer, did it. I decided to take an incomplete in my classes and leave the anthropology program. Dr. Oliver was shocked again, but he didn't fight my leaving. I found out that he had a divinity student living in his basement!

Over time I became aware of a major overlap between cultural anthropology and theology: both dealt with all dimensions of life and their interrelationships—one from a behavioral science point of view, the other from a theological one. When I embraced anthropology as my field of study, I felt it would give me the most inclusive understanding of human behavior. Now I had become aware that its very epistemology, the way it "knew" that behavior, both served and limited its knowledge of human reality. Theology in its origins and purity is the mind's reflection on the firsthand experiential knowledge of the deep Real shown to us through a different faculty of knowing: the intuitive, unitive awareness of what some of the early Christian desert elders and their successors called "the spiritual heart."

I still respected behavioral science–based knowledge and would continue to learn from it over the years. But now I would center on *theological* anthropology, an understanding of the human being in light of an intuited, personally and historically given, life-transforming "revelation" of life's source, purpose, and evolution. The revelation at its heart I came to believe is of an ever mysterious yet intimate guiding Love, "in whom we live and move and have our being," as St. Paul testifies in Acts 17:28.

Divinity School

The second semester found me going to classes in Andover Hall at the divinity school. The longer I was there (a total of three and a half years), the more it felt right to me, and I decided to register for the MDiv. At first I had a vague sense of going for a PhD after my MDiv (master of divinity) degree and becoming a college or seminary teacher of religion, as Bill Becker intended to do. But as Dr. Hartshorne said later, he could see that I had more of a "pastoral nose," and he could understand that I was likely moving toward pastoral ministry rather than teaching. Unfortunately, the divinity school's weight was strongly on the side of sophisticated, academic thinking—after all, this was Harvard—and very little on the side of pastoral ministry, much less on carefully cultivating living from the "spiritual heart."

The requirements for the MDiv degree were most unusual for a seminary (or "theological school," as more academic seminaries especially like to be called). First, we had to pass an English Bible content exam, which I somehow managed to do despite my limited biblical knowledge at the time. Second, there was only one course requirement for the whole three years of the program: public speaking. Since I had a college course in that, I asked the speech teacher to exempt me from the class. He said he would if he felt I spoke well enough from the pulpit of the university chapel.

He set a time to meet with me later in the chapel, which was a large church for the whole university in the middle of the Harvard Yard. The pulpit was high up over the congregation. When I arrived, no one else was present except the teacher. We had agreed on the text that I would read, and sitting far back in the last pew, he listened to me. I nervously did my best to project and animate what I was reading, not at all being confident in that setting that I could convince him to exempt me. Afterward he said nothing about my performance, except that he was exempting me from the class, and that was that.

I was able to take any courses I wanted in my years there, but there was a serious catch. To receive the degree at the end of the three years, I had to pass written and oral exams in church history, theology, ethics, scripture, and pastoral care. I ended up taking most of the courses that would have been required in other seminaries in order to pass those exams at the end.

The divinity school was in the midst of a renaissance due to the support of the new university president, Nathan Pusey, who sat in the front row of the university chapel every Sunday and read one of the lessons. That was a radical departure from the previous president, who I heard hoped the school would fade away. Some great scholars were brought to the school faculty in all fields, Paul Tillich being one of them. The student body in the various degree programs was very diverse: Unitarian Greek Orthodox, Roman Catholic, Quaker, and Evangelical, along with many mainstream Protestants.

The school had a student-run weekly service in the chapel of Andover Hall. You can guess that it wasn't always easy to agree on its content or even its environment. At one point the cross on the wall behind the altar in the chapel was removed by some students, only to be found back up the next week thanks to other students. We managed to have a Communion service, but it was hard to agree on whether to use grape juice or wine. The agreed compromise was to use Catawba grape juice, which tasted like wine but was grape juice! Occasionally we had a play put on by the students in the chapel. I was a cast member in one of them. I can't remember the play's name or theme, but I had the role of the angel Gabriel. That was the only time I remember ever performing in a play. I worried about remembering my lines, but I managed somehow.

For all our differences, we students shared a seriousness about our studies. The quality of the faculty was such that I think we were all intimidated and/or fascinated by our classes. All the faculty at that time were men, as well as almost all the students (one of the very few women was Beth Rhude, who I became close to). Religious leadership and scholarship were still primarily a man's world then (as it was in most every other field).

Few students were very serious about community or prayer together. It didn't help that a refectory hadn't been built yet, since eating together can make such a difference in fostering community. I had a fair number of individual relationships, though, with those who lived in Andover Hall with me. One year I was elected student-body president, although that meant little since so few students were seriously involved in student affairs. A number of students were married and lived off campus.

Finding a Church

If I was likely going to be a minister, I needed to think about joining a church, since I hadn't belonged to one since leaving Catholicism after high school. I attended the Cambridge Society of Friends Meeting occasionally and felt myself to be, as the saying goes, "a friend of Friends." I was even a member of the New England regional American Friends Service Committee because of my participation in the AFSC Japan program. But I wasn't drawn to become a full-fledge Quaker. Besides, Quakers didn't employ ministers in their predominant East Coast form of "unprogrammed meetings." The fact that the Korean War was still on brought a sense of urgency to my decision, since I was subject to the draft after leaving the NROTC program at Stanford and graduating from college. Especially with my pacifist leanings, I certainly didn't want to be drafted. Seminarians under the care of their denomination were exempt from the draft, as were ordained clergy.

I had also been attending the First Congregational Church in Cambridge on Sundays, which was walking distance from my dorm. I appreciated its liberal theology and social concerns. At one time, Congregationalists were the established church in most of New England, descending from the early Pilgrim immigrants. Congregationalism had long ago given up its original fundamentalist strictness and lost its central place in New England religious life, as many other denominations built churches there. The minister of the First Congregational Church in Cambridge (Reverend Foster, I think was his name) invited me to his home for Thanksgiving dinner in my first fall there, which made me feel welcomed and cared for. I had a meeting with him soon after that to talk about becoming a member, and not long after I did. I also became a seminarian under the care of the regional Congregational Conference of Churches. (In more recent years, almost all Congregational churches formally merged with the Evangelical and Reformed Church and today they are called the United Church of Christ.)

Tempe Mental Hospital

I didn't give up my Quaker connections, though. In the spring of my first year of divinity school, I received in the mail a list of summer volunteer projects that the American Friends Service Committee was sponsoring. I had such an amazing experience in Japan that I was moved to volunteer for another one. I was particularly drawn to one that would be held at the State Mental Hospital in Tempe, Arizona. Because Arizona has so much untaxable federal land, the state couldn't (or wouldn't) adequately fund and staff it. AFSC volunteers were to work in the wards assisting the staff in any way they could. I signed up, and after a little time at home that summer, I drove to Tempe.

Tempe is the home of Arizona State University, and the AFSC had arranged to house volunteers in an old fraternity house that was vacant for the summer. On the first day, under an older dedicated volunteer director and his wife, the small gender and racially mixed group of ten volunteers spent the day getting to know one another. No one was Quaker. We were hosted by the Tempe Friends Meeting once during the summer.

The next day we read materials that introduced us to the hospital and our work there. We were assigned by the hospital to certain wards. I spent most of the summer in a large, long-term care ward of about forty patients. Their beds were all together in one huge room. I was asked to do everything from cutting patients' toenails to befriending them as best I could. I have a vivid memory of a likeable young catatonic man who at times during the day would freeze in place, like a statue. Another patient was a middle-aged Native American. He never talked with words in my experience, but more than once he spoke his inner rage with his fist, smashing it through a window. Another patient was kept in a padded, locked room. Whenever I looked through the window of his door, I saw him relentlessly pacing back and forth, stark naked.

Once a week a psychiatrist came by, sat in the ward's little staff office, and handed out pills for various patients, most of which seemed to be tranquilizers. I don't remember him talking to any patients. He seemed to treat them as hopeless wards of the state, to be maintained until they died, with no hope or help for ever being mentally healthy enough to leave. The psychiatric aide in the ward was responsible for the daily maintenance needs of patients. Only one was there at a time, responsible for the whole ward. The aides were low-paid and basically untrained. As a result, they often didn't stay very long. Like the psychiatrist, they assumed the patients were hopeless and in the hospital for life. They were capable of giving patients only minimal physical care, which really is all they had time for anyway. I felt frustrated and helpless when I was there. All I could do was try to treat the patients as a chaplain might, respecting the dignity of their humanity as children of G-d and offering words and little acts that reflected that.

Occasionally I would be shifted to the medical ward for physically ill mental patients. Over the summer I became friends with Jerry, the young daytime aide there. He filled me in on what was going on around the hospital. It was the only air-conditioned ward there. In my usual ward, the heat (this was summertime in the desert) left everyone in a semi-desultory stupor during much of the day.

Each evening when I returned to the fraternity house, which also wasn't air conditioned, the heat-inflicted stupor would continue. During one heat wave, the daily temperature highs reached 106 degrees. The nights didn't cool off that much. I would sleep mostly naked with wet towels on me to try to bear the heat enough to get a little sleep.

Sometimes I wondered whether some of the vulnerable patients in the hospital were being protected from the tougher craziness of some people outside the hospital. It felt like there was a thin line between the culturally defined "insane" and the "sane."

The volunteers had many talks together about our experiences in the hospital and how it was affecting our views of mental illness and the kinds of care needed. We also did some fun things together to further our own little community (and sanity) for the summer. At the end, despite my frustrations, I left with gladness that I had had the opportunity for touching into the world of the seriously mentally ill, which was brand new to me.

I also left with clarity about how much more I felt could and should be done for the patients I had befriended that summer. I also was left more motivated to explore further psychological knowledge of our human condition in the future, including my own mental condition.

Friends at Harvard

When I returned to the divinity school in the fall, I roomed with my old high school friend Bill Becker in Andover Hall. We waded into what in hindsight was an early sign of a growing American social activist tide that eventually would swell into the social consciousness and conflicts of the nation in the '60s. We both felt that we needed to resist planned American nuclear testing. We saw much danger and no hope of ultimate reconciliation resulting from the present arms race and that we needed to take a public position against it. We asked ourselves how we could best do this.

We discovered that we weren't alone, that there was a planned "Walk for Peace" from New Haven, Connecticut, to the United Nations building in New York, which Bill and I decided to join. Over fifty people were on this walk, and we were joined by others at various points along the way. Sponsors included the New England Walk for Peace Committee, the Fellowship of Reconciliation, and the First Methodist Church of New Haven. I kept a list of the walkers, which included ministers, seminarians, college students, and laypeople from many backgrounds. It was quite an experience. I discovered what it was to be in a vulnerable, controversial, publicly witnessing posture walking on the side of the highway, with some passersby angrily shouting "Commies" at us along the way, while others ignored, supported, or just dumbfoundedly observed us. Being a group together I think gave us more courage and affirmation in our protest.

The other action Bill and I took was to wear light-blue armbands as a sign of protest around the Harvard campus, and we invited others to do likewise by making them available in our room. We were happy to find a front-page article about what we were doing in the *Harvard Crimson* student newspaper that helped to spread the word. The reporter quoted me saying that "students wearing armbands have wide ranges of opinion about methods of remedying present world tensions. Their sole common belief is in the futility of the current nuclear arms race. We want to encourage our government, as well as other nuclear powers, to abandon the confused policies which seek to found a just peace upon ever more lethal weapons of war."

Another former Hollywood High School schoolmate soon appeared at the divinity school: Charles Krahmalkov. Charlie thought he might become a rabbi, but finally decided that he was meant to be a teacher. He came to Harvard for a PhD in ancient Near Eastern religions and languages. He lived in the newly built World Religions Center across the street from Andover Hall.

One year we decided to eat our dinners together in the little kitchen-dining room that was part of his living quarters. Neither of us was into the time and motivation it took for cooking though, so we usually ended up eating TV dinners. I'll never forget the evening we listened to John F. Kennedy's inauguration address, where he uttered the famous line, "Don't ask what your country can do for you; ask what you can do for your country." We were both so moved by that speech that when it ended, we spontaneously embraced each other, feeling a new hope for the country's future. Indeed, it was a fresh start in many ways, but any romanticism about its prospects were dimmed by Kennedy's (and his brother's) assassination, among other political crises of the following years.

When Charles finished his doctorate in such a specialized historical field, there were only a handful of such teaching positions in the country. Basically one had to wait for someone to retire or die before a position opened up. Charles lucked (or better, graced) out: someone had just retired in that esoteric field at the University of Michigan at Ann Arbor, and Charles applied for the job and was appointed in his place. He spent his entire career there, where toward the end of his research he proved—at least to himself, it was controversial with other scholars—for the first time that Moses was not a mythical biblical figure but really existed. After retirement, with the inspiration of a Hasidic rabbi, he turned to serious study and embraced Jewish mysticism. He had read at least my first book and respected my contemplative turn. To this day we still correspond, probe existential issues, talk about our families, and reminisce about our long-ago years together.

While he and I were studying at Harvard, I once drove him there from our homes in Los Angeles. On that long, tedious trip he taught me a beautiful Goethe poem in German. He drilled it into me over and over, to the point that I had it in me forever after that. When I was with my dying brother-in-law Larry Lyon in San Francisco about fifty years later, that poem came to life again. He had been a professor of German literature at UCLA. I didn't know how I could comfort him, especially since he had no religious faith, until that poem suddenly came back to me. I began to recite it, hoping he might still be able to recognize it in his dying condition, despite my poor German pronunciation. He immediately recognized it, and as I spoke, he raised one hand in the air from his bed and conducted the rhythm of the poem, with an ecstatic smile on his face. Afterward he pointed to a book in the bookcase next to his bed, where I found the poem. That made me wonder whether, in the mysterious ways of the Spirit, it was for that moment that I had held on to that poem for so long.

I also drove Charles, along with John Watt, back to Los Angeles with me at the end of another academic year. Watt was a very learned and friendly Scottish doctoral history student I had befriended at Harvard. As with other European students I drove cross country over the years, he was awed when we came to the desert West, which so contrasts with European topography. It reminded me of what a vast and varied country I live in.

At Harvard, John was dating someone from an old Yankee New England family, whose sister I was dating occasionally. With my broken, scattered family, I was a bit awed by a family with such roots and stability. Eventually John proposed marriage and asked me to be his best man at their wedding in the university chapel.

One other person at Harvard became a lifetime friend until his death a few years ago: David Ruth. He lived in Andover Hall also. He was in

The Harvard Years: Further Opening and Clarity of Call

a new joint PhD program between the divinity school and the Graduate School of Arts and Sciences, bringing both behavioral science and theological perspective to the study of religion. Like Hans Hofmann on the divinity school faculty, David in his own way was a free spirit with a brilliant, rebellious mind.

When David completed his doctorate, he spent the rest of his life mostly as a professor of sociology in a number of universities. During those years he became the first single man ever to be legally allowed to adopt a Native American boy through an adoption agency. Tommy was seven years old when he came to David's house. He had been abused as a child, even abandoned in a railroad station, and it took David years of loyal care before Tommy was finally convinced that he wouldn't be abandoned again. David respected Tommy's Lakota Sioux ancestry and wanted him to appreciate it also. It wasn't until he was long grown up, though, that he came to a full affirmation of his ancestry. I was his godfather.

After retiring, David spent much of his time playing classical music on the piano, up to six hours a day. Early in his life he had contemplated being a professional pianist. He had an incredible memory: he could play a complicated Chopin etude for the first time, close the music book and play it by heart. One of his two cats, Gufus, was ecstatic about his music, and Gufus had his favorite pieces. Once, the cat climbed up on his shoulders in meowing ecstasy while David was playing one of them. After a long illness, Gufus died, under the piano. When David himself died, I felt a great loss, for myself and for my family.

Sadly, at Harvard I lost a living friend also. In my second year there, John Hill, my old "swearing" partner at Stanford, came to Harvard for a PhD program in psychology. He was a year behind me at Stanford and we had lost touch, so I was surprised to run into him one day near Harvard Yard. After our initial conversation I asked him if he would like to visit the famous chapel at the Massachusetts Institute of Technology, which is also in Cambridge, and continue our conversation along the way. He agreed. The chapel is in the round, surrounded by a mote of water. The entire bottom half of the circular chapel's wall was made of clear glass rather than concrete. The undulating waters in the mote reflected light throughout the whole chapel, providing a unique sense of aliveness.

On the ride home I made the mistake of talking to him with great enthusiasm about my newfound religious consciousness. I somehow had not first found out his views. As it turned out, he was appalled by my turn to religion. I didn't realize that until too late. When we returned to Harvard and got out of my car, he suddenly exploded, saying he felt I was proselytizing him, and he didn't want to have anything to do with me again. I was left standing there in shock as he rapidly walked away. I never saw him again. I learned a lesson captured in the popular line "Don't talk with people about religion or politics" (unless you know the person is really open to listening).

Summer Research, Church, and Monastic Experiences in California, New Hampshire, and New York

At the end of that second year in seminary I had agreed to do some summer research for Hans Hofmann's five-year NIH-supported religion and mental health project. It involved interviewing a number of clergy in the San Francisco Bay Area about the pastoral counseling and preaching they do, and gathering their ideas about what could be done to improve community understanding of mental illness and health.

I also had arranged to be a summer seminarian helping with the vacation church school and other things at the First Congregational Church in San Jose. I needed to rent a room for the summer, and I needed someone to rent it with me to make it affordable. As it turned out, Dennis Severis, a Greek Cypriot who was in the Lausanne pension with me, with whom I had retained contact, was doing some work in the Bay Area and also needed a place to stay. We found an apartment that was available for the summer and moved in. We both were gone so much that we barely saw each other, but it was good to renew our friendship in the time we had.

The church experience was good. Leonard Hildebrand, the senior pastor, was supportive of me and I learned a lot from him about being a minister in a church, which was so new to me and which my seminary had very little to say about. My most vivid memory of that time was being a counselor for high schoolers in the weeklong summer camp of the area Congregational churches in the foothills of the Santa Cruz mountains. Every morning began with a wakeup bell. After about a half hour for everyone to get dressed and washed, a second bell would ring, which meant it was time for everyone to walk out of their cabins in silence and find some place to sit in solitude for twenty minutes of reflection and prayer, at the end of which another bell would ring.

This was many years before meditative silence began to seep into the larger church's life. I was very moved by the impact it had on me and on the campers. Teenage life is so full of words, worries, and thrills. This daily twenty minutes of attentive silence was probably the only time in their lives that these teens ever shared intentional, opening, listening silence with others. My strong impression was that for many of them, this silent space gave them room to discover and claim a deeper, freer sense of self, intimately connected with letting in the love and callings of G-d. It would have helped if a camp leader had given them some guidance in how to let themselves sink beneath the busy surface of their minds and be open to what was given in that receptive space, but at least they had the intentional silence. The Spirit can do its own surprising teaching in that space.

I'm afraid my only memory from all my interviews with clergy was their answer to the question "What was the title of three of your recent sermons?" I was amazed how many of them couldn't remember! It made me realize that sermons are for the moment, not for posterity. I expect the people in the pews couldn't remember the themes of three recent sermons either, but that doesn't mean that at the time of their presentation, the sermons didn't leave some Spirit-influenced trace, however unconscious, in their psyches.

The following summer found me being a seminarian at a local church again, but this time in a much more central leadership position. I signed up to be the summer seminarian minister at the Congregational Church in Hanover Center, New Hampshire, a tiny village that had long ago been marginalized by the town of Hanover, where Dartmouth College is located.

When I packed up my car for the summer and went up into the hills inland from Hanover, I saw this classic old, white, steepled Congregational Church of Hanover Center looming ahead. In fact, as I remember, that's all there was to the village. The rest of the structures were just scattered houses for miles around the church. People went down into Hanover to shop. The church was open only in the summer, thanks to Wilbur Bull, a retired Congregational minister from Maine who lived in the village. I had arranged to meet him at his house the day I arrived. He was a big man with a calm, gentle demeanor. We had a good conversation about the community and the church.

At first I thought he was a little senile, because when I asked him questions, there would be a long silence before he responded. Eventually I discovered that he wasn't senile at all; it's just the way many people deep in old northern New England culture seemed to speak. It made me feel that it would be difficult to snow such a person, to overwhelm them with some view or demand. The silent pauses seem to absorb any such temptation; you could not displace the settled integrity of the person. His silences also calmed me down and gave me room to slow down and not try to force or impress or do anything other than just be who I am. Wilbur's very way of being present taught me a lot.

He would not be involved in helping me that summer. I was on my own, although I always could talk with him if I wanted to. It was my job to lead the Sunday service, preach, and visit everyone in the community that I could.

I didn't live in Hanover Center. Instead, it had been arranged for me to have a room offered by a retired letter carrier and his wife in their house a few blocks from the main square of Hanover. The letter carrier was well known because he had planted flowering plants all over downtown Hanover.

They were a lovely, caring couple. It was a very simple house with simple, old furnishings, my bed included. The mattress was so old and soft that it formed a U when I laid down on it—I had to cling to the top sometimes in order to turn over.

In the weeks that followed, I managed to visit a variety of people in their homes around Hanover Center. Many of them were isolated from one another in the gently rolling hills. Most of them didn't come to the church or any other church (which would have been in Hanover). That reality increased my sense of how alone and disconnected from any community many people there were, since there were no other public meeting places. Alcohol addiction had developed with some of them, I expect in part to soothe the loneliness. I did what I could to comfort them, pray with them, and help them to feel more connected with others and with G-d.

I came to be quite close to one exceptional family in the village. The mother was from New Zealand, the father had some job that kept him living away from home much of the time. He was Unitarian, but the mother and their two young teenage boys came to our church on Sundays. I remember watching one of the boys as he milked and talked to their cow. I helped them to fork hay out of their barn (at the price of an allergy attack afterward). Since their father wasn't there very much, I think I became a bit of a substitute father for the boys. I took one of them with me to New York City one weekend, staying with a cousin of mine, Larry Chelsi, who was an opera and Broadway musicals singer (not a famous one but dedicated to his career after leaving Portland, Oregon, to become a professional singer). Some years later, both boys called me at separate times, having grown up and were now into their professions. (The cow milker had become a medical doctor.)

In my Sunday sermons at the church, I tried to keep in mind what I had learned in a homiletics class at Harvard taught by George Buttrick, who was the "preacher to the university," although there wasn't much relevant to my little rural church situation. Previously he had been the senior minister of the huge Madison Avenue Presbyterian Church in New York City, with a big staff. He urged us to give twenty hours to the preparation of every sermon, ignoring the fact that most of us students would never be part of such a church as his, with a big staff, where we would have the luxury to spend as much time as he could afford to prepare a sermon every week. He was a great preacher, though. The huge university chapel was packed with Harvard students every Sunday, even during winter snowstorms.

Most of my other seminary classes were far too abstract and sophisticated to be relevant to my work in Hanover Center. I struggled to include concrete stories that people could understand and identify with, but even those seemed to be only tangentially connected with the daily life these people were living. People came on Sundays anyway, and they didn't complain—I think many were just starved for a little sense of community and spiritual meaning for their lives that they were willing to bear thoughts coming from my very different cultural world. Singing familiar hymns helped to make connections with them. The volunteer organist for the little foot-pump organ in the church helped select hymns that people would recognize.

After the service one Sunday late in the summer, we had what the people in the church there had every summer: a potluck dinner. A group of women in the community put it together, including cooking some of the food right there. I remember being awed by the tremendous energy and seriousness they put into the preparation. It was something they understood and knew how to carefully put together, and they felt valued in doing so. It expressed a form of service for the sake of the larger community that I expect was appreciated by all those who came a lot more than my struggling sermons!

A few people bypassed our church on Sundays on their way to other churches in Hanover. One family went to the Episcopal church in town. I visited the priest there once, Father McBurney. He invited me to accompany him on a retreat the next week at Holy Cross Monastery, an Episcopal monastery on the Hudson River in West Park, New York. I had never been on a retreat before, nor stayed in a monastery. I felt a strong magnetic pull to accept his invitation.

Father McBurney was in the Anglo-Catholic wing of the Episcopal Church, a wing that was born in the early nineteenth century in Great

Britain. It moved away from the more Protestant side that had dominated Anglican tradition until then, developing liturgical practices close to those of the Roman Catholic Church, and forming monastic communities that hadn't existed since Henry the VIII suppressed all of them in the sixteenth century.

When we arrived at the monastery, the guest master showed us to our individual rooms and gave us a printed sheet with the daily "horarium," the Benedictine-inspired schedule. It included the historical daily monastic rhythm of seven periods of corporate prayer spread through the day and night. It also included times for daily Mass, mealtimes, and the overnight Great Silence after Compline, the last shared prayer time of the day. The monks themselves had special times of the day between these prayer gatherings for work, study, and communal recreation.

This daily rhythm impressed me, assuring time each day for attending every dimension of needed community life. Some of it was in solitude, other parts were communal. It had been well tested through fifteen hundred years of Benedictine history. Monks took the traditional vows of poverty, chastity, and obedience. It was one way that radical Christian commitment could be lived out. Father McBurney was an associate member of the community, which meant that he committed himself to a serious prayer life, wore a small wooden cross as a sign of his commitment, came to the monastery for an annual retreat, and met regularly with a spiritual director.

Our three days of retreat were spent in silence. While walking alone in the woods on the edge of the Hudson River on the first full day, I suddenly was overwhelmed by a sense of benevolent radiant Presence that I could not explain; it caught up my whole being. It lasted for only a very few minutes, but it imprinted itself in my consciousness forever. I felt that the silence and rhythm of the day, together with my desire for a deeper spiritual awareness, helped to open the way for that experience. It was fed also by a fresh, positive sense of my Roman Catholic upbringing in the High Mass on one of my days there. I was transported to another quality of Presence when the thurifer (holder of the incense pot) swung the thurible (incense pot) as he processed down the main chapel aisle. It brought back to life what it was like for incense to pervade my consciousness, overwhelming any sense of distance or distraction from sacred Presence, as I experienced at times in my early Catholic Masses.

I rode back to Hanover in a daze at the end of the retreat. I had touched a mystical nerve in me that yearned to be fed, and I didn't sense the invitation to that spiritual food in Congregational practices. I pummeled Father McBurney with questions about the Episcopal Church, about which I knew little. I would bring back to Cambridge a new probing of where I belonged.

I had one other responsibility in Hanover during my time there. I was asked to be the summer chaplain at the small hospital in town. That was a brand-new experience for me. I hardly had stepped into a hospital since I was confined to one with the mysterious throat ailment I had as a child in New York City. My job was to look in on patients who were open to a visit and offer them comfort, prayer, and a listening heart. My one clear memory of those visits was walking into the room of a lady in her sixties, who had been diagnosed with terminal cancer. She greeted me with a confident smile. Her mind was clear. She talked with me from a place of deep, accepting, loving peace. She didn't really need my presence, but I needed hers. She left me with an indelible blessing of tasting her peace and the way it showed me that death was not to be ultimately feared. Death was part of life, and in a Christian context, a transition to a larger life. In an oblique way, that experience connected with my time at the monastery: this dying lady witnessed to a deep, trustworthy, living presence that transcends ego's fragile, grasping, confused, self-protective hold on my consciousness.

Finding My Spiritual Home in the Episcopal Church

When I returned to the divinity school that fall, I found myself seeking out the few Episcopal students there. The most influential one was Bob Mill, who was a priest getting another master's degree. He spoke of the Anglican tradition (as had others in that optimistic era) as a "sleeping giant," and spelled out all that he felt it offered. He had friends at the nearby Episcopal Divinity School to whom he introduced me. They were mostly in the Anglo-Catholic (also called "High Church") tradition. Some of them attended one of the highest "High Churches" in New England: Church of the Advent, located on Beacon Hill in downtown Boston. Little by little I made the decision to take the leap into membership. I didn't leave the Congregational Church with any antipathy; indeed, I left with some guilt. It had been good to me in the two years I had been a member. I respected much about it. But I felt that in the Episcopal Church I found what seemed like the rich side of the Catholic Church I had left, minus the authoritarianism and rigid views that turned me off in that still pre–Second Vatican Council era.

I was required to come into my new denomination through a local Episcopal parish. I set up a time to talk with the rector of Christ Church in Cambridge (just a few blocks from the First Congregational Church where I was a member). As it turned out, that was one of the "lowest" (i.e., Protestant oriented) Episcopal churches in Massachusetts. When the rector heard that I had been attending Church of the Advent, he was very reluctant to accept me; Church of the Advent was beyond the pale of acceptability in his eyes. I finally convinced him to reluctantly agree, though. In that era of the Episcopal Church, there was a great divide between High and Low churches. Fortunately, over later decades, these extremes diminished, and I think most Episcopal churches moved toward a middle ground. But that new era had not yet evolved.

In the next semester I found an Episcopal church in Marblehead that would accept me to do field work as a seminarian, working with its high school kids. The old rector there shared with me a lot of his practical parish experience (and some slanted views, too, to my mind).

In my final semester at Harvard, the required final written and oral exams for the MDiv degree loomed ahead. How do you study for exams that could ask *anything* about theology, church history, scripture, ethics, and pastoral ministry? And find the time to do it on the side of the last semester course work that I needed to do?

All the exams were given day by day during one agonizing week in May. I've never stayed up nearly all night for so many days ahead of and sometimes during that week. I remember going with Carl Straub, a fellow senior student involved in the same ordeal, to a nearby cafeteria the night before they began. We sat in a booth and while eating we talked about our nervousness. We began laughing. And laughing more. We couldn't stop. It was the steam valve for bloated anxiety. Other customers must have thought we were nuts—and in a temporary way, we were. We walked back to Andover Hall as ready as we could be to walk the plank and trust that the exam waters we fell into would be familiar and swimmable.

I have almost no memory of the exams themselves. All I know is that G-d was merciful, and I somehow passed all the written and oral exams. In hindsight I wonder why I didn't have a more "trust in G-d" calm attitude, knowing that whatever happened would be redeemable in time. You could say that that was the one exam I failed.

Pilgrimage to Inspiring Places in Post-World War European Christianity

In the summer of 1961 I joined an Episcopal group of clergy and seminarians for a two-week pilgrimage to a number of inspiring Christian sites in post–World War II Europe. The war had left many Christians feeling the need for a fresh start. The church's life and thought in and before that war had often been backward-looking or compromised by accommodation to rising dictatorships. Europe needed a church that looked to the future and not just the past, a church that could help inspire a deeper sense of Christian faith and life and whatever actions would make for a more peaceful world.

One expression of this aspiration showed itself in daring new church architecture that broke continuity with pre-war traditional architecture. One such expression was the new Anglican Coventry Cathedral built out of the ruins of the old one, which was destroyed by Nazi bombs. Some remains of the old cathedral were preserved for people to visit, to remind them of the destruction that happens when nations try to conquer other nations and when then the desire for revenge can lead to another round of destruction. Reconciliation—the need for forgiveness and developing new ways of living together in a just peace—was the key value held up by the very modern new cathedral. A new international spiritual community was founded there, the Community of the Cross of Nails, made up of people committed to continue the work of reconciliation around the world. I was very moved by our visit and prayer there. The large altar cross purposely left amid the ruins of the old cathedral gave me a stark sense of Jesus's words on the cross: "Father, forgive them, for they know not what they do" (Lk 23:34).

We visited other strikingly new churches in Europe, built by famous architects. I can't remember their names now. I only remember the "feel" of a side chapel in one of them in France, where the daylight streamed in through hidden skylights that lit up the walls and overwhelmed me with a sense of the mystery and light of G-d's presence.

Another church we visited in France was very old, but its liturgy foreshadowed the bold changes soon coming from the Second Vatican Council. This was the Church of Saint Severin on the Left Bank in Paris, where many university students live. Among other things, the church brought back the shared exchange of peace with your neighbors in the pews that had been missing for centuries in the Eucharistic services of almost all churches. It came after the people's confession of sins, as an affirming sign of reconciliation. The exchange involved clasping the hands of your neighbors in the pew and saying "The peace of Christ be with you." Another practice I experienced there for the first time was the offering basket. A big basket sat inside the entrance to the church, where people were encouraged to leave food and other items for the poor. The filled basket was brought up at the offertory, along with the bread and wine.

The pilgrimage took us to some new religious communities that had recently risen in Europe. One was the Taizé community near a tiny village in eastern France. It was founded as an ecumenical men's Protestant monastic community that would foster the post–World War II need for reconciliation among churches and peace among peoples in the world, with a special focus on drawing youth together to be inspired and contribute to the fulfillment of this vision. The new community reached out to Roman Catholics who shared their vision, and they were loaned a local Catholic church until they built their own. I was very taken by their simple way of life together and by their liturgy filled with silence, newly created Taizé chants, and abundant candlelight, with the brothers in their white habits sitting together in the middle of the congregation.

Over the following years, to this day, the community has attracted thousands of youth from all over the world to retreats and special massive youth gatherings. Some of these gatherings began to be offered in other countries in areas where there were ethnic and other forms of conflict. In these gatherings, the youth would process behind a cross from one part of a conflicted community to the other, seeking reconciliation.

Taizé songs have joined the hymnbooks of churches of all stripes. I remember participating in a Taizé chant gathering for over a thousand young people at the Washington National Cathedral some years ago, where the singing continued, interspersed with periods of silence, until 1 a.m. Many Roman Catholic, Anglican, and Protestant churches today have weekly Taizé song and silence sessions, in an atmosphere full of votive candlelight and a large icon cross. The cross is sometimes lying flat on the floor in front of the altar, where people can individually come forward and kneel before it in silent prayer, some leaning down to kiss the cross.

In my time at Taizé that summer, and in all my contacts in later years, I've felt that the Spirit was alive and bringing amazing renewal and reconciling power to individuals, churches, and the world. I've found it to be one of the enduring expressions of hope in an often-discouraging world.

Our European pilgrimage took us to another enduring center of hope for the church and world: the Iona community on the Isle of Iona, off the west coast of Scotland. Under the leadership of Church of Scotland Minister George McCloud, the ruined abbey founded by the Irish missionary monk St. Columba in the sixth century, was rebuilt and a nonresidential religious community was formed that gave special place to serving the needs and justice of the poor in Scottish cities, as well as inspiration for the renewal of the Church of Scotland's life and worship.

Iona is a tiny island (just three miles long) with a population of less than two hundred people, outnumbered by the sheep. To get there involves a long bus or car ride from Edinburgh or Glasgow to Oban, then a ferry across to the island of Mull, a bus or car to the end of that island, and finally a launch (more recently a small ferry) to Iona. People today come on pilgrimage from all over the world, from every Christian tradition.

We stayed at the restored stone abbey. When Communion is offered, everyone is invited to sit around an enormously long table. The community has developed its own hymnbook and daily worship services. In them I felt the ancient hallowed presence of St. Columba and his successors and the freshness of the Iona community's renewal. In a walk to St. Columba's Bay on the far side of the island, where by legend he first landed from Ireland, his presence also was palpable. St. Columba was one of a number of Celtic saints who helped bring Christianity to Western Europe.

In later years I returned to Iona, first with my family, then on the Shalem Institute's pilgrimages there. The pilgrimage always included a silent walk together to St. Columba's Bay. I remember being very moved by one pilgrim who brought the ashes of his recently deceased wife to be poured into the bay. The rest of us stood on the rocky shore in prayer and silence while he and a supportive other pilgrim walked forward with the ashes to the water's edge and offered them to G-d in this holy site. On another pilgrimage, a pilgrim buried her deceased husband's ashes in one of the ruins of the old abbey, joining the nearby graves of long-deceased monks.

Each time of the four times I have been privileged to set foot on that holy island over a period of fifty years, I found it to be a "thin" place between heaven and earth, full of a healing, hopeful, and living Presence, as have so many other pilgrims. Its unpretentious grazing land, few houses and small stores, and the stand-out abbey, full of reverent pilgrims, surrounded by a turquoise sea and penetrating light from the clear blue sky when the mists suddenly thin out, always leaves me tranquil yet not complacent. I always feel a call and empowerment to let the holy Presence pervade my being and draw me to my true nature and life in G-d.

The one "peculiar" note on the island for me always is a walk over its nearly invisible small nine-hole pitch-and-putt golf course. Golf originated in Scotland, and here it must be in its original form. Many people don't even recognize they're walking on it. There's no sign. It's just a continuation of the grassland, maybe a fifty-square-yard section of it, with no greens, and sometimes not even visible markers for the holes. It's kept cut by the sheep who graze on it. It's wonderfully Iona in its simplicity and lack of commercialism.

Iona was the last place visited on our European pilgrimage that summer, but it wasn't the end of the pilgrimage for two of us. Bob Mill and I had arranged to continue the pilgrimage together on our own for a week in order to visit a few more holy sites in northern England. We rented a car and spent our first night at a remote little hotel in northern Scotland. Late that evening, Bob received a long-distance phone call that brought him the news of his mother's sudden death. We left the hotel at once and drove the hours it took to get to the airport near Glasgow. The drive somehow matched the disorientation and power of that unexpected death. We drove in pitch darkness on unfamiliar, winding roads, drenched by a severe thunderstorm whose lightning lit up the heather-covered hills for a flash of time. We finally arrived at the airport and we sadly parted company. I had decided to continue the pilgrimage on my own.

After a night's rest in Glasgow, I drove east toward the first of three sites we had planned to visit: Durham Cathedral. That was long a pilgrimage center in honor of St. Cuthbert, another Celtic missionary saint, who was bishop there and is buried in the cathedral. The beauty of his special burial place was striking, including the preserved clothing and other articles of his life on display in the museum next to his grave. I felt the continuing holiness of the place. My prayer flowed easily there.

The next site was Lindisfarne, a tiny island off the northeast coast of England, another ancient pilgrimage site, because it was where St. Cuthbert had his hermitage. The road to the island can only be reached at low tide. When you arrive, you see offshore an even smaller little island where St. Cuthbert's hermitage once stood. The little living church on the island felt like an authentic place of prayer. A small Anglican religious community lives in one of the few buildings on the island. On the far end is a fairy-tale castle that was built by a nobleman after the Reformation that has no religious significance.

The third and last site I visited was the one that was most striking and enduring in my memory. It was a new friary of the Anglican Franciscan community, which at that time was the largest Anglican men's religious order with a number of friaries in Britain and other countries. The community had just bought a small, old inn on a cliff overlooking the North Sea in Alnmouth, Northumberland. When I arrived, the six friars there were hard at work renovating the entire building.

The only place fully renovated was the chapel. When I entered it, my mind instantly sank into my heart and I felt a transcendent Presence. The chapel itself was very simple, befitting Franciscan tradition of simplicity in all things. There was a small wooden altar, a vigil light, and an expansive view through a window behind them of sea and sky. The message it spoke to me: "This is all I need to ground my life and prayer: a simple space devoted to my deepest consciousness in G-d, and ideally an expansive view of sky and water that points to the mysterious yet palpable vastness of life in G-d."

In the few days I was there, I had long talks with Michael Fisher, the guardian (superior) of the community. He sensed a readiness in me for a deeper spiritual awareness. I was the first guest of this new house and so he could afford more time with me. I was moved to make my first formal confession in many years with him. I spent a good deal of time going over those years and reflecting on what I needed to confess. I brought a long, written list with me when it came time to meet Michael in the chapel. It was a relief to let it all go to G-d with a sense of repentance and to receive a sense of forgiveness and new life in my absolution. It wasn't a relief, though, to discover afterward that I somehow had lost the written confession on the grounds of the friary on the way back to my cell! I searched everywhere for it, but I never found it. After my initial anxiety about someone else reading it, I finally relaxed with a sense that in its mysterious disappearance the whole list of sins had literally been taken away from me and lost, taken away forever.

I later found out that Father Michael was a charismatic pied piper in the larger Franciscan community. He was a vessel of the Spirit's inspiration that led many new young men to join the community. In his presence I was tempted to join myself, but I never felt enough of a call to do it.

The religious community life has a way of symbolizing radical spiritual commitment. A community member years later told me that monks and friars are just another group of struggling Christians, but their symbolic power as a vowed community leaves them able to be an inspiration for many people who are not members. I maintained my relationship with the Franciscans by formally becoming a "companion" of the community, which involved a commitment to support the community and some basic Franciscan values in my life.

Mixed in with all the seriousness of my time at the friary were several lighter moments. The first was drinking coffee every morning with hot milk. I never drank coffee before then: I didn't like it. Tea was my morning drink. But I had never drunk a cup of half coffee and half hot milk. I loved it, and ever since coffee has been my morning wake-up gift. I remember once reading that drinking coffee began as a spiritual practice in Turkey many centuries ago, which added a special aura to it—a way of "waking up to G-d," if you will.

The other lighter event was a trip with the brothers to the mansion of the current Lord Earl Grey (of Earl Grey tea fame) in the nearby town of Alnwick. The daughter of Earl Grey was the patron of the new friary, which I assumed included giving it the money it needed for renovation. She also was the wife of the last British Governor General of Kenya. (Keep in mind that British colonialism wasn't quite dead yet in 1961, but well on its way out.)

The trip had a very practical primary purpose: to take a bath. The plumbing for bathtubs (which still were the primary way to get your body clean in Britain at that time, rather than showers) had not yet been installed in the renovating friary. Lord Grey and his daughter had generously offered their bathtubs to the brothers in the interim.

When we stepped out of our van before the imposing mansion and were welcomed into the foyer, a maid passed out a towel to each of us. Over the next hour or so we took turns taking a bath in the available bathrooms. What a contrast to the friary, where every room was torn up and strewn with signs of ongoing renovation! (I, as the only guest, was given the only room with a bed; the brothers slept on the floor.) The contrast continued as we sat around an elegant table after our baths and sipped tea with the elderly Earl and his daughter. Afterward, he took us on a tour of his prized rhododendron garden behind the mansion, which also included a variety of other plants and trees that gave a certain wildness to the garden that I think was in vogue at that time. In the middle of the huge garden was a lovely small stone chapel.

When our time there ended, we expressed our gratitude and departed. I felt as though the day had been a paradoxical experience of intermingling wealth, status, and simple Franciscan poverty that Francis himself experienced as he related to the Italian nobility of his time, without being compromised in his vocation. In Britain, with all its historical feudal self-indulgence and frequent sense of superiority, one strand of its nobility at least has been conditioned to believe that it is responsible for using its wealth and privilege to benefit the larger community and society. I think that matches an enduring strand of Christian tradition that justifies receiving or developing wealth only in so far as its main intent is to use the wealth to serve the common good.

When I left the friary, I drove south toward Heathrow Airport on a windy day where clouds sped across the sunlit sky in accelerated time. I stopped for my last night in Britain in a small hotel, getting up in time to respond to the bell of the village church for morning prayer. I was the only person present besides the vicar. I fumbled around in the English Book of Common Prayer trying to find the proper responses of the congregation, until the vicar gave up and just sped along with the service on his own.

I was reminded of an English sociological study in that time that spoke of the positive effect of a village church's bells on the mental health of the community, even for people who didn't normally attend. They in effect attended vicariously, wanting and even needing the bell to ring and the service to happen. In a village where the church had been closed and the bells stopped ringing, the mental health of the community was negatively affected. Ever since reading that study, I've been aware that there can be many more people in church than those who show up in person. Those who come in person in a sense stand in for many who do not come.

As an aside, my wife and I took another pilgrimage some years later which we extended by remained in Paris on our own for a few days after finishing an exploration of western France with a Road Scholar group. We visited the Church of St. Severin on the Left Bank that I earlier described. Its creativity continues. Now it has a big bulletin board along one wall near the entrance where you could pin written prayers for people and causes. On the other side of the church near the entrance I noticed a new large room with a clear glass wall facing the aisle; you can see a chair sat on each side of a desk. A sign pointing in the direction of that room said it was the confessional. What a different feel that confessional had from that of my childhood: the old, dark, tiny booth with kneeling space where a priest sat behind a screen to hear your confession! Here you were in a face-to-face encounter with a priest who would listen to your confession, counsel you as seemed called for, and pronounce G-d's word of forgiveness and offer the freedom for a new beginning.

We also visited a huge, old Jesuit church, St. Ignatius, hidden behind the façade of a modern apartment building. The Jesuits there focus on young working Catholics and have devised a liturgy that includes, after the gospel lesson is read, everyone going apart from one another to some chapel or other place they're drawn to sit in the huge church. For fifteen minutes, each participant silently reflects on the gospel along with the prayer it evoked in them, then returns to where they were. They meet for another ten minutes with several other people to share together what came to them. The liturgy proceeds at a slow, reflective pace, so much so that it's called "the Mass that takes its time." It provides a sacred spaciousness for urban young adults, many of whose lives otherwise are spiritually spaceless. Hundreds come each Sunday. Many also participate in pilgrimages to sacred places in France, such as Chartres Cathedral (where the ancient pilgrimage labyrinth built into the cathedral floor is found that has inspired its replication in hundreds of churches and retreat centers throughout the United States and around the world).

We discovered yet another old, large church in Paris that now provides much silence in its services, as well as chanting together. The church has been given to the New Jerusalem Community, which is made up of many young Catholic men and women who have committed themselves to work part-time in secular jobs and give the rest of their time to the renewal of the urban church in France. Amazing things are happening today in this possibly most secular of European countries! Similar new religious communities have arisen in other parts of Europe.

Deepening Community at the Episcopal Theological School

As a seminarian who had not gone to an Episcopal seminary, I was required by the bishop to enroll for an extra year at the Episcopal Theological School (ETS) in Cambridge, located just a few blocks from Harvard Divinity School. I enrolled in the special one-year Anglican Studies program.

Ironically, my assigned roommate for the year, Sarkis Sarkisian, was not Episcopalian but rather Armenian Orthodox. He was a recent escapee from Soviet Russian–controlled Armenia, where he had been a student in an Armenian seminary. He told me that at least one fellow student was in fact a Soviet agent, whose job it was to secretly spy on other students and report to the secret police any anti-Soviet conversations or activities. When he arrived in this country, there was no Armenian seminary for him to continue his studies, so his bishop decided to send him to ETS.

I learned a lot about Anglican tradition that year in my classes, as well as from talking with fellow students three times a day in the school refectory and with a small group of students whom I befriended and hung out with. Among my happiest moments were in the required daily chapel services. In my years at Harvard, only a few students went to chapel. Also, as I said earlier, at that time there was no refectory at Harvard where you could come to know fellow students and share ideas and experiences. There was little sense of shared life. At ETS, a sense of religious community and shared vocation was strong. Gathering together in chapel expressed the heart of such community.

All students had to wear an Oxford gown in chapel, and every student had an assigned place. I don't think either of these were important to most other students, but for me, who had experienced years of the lack of close community at Harvard, they were signs of belonging. The gown expressed a common vocation that transcended our individual differences. My assigned place in the chapel expressed my unique place in the whole. If I or others were missing or present, others would know it. It was not an anonymous gathering. It was a gathering of people in which everyone had a place that they alone could fill, and by inference, a community that shared a commitment to the well-being of one another.

A complementary community existed nearby ETS: an Episcopal monastery founded by the Society of St. John the Evangelist. It lives by a Benedictine rule (recently wonderfully revised by that community for our times). I participated in their services from time to time and in later years made a retreat there; once, I also led a workshop on spiritual direction. The monastery provided spiritual directors for Harvard and seminary students and many clergy and laity in and beyond Cambridge, and a year-round retreat ministry. My mind settled down there and my spiritual heart opened, especially when I joined the monks in singing psalms and in the living, intimate silent times together.

As I alluded to earlier, a monastery is archetypal: it represents to the human psyche a sense of what it is to be fully committed to the spiritual journey in community. Their very existence, even if you rarely go inside a monastery, carries a sense of the human yearning for a deeper in-reach and out-reach for wholeness, for a shared way of life centered on the wholeness of the Giver of life.

My other major memory of that year was of someone who did not belong to either community yet gifted me in a special personal way. Her name was Judy Green. I was walking through the marvelous Pitti Palace art gallery in Florence, Italy, the summer before, on that European church pilgrimage. I stopped before some famous painting, and someone else stopped in front of it at the same time. In a spontaneous moment, our eyes met. Her sparkling green eyes drew me in—indeed, really mesmerized me. Somehow words began to sound between us. She was an American student from Sarah Lawrence College in Connecticut, studying art in Florence for the summer. After only a few minutes of getting acquainted, I knew I wanted to see her again, but our pilgrimage group was about to leave Florence and there would be no time. I asked her for her address where she lived in Westport, Connecticut, and whether it would be okay to contact her when I returned. She said yes, and I floated away with Cupid's arrow in my heart.

When I returned to Cambridge, one of the first things I did was call her. She invited me to visit her at Sarah Lawrence College for a day, which I quickly agreed to do. We had a wonderful time together. At one point I saw a photo of her she had in her room. It featured her on the front page of a recent issue of *Look* magazine, leaning back on a chair planted in the shallow surf of an ocean beach in a bathing suit. Wow! What other word could convey her beauty.

I found out that she was Jewish, and she found out that I was a Christian seminarian, but that difference didn't stop us. When I returned to ETS, my room was across the hall from a pay phone booth. We spent hours on that phone together many times. I have no idea what we talked about now, I just remember wanting the calls to last as long as possible. Soon she invited me to spend the night in her family home and meet her parents. Then I invited her to come and stay at the seminary for a weekend. It was a very new and strange experience for her. Without really talking about it, I think we both realized the tenuousness of our future relationship, in light of her Jewish faith and her more secular orientation to life.

We kept in regular contact, though, that whole academic year. The following June she came to my ordination at Washington Cathedral. As close as we were, that did it. It was very painful and yet we both realized that we would have no future together. But I remained very grateful for the yearlong gift of my time with her.

The Call to Ordination and Ministry in Washington, DC

When I was moved to envision ordination as a priest, I had to find a parish church and a bishop who would sponsor me as a seminarian. Hans Hofmann, my old adviser at Harvard Divinity School, suggested going to Washington, DC, because he thought more people there than elsewhere have to face and deal with the country's and the larger world's problems and cultures. I took his advice and was put in touch with Felix Kloman, the rector of a large parish in DC. He agreed to interview me.

When I took the train down to DC, I stayed in the YMCA overnight, and I found my way to his office the next morning. He had many years of experience as a parish priest and with candidates for Holy Orders. Normally no one would sponsor you for ordination without your being a longtime member of the parish, and I was very unsure whether he would make an exception for me. He proved to be a very trusting man, though. Dr. Kloman had recently had a cancerous larynx removed and he could speak only in a whisper, but I managed to understand his questions about my background and sense of calling to be a priest. At the end, he said he would accept me as a member of his church and would send me for an interview with the Episcopal bishop of Washington, William Creighton.

I left his office relieved and happy. I immediately called the bishop's office and managed to get an appointment for the next day. After hearing my story, Bishop Creighton proved to be as trusting as Dr. Kloman: he agreed to accept me as a postulant (the first step toward ordination) if I was found mentally competent in a psychological exam, which I later passed. I was amazed. Today acceptance would be much harder: I would have had to go through a much more extensive and drawn-out series of background questionnaires and discernment meetings with a special committee in the parish and with a special diocesan committee as well, which can take over many months and even years.

The next step along the way was to take a series of "canonical exams" that showed sufficient grasp of such subjects as scripture, New Testament Greek, theology, pastoral ministry, liturgics, and church history. The exams are more standardized across the country now. But at my time of taking them, each subject exam was developed by knowledgeable priests in each diocese appointed by the bishop. I have a vivid memory of the setting for my Greek exam. The priest invited me to meet for lunch in a Chinese restaurant near his parish. After getting acquainted over our meal, he pulled out a Greek New Testament and pointed to a paragraph for me to translate into English. I managed to get it right, and that was it—exam passed.

The next stage was to find a parish that would accept a young, inexperienced, brand-new priest. I was invited to Washington, DC, in the spring to meet with the rectors of two parishes that were looking for assistant priests. One was a well-established and well-regarded traditional Episcopal parish, Holy Trinity, with a rector known for his great preaching. The other available church, St. Stephen and the Incarnation, was in the first year of a radical transition. Its inner-city residential neighborhood was rapidly changing from European American to African American. This was 1962, and most churches as well as so many other institutions were still in effect segregated by race. The vestry (elected lay leaders) of the parish had made the courageous decision the year before to invite a New York City social activist and inner-city priest, Bill Wendt, to become the rector of St. Stephen's and lead it into a new integrated era, a challenge he accepted.

When I arrived at the red-bricked church I was amazed at its size. It turned out to be the largest parish church building in the diocese (apart from the cathedral), built about 1929 as a merger between two Episcopal churches: St. Stephen's and the Church of the Incarnation. I met with Bill Wendt in his office. He told me he had been a fighter pilot over North Africa during World War II. After the war, he and a few other veterans went to seminary together with a shared calling to become priests dedicated to ministry with marginalized people in inner-city churches.

He folded his hands behind his head (a gesture I would unconsciously pick up from him over time) and asked me a few questions about my life and how I felt about working in a church that was losing most of its white parishioners and just beginning to attract black ones, with uncertainty about what the future would hold. He also pointed out his commitment to offer social services for the many poor and working-class black people who were moving into the neighborhood, whether or not they became members of the church. He needed help. Herbert Aldrich, a much older single priest who lived with Bill and his family in the rectory next door to the church, was still on staff, but Bill needed a young priest willing to bring fresh energy to the tenuous venture ahead.

He invited me on the spot to join him, if money could be raised to support me. Some weeks later, I was told that Bishop Creighton had managed to do that, barely. All he could offer in material compensation was a salary of $3,500 a year; the parish would give me a two-room living space in a church-owned house next door to the rectory, in which a retired church couple devoted to working with the poor already lived. Bill and his wife, Mary, would offer me meals with their family next door.

So my choice was clear for beginning my ministry: a fine traditional, well-off white downtown church (if its rector would accept me), or this rapidly changing parish with an uncertain future and a visionary, courageous new rector. When I brought the choice to prayer and discernment with the help of Dr. Kloman, I was strongly moved to choose the unpredictable future of St. Stephen's. I didn't even ask for an interview with the rector of Trinity. I called Bill Wendt and said, "I'm with you!" Over the next five years my calling there was powerfully confirmed.

Chapter 7

The Whirlwind Years at St. Stephen's during a Historic Moment in the Church Worldwide

In June I left Cambridge with a fully packed car of my belongings, drove to Washington, DC, and moved into the "church house" next door to the rectory. I was ordained that month as a deacon in Washington Cathedral (a required step before ordination as a priest, which would come the next December). Thus began the most all-around challenging years of my life.

What did I bring to meet that challenge, beyond a sense of calling and a dedicated energy to learn and give what I could? In hindsight, I think I brought an empathic sensitivity to people that I had shown since early childhood, although there were some people I just couldn't easily identify with. I liked to please people (sometimes too much—I often avoided conflict when I should not have). I liked to look good to people, especially as a priest, but that could lead me to hide my dark and incompetent sides and look better than I really was. I obsessively embraced responsibility for whatever I took on. I liked being on a creative frontier and working collaboratively. I liked teaching and preaching, even if I was such a novice and so cerebrally conditioned theologically at Harvard that I'm sure I missed communicating with many people on a simple, more concrete level. I held a biblical vision of Jesus's evolving kingdom of G-d on earth that valued human inclusiveness, justice, peace, and the interwoven love of G-od, neighbor, and self, but that vision could be compromised on the firing line by my ego, fears, and limitations.

In summary, I brought to the church my strengths and weaknesses, which I hoped could complement all the other church leaders' own light and dark sides. I was clear that together we offered so much more than we could alone.

Bill Wendt wanted a "team ministry" where we shared leadership of church services, along with special responsibilities for each of us. Every Saturday morning the team met together and reflected on what had been happening and on creative possibilities for the parish. Every winter we would have a two-night retreat together at a motel in Ocean City and let our prayerful imaginations sore as to what more we could do. Because of the exodus of so many white parishioners and the arrival of both white and black people who liked the new directions of the parish, we felt that we were limited only by our inadequate awareness of the Spirit's imagination as to what could be done.

A new young priest, Barry Evans, joined us the year after I came. His special strength was liturgical reform, which was invaluable at a historic moment in the church worldwide, where there was growing openness to a less rigid, simpler, and more alive liturgy and more intimate sacred space. He helped oversee a major architectural change of the chancel that, among other things, brought a striking new altar closer to the people, which made it accessible for Communion and prayer from all sides. I brought into the main Sunday Eucharist two elements that I had learned in my visit to the parish of St. Severin in Paris: the exchange of peace with one another after confession, and a basket placed at the church entrance in which people could place material items for the poor. As at St. Severin, the basket was brought forward and offered up at the altar along with the bread and wine.

Christian education was my special work, especially teaching the Confirmation classes, which were full of an interracial mix of new people who were attracted to the church.

The First Summer Camp

The first summer I was there, Bill put me in charge of overseeing a Monday-through-Friday, two-month-long, full-day camp that had begun the summer before. It attracted two hundred mostly poor African American elementary and middle school children in the neighborhood. It was an all-consuming and exhausting responsibility, eye-opener, wonder, and joy. The interracial volunteer staff each year included about five young "Clayton Volunteers" from Great Britain; an Anglican priest from Nigeria, Singapore, or India; college and seminary student volunteers from across the country who served as class leaders; local high school students who assisted them; and qualified volunteers for music, arts and crafts, Bible study, and recreation. A volunteer program director supervised the twenty-three staff members. Those from other states and countries stuffed the extra rooms of the rectory and the church house, spilling over to the homes of parishioners. For many of the staff it was the first opportunity they ever had to develop personal and working relationships across racial and nationality lines.

Each day began at 9:00 a.m. with all the students and teachers sitting together in the church nave for a half hour of prayer, song, and scripture, led by me. The day ended at 2:45 p.m. with everyone singing and praying together in church again. I felt these were really valuable times that kept before everyone a larger vision of who we are as dignified, unique images of G-d, meant to live out creative love, justice, and joy together, as Jesus did, and to challenge whatever gets in the way of that purpose.

Parents came to special meetings during the summer in order for the staff to show them what we were doing and to air various neighborhood concerns. In addition to the daily program, an older neighborhood teenage group met for three evenings each week.

The staff was invited to weekly evening sessions led by challenging and visionary social, religious, and political leaders. On Friday evenings the live-in staff were invited to a particular layperson's home for dinner and conversation. Usually these hosts were white people anxious to find and foster personal connection with black and brown people in a still very segregated society. Often it was the first time a person of another race had ever crossed their door in a social capacity.

I vividly remember one of those evenings spent in the home of Gerry Lanigan. She was a beautiful woman whose magnificent singing voice beguiled anyone privileged to hear her sing. She had lit countless candles in the living and dining rooms that evening, turning the house into a flickering wonderland. After dinner, Bill Wendt spoke for all: "Sing for us, Gerry!" We gathered around her piano and for close to an hour she sang to us songs of love, sorrow, beauty, nature, G-d, and community. I was reminded of how song heard and sung can bring people together in a uniquely powerful way, transcending human differences. No wonder heaven is so often portrayed as full of singing!

The summer program ended with the annual "Day of Witness." The children were decked out in different national costumes representing the theme: one family in Christ. They walked in an ecumenical procession through ten neighborhood blocks, accompanied by several bands, a float, clergy wearing vestments, and laypeople. It ended in the church with a Eucharist dedicated to the world mission of the church that included outreach to the whole human family, celebrated by a Nigerian Anglican bishop. The church was packed with about seven hundred people from the neighborhood and from all over the Washington area, a marvelous assortment of humanity finding common cause together.

The grand finale of the day was a gigantic festival that took weeks of preparation and everyone's involvement. In effect it began the day before the festival with an organized neighborhood cleanup, including a rat hunt. Special recognition was given to the person who killed the largest rat. Rats proliferated in alley garbage cans; and rat bites, particularly to babies, were common.

Parents and other neighborhood adults whom staff had met through visits and special programs were asked to use their personal skills to help the children and staff with the festival. Together we devised contests and made booths, costumes, floats, banners, and arrangements for food and music.

I can remember the transcendent moment when it all came together for me. The festival day was half over. I knew the suffering and joy, the gifts and scars of so many of the people present. There were many others about whose life experience I could only guess. While resting alone on a bench in the churchyard for a few minutes, watching it all, I suddenly felt the deep "rightness" of everything happening there. Divine Spirit energy was moving through all of this, affirming not just our efforts but also ourselves just as we were—in and beyond our actions. I felt part of a great "happening" where boundaries dissolved and a common bond showed itself. It was a truly blessed day. A soft smile came to my face. At that moment there was nothing to do but sit there in awe, appreciating a glimpse of the kin-dom of heaven.

The overall intent of the summer program was to bring together the gifts of a wide range of people on behalf of the neighborhood whose residents in turn would realize and share their own gifts with one another and with those who came. For the staff, our hope was that they would take away learnings and friendships with one another and with the children, which would foster a vision of the goodness of a pluralistic society that cared for one another. The summer lingered into the rest of the year, with children and adults coming for baptism, Confirmation, church school, social gatherings, and for material help and counseling.

A Widening Civil Right Struggle

These things were occurring in the early stage of the widening civil rights struggle of that time. Very different people were discovering one another in fresh ways, with a certain mutual vulnerability. It was a particularly personal and in some ways romantic phase of the struggle, marked by a frequently common desire to let down the boundaries across racial, class, and ethnic lines as much as possible in order to learn from and care for one another. We agreed to let a behavioral scientist from NIH, Dr. Ivor Kraft, observe our staff interactions during the program. I remember him saying that we have a new, precious period of vulnerable opening across many lines, especially racial, before the door may begin to close again and the lines between racial groups harden

Adventure on the Road

Early that summer we decided to add a new dimension to the program: field trips. We needed a bus to do that. Getting that bus was an amazing, humbling personal story. We put in a closed bid for an old army surplus bus, and we won it. It fell to me to get it. Mr. T, an older neighborhood volunteer, agreed to drive me about an hour and a half north, beyond Baltimore, to Fort Meade, where the bus was sitting. When we arrived, Mr. T dropped me off and headed back to Washington. I was left standing amid an assortment of ancient buses that the army had very sensibly retired from active duty.

After signing the necessary forms, I was taken to one of the buses, given a key, and waved off. Here I was, wearing a clerical collar, sitting behind the wheel of an old manual-shift army bus, with a fast-beating heart that knew I had never driven any bus before. I felt the incongruity of a civilian cleric driving down the highway as though he had joined the army. The bus still had all its army markings.

I managed to get the bus started (that was the only guarantee that came with it). After testing my capacity to turn the bus around corners while still at the army base, I pulled onto Route 95, the main, multilane East Coast north-south highway. Once in the far-right lane I figured I could make it to Washington. All I had to do was go straight and fairly slow.

Everything was fine until I entered the Baltimore Harbor Tunnel during rush hour. In the middle of the tunnel, the bus suddenly died. While I sat there desperately trying to get it started, I heard loud sirens go off. The entire southbound tunnel was closed. Then I saw a tow truck come up to what was now a lonely bus in the middle of a deserted tunnel. The driver wordlessly gave my clerical collar and the bus a strange look, towed me out, and deposited me in the Tunnel Authority's parking lot. He told me that the bus probably had a vapor lock. He sent me to the Tunnel Authority office. Expecting some huge fine, towing fee, and a frowning look, I was surprised to be given a slip of paper by a grinning official and sent on my way. The paper simply read, "We are sorry that you were inconvenienced!" I could hardly believe it, but not wanting to press my luck, I went back to the bus, happy to leave this embarrassing scene.

I held my breath as I turned the key in the ignition, and I breathed again as I heard the motor start up and idle. I pulled back onto the highway, hoping the worst was over. But about a half hour later, in the middle of nowhere, the vapor lock suddenly returned, giving me just enough time to turn onto the shoulder. By this time dusk had fallen. I began to worry that I would be stuck there in the approaching darkness without help. I climbed up the bank into the woods to see if there was a house in sight. There wasn't. I went back to the highway, stood in front of the bus, and stuck out my thumb. Surely someone would think a priest was safe to pick up. The cars whizzed by. The story of the good Samaritan passed through my mind. It was getting darker. Then a white sports car that had passed by pulled over and backed up. Out of the car stepped a beautiful young woman. She leaned on the fender, looked at me and said, "Can I help you?"

It turned out that she was a stripper on her way to work at the Silver Slipper in Washington's red-light district. She said she had once been in love with a man who decided to become a Roman Catholic priest. Out of those fond memories she had stopped when she saw me. While driving me to a gas station for help, she told me her story. A hidden goodness ran through it, along with tragedy. She told me never to come to the Silver Slipper. It was just a job for her; she wouldn't justify the place for anyone. When we found a service station, she dropped me off. I thanked her for the gift she had been for me, in her story and her stopping.

The station's tow-truck driver who took me back to the bus was a Baptist who spent our drive telling me about his own struggles and faith. Since I now had help, the bus, contrary to the end (it wouldn't start for me), came alive for him. This time I made it all the way home.

Responding to Social Concerns at the Time

A few days later we transformed the bus's drab army green into a bright civilian blue. Mr. T, who became our bus driver, carried students and staff throughout the summer program on many experience-expanding adventures: to beaches (some students had never seen the ocean), museums, parks, plays, and civil rights demonstrations.

The need for a sense of self-worth in G-d's image was vividly brought home to me later that fall. One afternoon in St. Stephen's after-school program, I ran into two little black sisters who were crying together in front of the church hall. Inside, a film about contemporary African people had just ended. When I asked them why they were crying, they blurted out that their mother had told them that Africans were savages. They didn't have to say any more. It quickly dawned on me that they knew those Africans looked like and were related to them, and they were ashamed. I tried my best to help them disabuse themselves of such a view, but I knew how reinforced it was in the culture of the time, grounded in historical white racism.

For many years I had it drummed into my head when I was studying anthropology that there was no such thing as a "primitive" people. There were only literate and nonliterate cultures. The latter often were as or more sophisticated than the former in all but technological know-how. But who knew anything about anthropology in 1962? Not many people. The mid-century civil rights movement and its advocacy of the equal dignity and rights of all G-d's people was just taking off, but it hadn't yet reached the parents of those girls.

The closest I remember having a little "taste of heaven" like the one I was given in the end-of-summer carnival was on the day of the great March on Washington to the Lincoln Memorial to hear Martin Luther King Jr. share his dream on a hot August day in 1963. I and others helped to organize a march from the church for everyone in the church and neighborhood who wanted to join us. We wanted to make it as much a witness to the values of the socially conscious church as possible, so we decided to walk behind a processional cross and several gospel-expressing banners.

Just before setting out, I walked through the nave of the church and ran into Moses Oyenladi, the Nigerian Anglican priest who was working with us that summer. He had been adamant about staying behind, feeling that what we were doing was an American affair in which a foreign national shouldn't get involved. Now he suddenly was looking very excited and rushed toward the door to join us. He said that he had just been strongly moved by the Spirit to come—this was *his* battle too.

A solemn, motley crowd of hundreds started down 16th Street, which normally is full of traffic and pedestrians. That day it looked almost deserted. Many people were terrified that a riot might break out and hunkered down in their homes. As we walked past other churches, we were joined eventually by hundreds of others. When we arrived at St. John's Episcopal Church, across from the White House, we paused. I walked up the church steps with a bullhorn and led a litany of prayer for this special day. The crowd spontaneously sang together "We Shall Overcome." Then we were caught up in waves of people coming from all directions as we continued toward the Lincoln Memorial and found a spot to stop in front of the reflecting pool, surrounded by banners and what looked like an endless crowd of people filling every square foot of space around the pool in front of the memorial. We were silenced and bonded together by the clearly inspired speech of Martin Luther King Jr. He expressed my dream and the dream of all of us gathered. I sensed G-d's opening Spirit energy coursing through the hearts of that massive crowd. I felt *G-d's* dream flowing through us and a rising hope that the dream would become reality in time, beyond whatever obstacles would show themselves.

One obstacle that Dr. King increasingly realized was the war dragging on in Vietnam, devastating the land and people on both sides of the war and costing many thousands of American and Vietnamese lives. The pursuit of peace needed to join the pursuit of racial and economic justice. I remember giving my first sermon at St. Stephen's against the war, before there was broad scale public demonstration against it. At that time, I would have been thrown out of most parishes other than St. Stephen's for my criticism, especially in an area with so many military and government personnel. Support of the war effort was considered a patriotic duty by a great many people. Among other things, I spoke of the devastating immorality of napalming peasant villages. At the large parish forum after the service, Gerry Lanigan (who I earlier mentioned as a host to the summer staff) stood up and publicly excoriated me for focusing on the poor peasants in Vietnam and not mentioning the danger to our troops there. Her husband was a marine colonel in Vietnam.

She was right. I should have expressed more concern for them. Even though the Vietnamese suffered much more dramatically, American troops also suffered terribly—not only the troops but also their families. The war was no good for anyone.

Speaking of the military, a few years later I had a revelatory meeting with some military officers at the Pentagon. I was invited to be part of a team of clergy who were change agents in the church's life, meeting with a team of Pentagon officers who saw themselves as change agents in military life. When we met, I expected we would find little in common. I was amazed to discover that we had some fundamental things in common:

1. We both were serving in institutions that were grounded in a particular founding document to which we proclaimed loyalty. For the church, it was the Bible. For the military, it was the Constitution, which expressed many overlapping assumptions about human nature and communal well-being with those in the church.
2. We both valued a shared, overlapping "discipline" woven into our way of life. For the church that included (ideally) the practices of prayer, study, personal and social moral commitments, and the willingness to sacrifice our private ego wants to a higher communal purpose. For the military, the discipline included physical and mental fitness, training and preparedness to work together to defeat an enemy, care for one another, and willingness to sacrificially defend the country.
3. We all felt that our sense of purpose and disciplines to fulfill that purpose were essential to the communal "salvation" of people— in other words, what we stood for and did were needed for the full communal well-being of the nation.

When I left the meeting, I realized for the first time why a number of early-retired military personnel become clergy and why a number of clergy commit themselves to being military chaplains. Consciously or unconsciously, they recognize their overlaps in values.

The exception, of course, is pacifist conscientious objectors, who have an ideal of human value and community that does not believe violence should be legitimized. I remember a cadet at the Naval Academy in Annapolis taking me aside after I taught a form of meditation there once. He told me of his struggle to accept the killing of other people in warfare as ever morally right. He exemplified a resistance to killing that is built into morally conditioned human consciousness, reflected in the Fifth Commandment. That showed itself in my leaving naval ROTC in college. The controversial theory of a just war challenges this view, but that view at least recognizes that any war is a last-choice reluctant option that must be subject to many restrictions.

Since my years at St. Stephen's coincided with powerful, challenging national social movements that needed to be addressed on many levels, a fair amount of my time was caught up in supporting them. At one point I was moved to join others from the Washington area on a chartered plane to a national racial justice demonstration in Montgomery, Alabama. As we were landing at the small Montgomery airport, I looked out the window and saw that many other chartered planes were lined up along the runway, from all over the country. We left our plane and joined thousands of other marchers, walking there through an African American neighborhood where people were on their porches looking at us in amazement and cheering us on. After hearing many speeches in front of the state capitol, the crowd slowly dispersed. We had a little trepidation that there might be a counterdemonstration or even attack, since we knew we were not welcome by many white people. Nothing happened though, and we managed to walk the miles back to our plane and return to Washington, feeling a special kind of solidarity and hope together.

Life as a Parish Priest in Changing Times

Attention to the volcanic national happenings were complemented in those years by a range of church pastoral duties. As a new priest serving an increasingly interracial and interclass community, complemented by street people in various states of mental difficulty, I felt like I was on a frontier most every day. Recently I found a copy of a letter I wrote my father early in my time at St. Stephen's. Here is a little excerpt contrasting my long academic life with this new context of being a priest in an extremely diverse community in a time of great societal change.

> I'm being forged here at a foundry whose fire will brand me forever. I hope in time I will have attained enough guts and experience to be able to serve people with some good effect.

Bill and Mary Wendt were committed to an open-rectory policy, where people in need could come to the door at any time. Mary was never afraid to speak her mind to anyone. She was full of strong moral values. Her energy and ability to cope with every kind of crisis never seemed to flag. She was a stable anchor for all of us, including her three young children. The rectory was a big old Victorian house with huge windows. One of many unique experiences there was seeing a man suddenly climb through one of the open windows one summer, run across the living room, and go out another window, as someone chased him from behind. We watched dumbfounded. We had no idea who they were.

The open-rectory policy stretched to the church offices during the day. We had a food closet that served many people. Others would come wanting money, sometimes with sad stories such as "I lost my money and need to get to New York with my family; can you help me?" My desk was next to Bill's, and I can remember more than once his listening to a story that he almost certainly knew was false. A smirk would come over his mouth to let the person know he didn't believe them, but then he would take out a ten-dollar bill from his pocket and offer it.

Several people were given permission to live in the basement of the church at various times. One was Pete. He was a gentle alcoholic who would try to sober up and get help, but then he would disappear and return drunk. Another one was a middle-aged homeless man, also an alcoholic, who moved into the basement with his wife.

One time when Bill was away on vacation, during a church service that I wasn't part of, a layperson came rushing out to me as I stood outside the church and said a woman in front of the altar had stripped off all of her clothes and wanted to publicly confess her sins. Someone else had managed to come up and put her coat over her and bring her outside to me. I whisked her downstairs, but before I had a chance to talk to her, her sister showed up to take her home. I had no idea who she was, and we never saw her again. Actually, I sort of appreciated what she had done. If you're going to make a public confession, wouldn't becoming naked outside complement your wanting to be naked inside, and let go your sins in front of the altar and the congregation? The Bible speaks of publicly repenting with sackcloth and ashes. I realize, though, that any form of full disrobing in public for such a purpose is just socially unacceptable—at least put on sackcloth!

Another time when Bill was away on vacation and I was the priest responsible for the church, I saw through my office window a big bus emptying a large number of people in uniforms and carrying band instruments. Bill had failed to tell me that he had earlier agreed to let the parish hall be used by a band from the Royal Order of Moose on that day. When they arrived, the parish hall was being used for play rehearsal and a service was being held in the church sanctuary. The only place left for them to play was on the large flat roof of the parish hall. Writing this now, I'm wondering if I'm hallucinating a bit; I can't conceive of the band playing there. But the event is branded in my memory.

The church had several shut-ins who were part of the old church congregation before Bill Wendt arrived. He divided them up between me and the other priests to visit and bring Communion once a month. I had about five people to see. I remember one of them, an older lady living in a nearby apartment house, who interrupted my prayer as I was giving her the Communion host to blurt out, "What does this mean? I never understood it." I tried to explain it in terms I thought she could understand, and that seemed to help a little. She relented and took the host and consecrated wine. I left sad that it had been so meaningless to her in her long life in the church, but happy that she could finally admit it and maybe feel a little more appreciative in the future. The shut-ins on the whole were old enough that they could be frank about their lives and "tell it like it is" to me.

Dr. Campbell was a conservative member of the "old" church who gave free medical help to the parish clergy. I had seen him several times. He was an old-fashioned family doctor in ways. Once, when a parishioner I knew went to him with a boil on her arm, she told me that he took a big book and smashed it open.

Once, I received a phone call from him asking me to come to his house and give last rites to his deceased mother. When I arrived at his house, he took me up three flights of stairs to the sunroom where his mother had just died. In a single bed next to her was his father. I realized he had been caring for his very old parents there for years. I said prayers over his mother. When I finished, I notice her very old husband was awake and speechless, looking over to us with a puzzled look on his face. I gave him a reassuring smile and left. Today I still feel guilty for not going over to him, holding his hand, and comforting him. He may not have been in a mental condition to understand, but I should have tried. I was too inexperienced and intimidated at that unprecedented moment. I was numb to what I expect was the Spirit's call to go over to him. Hopefully Dr. Campbell filled in for me afterward.

Another pastoral blunder that still clicks off residual guilt was when I refused to allow twelve-year-old Linda to be confirmed. She came to the service ahead of time, excited about being confirmed. But she never would come to Confirmation class, even though she lived within walking distance to the church. It didn't seem fair to the others or to her own dignity to let the rite be so cheap—or so it seemed to me at the time. I told her she would have to wait until next year and attend the Confirmation class ahead of time. Later I understood a little better at what cost her life with a poor, struggling mother was lived. She had come to present herself for what she must vaguely have sensed as a rite that affirmed her belonging to G-d and the church community. Today I would have asked her just one question: "What does Confirmation mean to you?" and let her be presented for it if there was any positive awareness of G-d and the church in her life at all. As it was, law won over gospel in my denseness. She was crestfallen, and she never would return.

My worst fault of all to confess was a time when I received a phone call asking me to come to the hospital because Nancy was near death. Nancy was a young teenager from the poor white community near the church who had contracted a deadly form of cancer. I was in the middle of some serious religious book and I obsessively decided to delay going for a few minutes while a read a little more. When I arrived at the hospital and found her room, she had just died. Gerry Lanigan was there with her when it happened, which at least meant she didn't die alone. I don't know if she was even conscious in those minutes I could have come if I had immediately left for the hospital, but I should have been there; it was the clearest priority.

Praying Together: Liturgical Life at St. Stephen's

As an Anglo-Catholic (High Church) parish, we had morning prayer at 7:00 a.m. every day followed immediately by Mass in a side chapel. The priests of the parish took turns leading the service. I'm not a morning person. When it came to be my turn, I usually would just barely make it to the church on time. I remember oversleeping one day and when I arrived in the chapel, one of the regular daily lay participants, Ed Farrell, had gone up and led morning prayer in my place. I was both grateful and embarrassed. Bill Wendt once fell asleep while standing at the altar leading the early Mass. Words suddenly ceased, and it became an unscheduled silent meditation time for a few minutes. Maybe that was a movement of the Spirit that gave everyone a chance to be more fully present!

The liturgical calendar, including saints' feast days, was followed scrupulously. I came to deeply value the ordering of life these services and seasons gave to the day and week. I had come to the parish after many years in a very ordered academic world. It didn't take long to realize how much real, everyday life in a crowded, wildly heterogeneous neighborhood was lived on the edge of unmanageable chaos. I was brought to tears more than once as I realized my own limitations of energy, understanding, and compassion.

Daily involvements gyrated, often unpredictably, between hospitals, shut-ins, pleas for material help, alcoholics, near suicides, hustlers, robbers, conflicts between people, suburban people wanting to help as they struggled to understand the different world of inner-city experience, teenagers wanting to destroy and create, and children wanting a safe and sane place to play and learn in the summer and year-round after-school programs. Bewildered adults and children filled my Confirmation classes who I tried to help understand the new theological views and spiritual practices introduced to them. My oversaturated mind and tired body brought me to the altar again and again, seeking my true center in prayer.

My first sermon at St. Stephen's at the main Eucharist on Sunday morning was a humiliating beginning. The pulpit overlooked a huge nave that could hold close to a thousand people. The new sanctuary with its good sound system hadn't yet been built. There was no microphone at all in the pulpit. In the middle of my sermon I saw a woman stand up, leave her pew, and walk up to the pulpit. In a sweet, low voice she said, "We would like to hear you, but we can't. Please speak up." I was flustered. If they hadn't heard the first half of my sermon, how could I just keep going with the second half? I fumbled around and somehow put together some semi-coherent sentences, then I left the pulpit hoping the people might have heard a few words of value to them.

In my more mature later years of preaching and teaching, I've continued to carefully prepare what I would say, but I've learned that speaking what I've prepared is not what's most important. My sermon preparation really seems at best a way of being taken beneath the surface of a subject, listening for fresh insights that I might be given, and connecting them into a coherent talk. When I deliver the sermon or talk, I am so familiar with what I am about to say that at some point I find myself suddenly given deeper spontaneous insights that don't seem to come from me at all. I feel open to letting the Spirit come through in its own way.

People often tell me that the best part of anything I say is what suddenly erupts in me and speaks heart to heart. I'm further humbled when I realize that whatever I say will be received by different people in the ways they need to hear it. My words are more like a background mantra that gives people an openness to hear what the Spirit wants them to hear, sparked by my words, but not in my words. What they really need to hear I don't know, but the Spirit alive in them knows, and it may have nothing directly to do with what I'm saying.

At High Mass on Sundays, the presiding priest would chant rather than speak the words of consecration. Since I was kicked out of the choir in seventh grade when my voice began to change, I've never been a good singer. I tried my best when it was my turn, but I always felt humiliated. People were indulgent and didn't usually comment on my struggling voice, but I know my singing wasn't doing the kin-dom any quality service.

During the Good Friday service every year, we had a moving tradition of taking the congregation out of the church and having a procession around the neighborhood. We stopped for special prayers at places of suffering, such as places where someone was shot, where drugs were sold, where someone died, where beggars begged, symbolizing the troubles of the area. The sacrificial, suffering love of G-d in Christ for us was held up at each place as a current station of the cross, enfolding all the suffering in a mysterious yet very present larger Love.

On Easter Sunday, the Day of the Resurrection, the congregation would write special messages of loving hope on small pieces of paper and stuff them inside helium balloons that members then blew up at the end of the main Eucharist. Then we would all go outside and release the balloons. As they soared into the sky I felt great joy, knowing that the balloons would find different people who would get the messages of hope that Easter expressed. At the highest level, I think the Resurrection reveals to us that G-d's love soars through and beyond every form of suffering we ever could encounter. It offers us an undying hope for life's redemptive movement toward fullness of life in that mysterious, eternal love.

Such hope showed itself in a different liturgical context once when an integrated group of ten of us from St. Stephen's participated in a demonstration for the integration of an amusement park near Baltimore. During a period when other demonstrators were milling around there late in the afternoon, we gathered in a circle and began to read evening prayer from the Book of Common Prayer. Other people gathered around us and participated in the parts of the prayers that were familiar to them. The staid old words, so often repeated on my lips, came alive in a fresh way. Confession and absolution of sins, petitions, intercessions, thanksgivings, praise, scripture—all of these incarnated themselves in this moment of risk, witness, and hope. Some of that shared prayer made it into an evening TV news report. I was very glad for that. Somehow it gave a larger perspective and depth of motivation for such a demonstration—perspective and depth needed to offset the heated, narrowing polarizations that are so tempting at such times for participants and viewers alike.

A later liturgical highlight at St. Stephen's reflected the influence of another major social movement gathering steam: the liberation of women from restrictive and subservient social roles. That movement spilled over to the church and asserted the right of women to be priests, not just men. After years of struggle, the Episcopal Church was finally on the verge of supporting that right, but its final decision was slow in coming. Eleven women who felt called to priesthood decided they had long been ready and did not feel it was right to wait any longer for ordination. Three retired bishops agreed and ordained them together in Philadelphia. The bishop of Washington, DC, along with other active bishops, declared that these irregularly ordained women could not celebrate Communion in any parish until the national church had formally approved that women could do so.

Bill Wendt decided to defy that ban (and later paid the cost of formal censorship in a canonical trial initiated by several upset priests in the diocese). He and the priests and vestry at St. Stephen's were ready for one of those women to come to St. Stephen's and celebrate Communion at its main Sunday service. When word got out of that happening, the church that morning was packed with a standing-room-only congregation of about a thousand people from all over the metropolis and well beyond.

I will never forget seeing Australian-born Allison Cheek standing behind the altar in priestly vestments, raising the Communion host and chalice during the prayer of consecration. My conviction about women's ordination before that moment had been primarily intellectual. Now it became fully embodied. I deeply felt the rightness of a woman complementing and compensating for the overwhelming masculine imagery of G-d and church leadership at that time. I went home that day with fresh respect for the full place of women in spiritual leadership and indeed the right to such leadership in every other sphere of human life.

By my fifth and last full-time year on the staff of St. Stephen's, much had changed. People had come and gone from the staff. The situation no longer made it feasible for the staff to eat together. The parish still was a very unique, dynamic, growing place. Leadership related to race relations began to shift to black leadership and identity apart from whites (Asian Americans, Hispanics, and Indigenous Americans weren't so publicly visible and sizable at that time in Washington, DC). This shift was symbolized in a "black power" sermon given at St. Stephen's by the prominent civil rights activist Stokely Carmichael. It was a wrenching time as people struggled to try out new ways of relating and separating, leading and following, across racial lines.

St. Stephens's continued to be a center for a great variety of civil rights and anti-poverty activity and envisioning (including gender and sexual orientation concerns). Being in the heart of the nation's capital, there was the added burden and privilege of the church being the organizing and sleeping ground for all kinds of oppressed groups who came to Washington, DC, to place their grievances before the powers that be. That is true to this day.

Personal and Family Life in the Later St. Stephen's Years

I felt a growing need to be master of my own space. I moved to an apartment nearby and felt the constant amazement of returning there each day to a predictable sanctuary. My turn to such a personal space echoed what I had heard from other people who had been involved in an intensive and demanding communal life in those days. I didn't regret such a life in my early years at St. Stephen's, but a personal sanctuary was a called-for new dimension of my daily life now.

In that era of open social experimentation, about fifty communes blossomed in the DC area (most not related to any particular religious grounding). As I recall, most of them died within a few years, in part I think because of the demands and conflicts of communal living that left little or no space for solitude. Those few that survived longer shared the characteristic of a shared calling to some mission of service that transcended an end-in-itself experiment in communal living. Our little community of clergy and one family living together qualified for such a more durable community, but even the other people in such communities often moved on to other places eventually.

I began spending more time reflecting on my psychological condition. The appreciation of psychology had grown to new heights at that time in American culture, including among clergy and congregations. At the summit of personal psychological understanding at that time seemed to be psychoanalysis. Other forms of therapy were alluring, but psychoanalysis at that time seemed to have a reputation as a particularly serious and thorough way of understanding and better coping with your inner psychological responses to life. Most forms of therapy at that time, including psychoanalysis, were segregated from one's inner spiritual life and practice. I wrote a paper in seminary challenging Sigmund Freud's dismissal of religion as illusory, and yet here I was in awe of Freudian analysis. In the mindset of that time, it had an intrinsic value that didn't have to mesh with anything religious.

I was aware that the traumas of my early life had left their mark on me. I was ready to try to better understand their impact on my feelings and behavior and to reduce their negative qualities as much as possible. After meeting a psychoanalyst, who was a church member, at a diocesan committee meeting on clergy mental health, I felt he was someone who could respect my religious vocation and hopefully help me. I called him and asked if I could become his patient. He agreed.

I remember my first meeting with Dr. Bob. (I won't use his last name, although I'm sure he's long deceased.) As a classic Freudian analyst, Dr. Bob had a procedure that involved my lying down on his couch, with him sitting a few feet behind me, notebook in hand. He said nothing. It was up to me to relate whatever dreams, thoughts, feelings, motivations, and behavior came to mind. At the end of the hour, I would get up to leave, and he would get up and silently change the cloth under my head for the next patient. The same process continued for years (a full Freudian analysis needed a long commitment). It's astounding to realize that I can remember him saying only two brief sentences to me in response to what I was saying during those years. Besides those two sessions that evoked each of those sentences, every other session evoked nothing but silence from him.

At various points I found myself doubting whether there was any good coming out of this process and whether he was the right therapist for me. This was reinforced by a research article I read that said there was no evidence that psychoanalysis led to any substantial therapeutic results. I was too intimidated by psychoanalysis's reputation, though, to trust my instincts, so I kept going, hoping that some important breakthroughs would happen. Two things of potential value came to me: developing the habit of noticing what was going on in my mind and where it seemed to be coming from, and learning to trust my own insights (since I had virtually none from the doctor!).

When I finally quit at my own initiative, I felt like no transformational insights ever came, either because I was too dull to receive them or because the psychoanalytic process was not meant for me. I remember feeling that the doctor thought the process was a failure also, but he never said so. At times I felt a little sorry for him, having to spend his days in long silent sits with me and others. He fell asleep once while I was talking, and I felt I must have become very boring (even to myself). Much later in life I found a very different and truly valuable form of therapy that I'll mention later.

Another dimension of my personal life was my discovery of Ann Austin in 1964. She was a member of my adult Confirmation class. When the class ended, I invited her out for dinner with me. I found her uniquely alluring yet very quiet and self-contained in ways that left her a mystery. We continued dating and feeling ourselves drawn together, then apart, then together again over many months. We were very different from each other in ways that led to the "in and outness" of our relationship. I remember when I crossed the line from ambivalence to a special love. I preached an ecstatic sermon that Sunday on love, never mentioning my relationship with Ann. Mary Wendt, though, who was sitting in the congregation, picked up the extra passion behind my words. Right after the service she smiled and said to me, "Tilden, I think you're in love." Indeed, I did feel that, and since love with another person often has a way of spilling over to deeper love for creation, other people, and G-d, it was a very natural and easy homily.

Ann and I became engaged and were married at St. Stephen's by Bishop Paul Moore before many church members, with some old, close friends of mine as groomsmen. We rented an apartment where we lived for a year before renting a house close to Rock Creek Park. A year later, Ann became pregnant, and we were ready to find a house where we could stay a long time and raise a family. In what kind of neighborhood did we want our family to live? How could we balance personal values, safety, convenience, mix of people, and affordable price? With a memory of Jeremiah's purchase of a plot of land in a wobbly Judah as an encouragement to trust, we confirmed our desire to stay in the heterogeneous Kalorama Triangle neighborhood where we already were renting.

The violent riots after the tragic assassination of Martin Luther King Jr. happened just a little before that time, coming close to our neighborhood. Some people who lived near to the riot area sold their houses and moved out of the city. The price of homes in our neighborhood plummeted. We found a row house just right for us on Biltmore Street with an asking price that we could afford. We moved in with a menagerie of cats and a collie dog rescued from the pound, soon to be joined by a baby boy.

When Ann was ready to deliver, we quickly called her gynecologist and I rushed her to Columbia Women's Hospital in downtown DC. We hadn't arranged for me to be in the delivery room with her, so I was left in the waiting room. After some minutes, the doctor appeared at the door, his white coat showing blood stains. He told me that he was having difficulty with the delivery—the umbilical cord was wrapped around the baby's neck; then he disappeared. I was a nervous wreck. Why did he come out to tell me that if it wasn't really serious? My prayers doubled in intensity.

After what seemed like an eternity, the doctor reappeared and said it was a baby boy and in good condition, and I could visit him and Ann in about an hour. I took the biggest sigh of relief in my life. I left the hospital during the wait and crossed the street to a bar on Pennsylvania Avenue. It was the first and last time I ever was in a bar alone. I sat at the bar and nervously blurted out to the bartender, "My wife just delivered our first child; give me a shot of Southern Comfort." That was about the only hard liquor I could think of in my jumbled mind, something I almost never drank, and the name sounded right. The bartender was sympathetic and gave me an unasked-for second glass on the house. I stumbled back to the hospital and was taken to the nursery. I will never forget my heart leaping when I was shown my son's crib through the nursery window. Then I found Ann's room and we celebrated together. We named him Jeremy Austin.

We took Jeremy home and began a new phase of life together. I'm reminded of what Jeremy later smilingly told us after leaving the hospital with *his* first child: "They turn you out on your own with no set of instructions for raising a child!" We felt that also. We tried to be so carefully attentive to this precious new human being who was our responsibility alone (at least on the human level). He and his sister, Jennifer Gabrielle, born fifteen months later, were raised in that house through high school, in a neighborhood that remained one of the most mixed (ethnically, racially, vocationally, economically, and politically) in the city.

Chapter 8

Ministry beyond St. Stephen's

A number of seminarians worked with us in my years at St. Stephen's. Seminaries at that time were not equipped to provide adequate preparation for the socially challenging world in which budding priests and ministers would be living, especially in urban environments. Bill Wendt and I, and a few others, pondered what we could do to help. The upshot was the creation of the Washington Urban Training Program (UTP), approved for students eventually by two Protestant and three Roman Catholic theological schools in the metropolitan area, with me as part-time director.

This was my first step away from St. Stephen's, even though it involved only a day a week of my time. It gave room for my experiential educational instincts to expand. I threw myself into its organization with a passion. The seminarians who chose to enroll were allowed twelve hours a week by their schools for a combination of field placements and seminars. I arranged field placements in a wide variety of settings, from local grassroots community organizations to socially focused government agencies to riding in police cars.

The interdependence of the metropolitan area grew in our consciousness to the point that we came to see the inadequacy of looking for positive enduring change in the city without complementary change in the suburbs. Their neighborhoods, schools, social centers, and often workplaces were insulated from so much of the life and varieties of people in the city. More informed clergy leadership in suburban (as well as urban) churches had a potentially vital role in fostering relationships, understanding, and actions across racial and class lines that could lower the walls.

UTP seminars were held at the Institute for Policy Studies in DC. The institute leaders included a number of visionary societal and political thought leaders in Washington, none of whom were particularly "religious," but all of them were passionately concerned about building a just, creative, and inclusive human community. The students were inspired by their prophetic and well-informed minds.

One institute leader, Dr. Robb Burlage, a young, brilliant economist, particularly inspired me. I saw him as a secret friend of G-d, never giving up hope in high human purpose and possibilities. I remember him saying to me that if those of us in the church had something to bring to the table of social vision, then we should share it. If not, then just forget the church and join in helping to implement and enhance the vision he and the other faculty members were fostering.

What did the church have to bring? What came to me was that it brings an underlying trust in G-d as just, loving, and creative, drawing humans toward an overarching and universal vision of the kin-dom of heaven. Everyone has a place in its evolution. That vision is more substantial and enduring than any of the forces of sin, evil, and confusion that resist it. With that transcendent trust, when we involve ourselves in difficult societal struggles, we will not easily give up in the face of long-term resistance and failures. We won't ultimately despair as we continue to encounter seemingly overwhelming obstacles. We can "last" through whatever is thrown against the vision, trusting that in the end the vision will be fulfilled, even if that means a fullness that will not exist in our lifetime.

UTP received a small grant to evaluate its usefulness for seminarians. One clear discovery was that seminaries were constantly tempted to give it low priority because they did not reward the students' program involvement in the way they rewarded normal academic course work. John Fletcher, a theologian on the faculty of Virginia Theological Seminary, was on the faculty steering committee for the program. As he and the rest of us reflected on this seminary attitude, we expanded our reflection to the need for better preparation of seminaries for ministry in the local church and synagogue. Over the following months we evolved a vision of a new model for seminary education, which John tested with many religious bodies and found their willingness to support such an experiment. John became the director, lined up staff, including some mature pastors and rabbis, and the Interfaith Metropolitan Theological Education—or

Intermet, as it came to be called—was born. It eventually included students from six Christian, Jewish, and Unitarian faith traditions. I stayed on the fringe of the new seminary's life as a preceptor while I continued heading up the UTP and working at St. Stephen's.

After seven valiant years, Intermet died in 1977, largely for financial reasons. It was born at a time of much dissatisfaction with educational and other institutional structures all over the country. The experiment represented one more "larger possibility" of the heady years of the late sixties and early seventies. Although Intermet's brief flame burned out, it helped inspire a reconsideration of pastoral preparation in many other seminaries.

During this time, the bishop appointed me as chairperson of the diocesan youth committee for several years. At one point we decided to invite a number of local youth bands and folk singers to play and sing on the grounds of the Washington National Cathedral in an event titled "Spirit and Sound '67." About twenty bands were lined up to play a designated Sunday evening in multiple locations on the cathedral grounds. It was advertised broadly as a great celebrative event for youth. Heavy rain predicted for the day of the event, so we rescheduled for the next Sunday.

The bands came that next Sunday and were spread out on the grounds, but it unexpectedly began to rain steadily. We received wary permission to move some of the bands into the cathedral itself. The cacophony of the bands playing at the same time was unbelievable. Several young women decided to dance in front of the high altar. Someone else climbed onto Woodrow Wilson's tomb, a photo of which was confiscated by a cathedral official, who also called the bishop and told him to come immediately and do something about the bedlam. The bishop came, but he felt it best to let it keep going until the scheduled ending time, which wouldn't be long. The next day, the front page of the *Washington Post* had a large photo of the women dancing in front of the main altar. The dean of the cathedral later said that he had lost $600,000 in pledges as a result! Somehow the youth committee wasn't reprimanded. I felt some guilt about the cost to the cathedral, yet at the same time I hoped that the Spirit really was involved in the youthful ecstasy of that amazing event.

The Metropolitan Ecumenical Training Center: A New Ministry Is Born

In 1967, an interdenominational group of executives gathered to affirm what had been evolving in the tumultuous Washington, DC–area social action scene and to resist any conservative pullback. They felt that the evolving societal changes of recent years were good and would endure, and their implications for the religious community needed to be better understood and responded to in congregations by laity and clergy alike. They saw that this could best happen ecumenically. They represented a dozen DC-area faith traditions: Roman Catholic, many Protestant ones, and one Jewish. They banded together to form the Metropolitan Ecumenical Training Center (METC) and asked me to be its full-time executive director.

This was a big discernment for me. My years at St. Stephen's were so rich, yet I already had pulled away partly to lead the Urban Training Program. I shared these religious leaders' vision for a new center, although the vison was very sketchy, with no clear content. There was no real guidance for what I was being asked to do or how to go about doing it. After prayer and reflection with Ann and Bill Wendt, I decided to take a leap into the dark. I would wrap the UTP into my new job for another two years, and I would continue to be an occasional celebrant in worship services at St. Stephen's.

The executives on the METC board of directors had raised a little start-up money from participating denominations, enough to last just six months. My office was one of the two bedrooms in our apartment. I hired a part-time secretary, Dedi Whitehead, who was essential and supportive. I felt very much on my own, which threw me into prayer and the need to trust that G-d was with me on this frontier and grace somehow would flow. Much needed to be practically thought through and developed, and fast, or the whole effort would quickly lose its support.

I came aboard in the late spring. With the help of a curriculum committee of experienced friends that I rapidly brought together, METC launched a two-pronged summer program. The first was a weekly summer forum, each led by a well-known local religious or political leader, focused on various social issues in the area. The second prong was a weekly seminar for clergy concerned with social issues in their work.

The fine mix of clergy who attended that summer seminar laid seeds in my mind that continued to bear fruit during my succeeding ten years with METC. It was a group willing to be very honest about what was really going on in their congregations and their hearts. No one wasted time posturing, defending, or hiding. They were also free in sharing their bewilderment about what was happening in the volatile societal arena and how they were called to respond, and at what price in terms of congregational reaction to what they would do.

Over the ensuing years, I did a great deal more work with clergy and their congregations. I became aware of how much clergy needed to prayerfully help shape a congregational community that was just, honest, able to resolve its conflicts, respect differences, and show care for one another. Such a congregation can more truly model the way a human community can be life-giving, which in turn becomes a gift to the larger community.

I immersed myself in the applied behavioral sciences that many mainstream religious leaders ingested in those years. This included organizational development, a rapidly emerging field at that time focused on the systemic connections of structures, roles, and values in an organization's life, and ways of assisting these to move toward more open and managerially effective systems.

The gift of persons drawn to social prophecy often seems to be that of shocking and inspiring people into attention to what belongs to the common good that has been neglected. But then a second step, and a second kind of leader for it, is vitally needed: the hard, slow, collaborative work of institutionalizing the needed changes others have inspired, a step that the field of organizational development fosters. Without that, the initial prophetic promise can fade into a morass of incompetent and oppressive bungling that no amount of inspired rhetoric can rescue.

My awareness of the importance of institutional life as an arena needing careful attention led me to spend more time on race relations *within* organizations. It's within them that most people spend so much of their waking hours outside the home, especially places of work, play, and study. Here people must live together with other people of many kinds. They are the basic ongoing testing ground for heterogeneous human relationships.

In 1968 we put out a call for people who were concerned with race relations and justice, and who had some relevant experience with social psychology or organizational development. A large turnout for the meeting at Howard University revealed how much race was on the minds of many people in the psychological and applied behavioral science community at that time. An amazing cross section of people came, some of whom had a lot more concern than experience. The majority of them were white, but it was encouraging at least to see many whites willing to offer their concern and skills, and some of them already had credibility with many organizations that might be open to calling on them for help with racial discrimination and relationships. Out of that meeting grew a training program and a network of fifty-five people organized into the METC Race Institute, available to help organizations engage in concrete ways of identifying and eliminating institutional racism. Today I think such an institute would need many more non-white trainers to lead such work.

Over the next eight years these people worked in teams with schools, businesses, churches, government agencies, and volunteer organizations who sought our help. Two lessons stand out above all the others from that rich time for me. First, it seemed far more productive to focus on widespread *structural inequities* and what could be done about them than it was to focus on *attitudes*—in other words, to focus on institutional more than personal and culturally conditioned racism (although that was a vital dimension of what was attended to as well). As long as you have a modicum of goodwill (along with helpful legal mandates!), you can get somewhere together in recognizing built-in forms of discrimination in the overt and subtle ways that an organization is put together and functions. Action plans for change can be undertaken.

Personal prejudicial attitudes, which are harder to change, hopefully will be affected positively over time, but whether these changes adequately occur, organizational policies that help to assure more justice and dignity can be fostered and enforced. I came to feel that changing prejudicial attitudes needed long-term help from the way parents raised their children and teachers and religious leaders taught children to treat all people as fully equal and valued children of G-d. Aid also was needed to help white people recognize how many subtle white cultural assumptions about race have been subconsciously absorbed, even by whites who feel they are not racist, including an awareness of white superiority and privilege. Changes also can come from providing opportunities for honest, caring firsthand relationships with one another across racial lines.

I happen to be writing this page on the four hundredth anniversary of the arrival of the first involuntary American immigrants to this country: the first slave ship from Africa. The dehumanizing history that followed, together with the continued horrible oppression suffered after the emancipation from slavery, and the stubborn continuation of racism to this day in subtle and destructive ways despite the successes of the civil rights movement, has left an enduring wound on this country; some have called it the nation's original sin. We all need to be involved in an ongoing process for fuller awareness of the living forms of racism; of serious paths toward justice, healing, and reconciliation; and for the sharing of one another's gifts in an intentionally inclusive society.

Many Asian, Hispanic, and Indigenous American people have their own long history of such marginalization, suffering, and discrimination. Many whites have their own stories of debilitating *class* oppression by European elites that brought them to this country, but they came here voluntarily.

Jews and Christians Together

The last special opening of relationship in those METC years for me was between Jews and Christians. The American Jewish Committee was one of METC's official members. I can remember a young rabbi who participated in our annual program for clergy new to the area. It was a great sign of opening in itself for a rabbi to participate in an intimate continuing education program with Christian clergy. Part of the program included small groups focusing on personal feelings about one another. At one point the rabbi burst into a torrent of anger, aimed at a particular pastor in the group. It was a long pent-up anger at discrimination he had experienced with Christians that he had never expressed before to a Christian. As it turned out, there was great healing in that time; the two became close and lasting friends.

Annually we held special Jewish-Christian dialogues focused on various issues. These times of special openness were climaxed by a shared METC pilgrimage to the Holy Land together: Jews and Christians, blacks and whites, males and females, clergy and laypeople. At one point on the pilgrimage we each planted a young pine tree in a new national Israeli forest and formally dedicated that section of the forest to Martin Luther King Jr. Standing in a circle, holding hands, we sang "We Shall Overcome" together.

One of many learnings from that time for me was to realize how holy the Holy Land can be in Jewish consciousness. I remember riding next to a rabbi on the bus as we toured various sites in Israel. In the countryside, as we would pass what to me were nondescript barren hills, he would point out to me at various times that that was Mount so-and-so, where so and so happened historically. He deeply identified with the land as G-d's land gifted to the Jewish people. He belonged to that land and cared that it be respectfully honored.

That experience led me to ruminate on the meaning land can have for all peoples. We belong to the land of a particular country, state, and local community with their particular histories and sense of responsibility for the land and appreciation of it. Sometimes that might include a sense of divine gift and purpose, as with the Pilgrims in New England. It's such a different sense of land than one of seeing it as a meaningless commodity to exploit for material gain.

On that pilgrimage we had little contact with Muslim and Christian Palestinians, but on a later pilgrimage to the Holy Land based at St.

George's College in Jerusalem, I was happy to have much more opportunity for that. They have their own experience and sense of the Holy Land. They see that the greater power of the Jewish community has led to losing control of much of their land.

A Mission in Guyana

During those METC days, I was invited one summer to join three other church educators trained in organizational development to go to Guyana, a small, poor country on the Caribbean coast of South America. Our mission was to help the Anglican archdiocese in Guyana empower laity to be less dependent on priests and more involved in the leadership and outreach of the church, as well as to offer some community development skills for people in an inland bauxite mining town.

Guyana is on the equator, and its weather is very hot and humid year-round. We were housed in people's homes, none with air conditioning, all with mosquito nets over the beds to try to keep out malaria-causing mosquitos. Most of the population of Guyana hugs the coast. In working with a wonderful group of laypeople (mostly of South Indian and African origin), we discovered that many of them yearned to go beyond that coast and migrate to the United States, which many Guyanese have done over the years. We found the same yearning when we were flown to the inland bauxite mining town in the middle of the dense jungle that covers most of the country.

Toward the end of our week there, we were gifted with a day trip to the border of Guyana and Brazil, traveling in a chartered very old, noisily vibrating DC-3 plane. It left us at a deserted small landing strip on the border and flew away. We were alone. No other human being lived in the area. We had been told to walk some distance to a lovely waterfall with very cold water in which we could bathe, if we dared. Only one of us did so. After a few hours on the edge of the jungle, we walked back to the abandoned hangar next to which we had landed, cautiously trusting that the plane would eventually come back and take us away. After an hour or so waiting, it was a heart-warming sound to hear its old motor sputtering in the distance and landing to pick us up.

I have never felt so homesick in all my years of traveling. The ceaseless heat, the jungle atmosphere, the many people who wanted to leave the country, and an unpopular government all combined to create a sense of isolation and sadness. Surely G-d must be alive there. We met and worked with people who had learned to make the best of what they had and who had tasted G-d's goodness. We did what we could to help them believe in their own G-d-given gifts for leadership.

At the party community participants gave us on the last day, they drew us into a rhythmic round dance where one of them at a time would move to the center of the group and imitate one of the four of us Americans. They expressed every quirky gesture and characteristic of each of us incredibly well. We were left feeling naked—they had come to "know" us much more intimately than we knew, just by intensely watching and listening to us. I felt sorry to leave them. I could feel the sad resignation of some of them that they could not join us as we left the country.

Six months later, we returned to work with them for a week. The winter weather was only two degrees cooler than the summer heat. This time I felt more at ease and positive than the first time we were there. I really cared for these people and their struggles to shape a good, G-d-grounded personal and community life together.

Chapter 9

Deepening Contemplative Awareness

In my book *All God's Children*, I write more about what happened in those late years of Metropolitan Ecumenical Training Center and what I saw as their implications for the life of congregations, interfaith and interracial relations, and for myself personally. I valued all that METC was doing, but I increasingly felt that something was missing, something in my interior spiritual awareness. It wasn't the mind's "lines" that were missing—the theological words and their prescribed loving way of life were there, and I trusted them. In hindsight, I know it was awareness of the spaces *between* the lines, awareness that I came to realize arose from a faculty different than the mind: the spiritual heart. There I touch the receptive, unifying, intimate, preverbal, open awareness of my deepest self in G-d. Flashes of that awareness had spontaneously arisen in the past, especially during times of meditation, but now I was moved to let myself become more available to the widening of that awareness and its vulnerability to the transforming power of the Spirit. Such transformation moves my center of identity from a separated ego sense of self to being a unique carrier of communion in G-d.

I was not alone in my yearning for such deeper grounding. In my work with congregations and clergy, I ran into an increasing number of people who felt something was missing in their own interior lives and in the congregation's life, something more they were being invited to. They had a very hard time labeling it. Whatever it was, it was not satisfied by their current experience of fellowship, liturgy, preaching, study, verbal prayer, or social action. All of these offered "lines" of faith visible to the conceptual mind. But the nameless space out of which those lines at their truest emerge were an unexplored mystery. That discovery rang a bell with me and others and pointed toward what needed attention. When you're given a glimpse of that space between thoughts, how can you abide there and be receptive to what's given? Can you trust a sense of the liberating Spirit enough to let it strip you over time of the idols, illusions, and fears that divide you away from your truest being?

My first glimpse of addressing the yearning for deeper ground came unexpectedly in the summer of 1972 at a conference of the Association for Religion and the Applied Behavioral Sciences. The heart of the three-day conference was given over to forms of meditation led by Toby McCarroll, a renegade Roman Catholic who had formed his own little religious community in California. He guided us in a variety of Christian and Eastern forms of contemplative presence. I faintly began to glimpse what it is to be attentively present between thoughts. I noticed how boundary-less that space is, taking me beyond the confined world of my ego identity and conceptual mind. I now see where such embryonic awareness would lead me in the following years: to what felt like the very heart of my true identity and the elusive true heart of the church, in G-d's Heart. I saw that the vast, mysterious yet intimate divine Heart cannot be confined to any institution's view, for its beat sustains creation itself.

After that experience I was strongly moved to find further support for evolving this dawning awareness, but I was caught up in many responsibilities at METC, and further mature resources for such support seemed very thin. In the spring of 1973, I sponsored through METC a retreat that explored in an elementary way some Christian and other forms of meditative practices that cultivated prayerful presence between thoughts. I sensed that I and the other seekers in that retreat were being led down an obscure path that we were called to walk on without yet understanding all that it would entail.

Deepening Surrender

Over time I came to see that the very nature of the emerging path involved ever deeper surrender of the dominance of ego identity and definitive understandings. To go further would be far different than accumulating a few new skills and insights to stick to my flypaper mind and ego pride. The path would require letting go and emptying rather than taking on, filling up, and holding on. In Christian contemplative tradition, I learned this was the path of *kenosis*, the self-emptying seen in Christ described in Philippians 2:6–11. This new direction promised a disorientation of my way of seeing and acting. It required trust that a graced reorientation would come, even though its price would be the dethroning of fully autonomous ego-based identity and action, and of grasping, mind-based-knowledge. I still see both ego and mind as G-d-given gifts, meant to be facilitators of our deeper identity in the receptive spiritual heart, where we find the ground of our being and calling.

I had a three-month sabbatical leave coming up that summer, and I desperately sought to find a place and spiritual guide who could help this novice seriously progress on a path of deeper interior receptivity. Christian contemplative tradition and practice had been largely marginalized or buried since the Reformation and Counter-Reformation, replaced by the dominance of rational thought and affective piety. Serious contemplative life was mostly left for cultivation by certain monastic communities and the Religious Society of Friends (Quakers).

A member of such a contemplative community told me that even there, a careful oral tradition of contemplative practice and understanding, adapted by a mature guide to a particular seeker's evolving experience over years of time, was rare. The writings of great mystics were read, but that was different from the unique living "book of life" evolved between a particular guide and seeker. Of course, the true "guide" in Christian tradition is the Holy Spirit vibrating in each person's and community's life, but who is equipped to help you discern what the Spirit is bringing to life in you, and what can help you attend to that guidance over time?

I felt a little like an orphan in a large Christian orphanage where we weren't raised by adequately spiritually mature parents to help us move beyond an elemental level of spiritual awareness. The Spirit still has ways of getting through to us in flashes of experience and illumination, but oh, to have someone over an extended period of time who can selflessly sit with us in a way that gives room for probings that help us see and do what is needed to sink further into our calling and true being in G-d!

When my sabbatical leave crept up on me, I had made only one decision. I would go to California, that alluring symbol of the fresh start, where so many spiritual resources seemed to exist in proximity to one another. But where in particular to go? Whom to see? Being unsure that any satisfactory answer would come, I flew to San Francisco and contacted a few contemplatively concerned Christian leaders whose names had been given to me. I asked each of them the same question: "Whom do you trust as a deeply developed Christian contemplative spiritual leader who might help me during my sabbatical?"

Their answers were surprisingly consistent: there was no one they could unqualifiedly recommend, especially not anyone proficient in contemplative awareness and practices. Each echoed in their own way the chorus I had become familiar with: the church had strong guides in biblical, theological, and moral concepts; liturgical practice; ;pastoral and societal care, and the early stages of spiritual development. But there were extremely few mature guides for attending the Spirit's invitations to deeper interior spiritual awareness and practices that fostered such awareness.

Eventually it became clear that I needed to stop restricting my question to *Christian* spiritual leaders. One of the Christians, a psychologist, who I put my more open question to, responded to me with a pointed question of his own: "Are you really ready to roll up your sleeves and go to work, regardless of where it leads you, or do you just want to play games and not risk real change?"

I froze a little inside. Gnawing at my defensive edge was the desire to keep anything at bay that would threaten my ego control and identity. But a deeper voice inside said, "Yes, this is what I came for." Straightening up in my chair, I finally responded, "Yes, I'm ready." I felt the Spirit had shaped a fresh vulnerability in me. My ego defensiveness was at a record low level. I sensed my willing openness for whatever would be given.

Discovering Tibetan Buddhism at Nyingma Institute

Then my new psychologist friend told me that the next week, one of the few authentic spiritual masters of Tibetan Buddhist meditation and understanding in this country would begin an intensive two-month program for people in the helping professions who were not Buddhists. For those with less time, it could be entered for just two weeks.

This was a very unexpected and unknown basket to put all my sabbatical eggs in. I decided to register for just two weeks and then maybe move on. I had brought my wife, Ann, and our two very young children with me to San Francisco to visit my family in San Jose for a week together, as we had done every summer. Ann was willing to fly back to DC with the children after that, and if it was important to me, she was willing to accept my remaining in California for most of the rest of my summer sabbatical. Our relationship was struggling at that point, so the separation also would be an opportunity to see what it was like to live apart for a while.

The next Monday I found myself at the entrance to the Nyingma Institute's building in Berkeley, founded by Tarthang Tulku Rinpoche. The building was an ex-fraternity house overlooking the San Francisco Bay on the edge of the University of California campus. It was painted in distinctive Tibetan colors and topped with Tibetan prayer flags flapping in the wind. I was amazed to be there. My search for contemplative spiritual help had thrown me onto this strange religious shore that owed nothing to any of the three Near Eastern–originated Abrahamic faiths or to Western civilization.

Before arriving at the institute that first day, I offered a prayer asking that I would stay open to the truth, stay in touch with the best of my own Christian roots, and be saved from becoming lost in mere exotic trappings. (What could be more exotic than Tibet!) In hindsight, today I would say that I came seeking ways of purging the clutter of my psyche and becoming more open to the true indwelling radiant compassion that I trusted is the heart of the deepest reality. In specifically Christian terms, I was being moved by the Spirit to embrace more fully the Light and Love that the Gospel of John declares to be the core names of G-d. I prayed for the empowerment of G-d's Spirit in Christ to further my realization of the deep Real, with the help of the "skillful means" that to my speculative Christian mind had been evolved by the Spirit in Tibetan Buddhist tradition.

My walk up the steep hill and long staircase to the main entrance of the Nyingma Institute felt like a small pilgrimage in itself. I was greeted by a great pile of shoes just inside the front door. Adding mine to it, I entered the building that much lighter, quieter, and humbler. I remembered Moses's experience of G-d in the Burning Bush when he was instructed to take off his shoes, "For the place on which you are standing is holy ground" (Ex 3:5). The commonality of this practice in other great religious traditions came to mind as well.

I was shown to my room, which was a cubby hole that could only be reached by going through someone else's room. That added to my humility. No frills here! It was probably the smallest room in the building, but it would be good enough. Some of the other fifty-odd participants in the program lived in the building with me. Most of them were therapists, with a scattering of teachers, artists, and others. I was the only Christian clergy person. Actually, I think I was one of only a very few, if any, participants who were active in any Western religious path.

The one commitment held in common was the desire to spend time with Rinpoche (a title of respect for a high lama). Rinpoche had a monastery about a mile away in Berkeley that involved much more extensive commitments. The Nyingma Institute, on the other hand, is more of a secular study center, for those who do not necessarily want to undertake a commitment to the Buddhist path.

This lack of a shared, deep commitment together both relieved and plagued me. I felt ego relief in being an anonymous person who could come and go as I pleased, do the study and meditation work assigned by Rinpoche or not, and speak to or ignore other participants. This comfortable ego-in-charge looseness, reinforced by others, had a price: there was no reinforcement or security for really letting go; for allowing the patient, hard work of opening and emptying to happen, a work of willingness to live vulnerably from a deeper place that I felt was a called-for response for me to an invitation of the Spirit in being there.

I became vividly aware of the impact of community on where and how far one usually goes in spiritual evolution. Looking back through Christian spiritual history, I saw why there has been such emphasis on the value of shared discipline, long-term commitment, and mutual support. At the same time, I understood why many contemplatively grounded members were moved to leave human community altogether for an extended period of silent solitude, where they could give themselves totally to their desire for fuller conversion into the realization and embrace of their true being in G-d. Buddhists are silent about G-d. Perhaps at the deepest levels of graced consciousness, Christians and other theists are also silent. They realize firsthand the living sacred Silence, the radiant Love, that is beyond the naming in its vast intimacy. John of the Cross calls Silence the first name of G-d. Meister Eckhart says there is nothing so like G-d as silence.

Paradoxically, when I have been in solitude and graced to be deep in that Silence over the years, I have found myself in community. I don't feel alone. Everyone, everything eventually seems to show up in my consciousness then. I realize my inextricable belonging within a larger communal wholeness that always is; an interwovenness that dispels any sense of an ultimately separate self and reveals my being as a unique pinprick of light integrally connected to a vast sea of lights, all streaming from a mysteriously intimate Light. Recognition of that Light and opening to its creative beams of Love may be one way of embracing what it means to be created in the image of G-d.

The one great stimulus for all of us that summer was Rinpoche himself. His background in deep spiritual community and solitude, together with his intelligence and command of all aspects of Buddhist practices and understanding, as well as his energy, warmth, and ways of being intuitively present to us individually and together, combined to make him a powerful magnet for those seeking a guide into the deeper reaches of human consciousness.

Born into a lama's family in eastern Tibet, he was "discovered" as a child to be a reincarnate high lama, a *tulku*, and as such was given twenty years of the strictest and most careful education with some of the best teachers available in Tibetan monasteries. That education wove together art, psychology, meditation, devotional practices, philosophy, and forms of physical alertness and healing into a single fabric of awareness, understanding, and behavior. Great weight fell on the development of firsthand direct awareness (deeper than conceptual awareness) that cut through layers of illusion, fear, and desire. Such development included months alone in caves, paying attention to the movements of the mind at very subtle levels, and learning to see and reduce its scatteredness and grasping to realize the mind's basic nature and to cultivate a deep compassion for all sentient beings.

Such intense discipline over time could lead to certain psychic powers, which were considered by-products not to be sought after lest they become subtle ego power trips. Rinpoche would never speak of or admit to having such powers, yet a number of persons in the group had clear evidence of his knowing things about them that he could not have known without the capacity to directly be in their minds. This is not to say that he was "all-knowing"; he was subject to the limitations and failings of all mortals. Yet his gift of direct perception clearly was developed beyond those of us sitting before him that summer (and some of those sitting were internationally well-known psychologists who were not easily duped).

Such purported powers created a certain aura of mystery and fascination around him. That Rinpoche did not exploit this fascination led me to trust him more. In fact, he projected a very everyday personality, marked especially by an earthy humor. He never tried to sound dramatic or awesome. He always seemed to accept where you were, to speak on your level, to mirror your situation, to be "with you" in a way that helped you relax and loosen up. At the same time, he always gave you a subtle challenge to let go of your own laziness, selfishness, lack of confidence, complacency, or egotistical seriousness, whichever he perceived was blocking your awareness. His ultimate challenge was to let go of everything, or as he would put it, "Nothing holding anything anywhere," in mind or body. Everything he taught was a means to that end. He offered a great range of meditation practices for lightening emotional attachments and cultivating awareness, along with philosophical concepts for the mind's understanding, all aimed at a fully present-in-the-moment inclusive awareness with nothing left to cling to—free to receive directly from the deep Real.

I noticed how differently he dealt with each student who came up to him during break times to question what was happening in their meditation and what they needed to do. I sensed he could spontaneously bypass an intellectual and ego way of listening, freeing him to be inside the person's mind, intuiting directly what was going on and what was needed. For example, one person he would give a particular mantra to chant; another he would give a broom to sweep the floor; another he would gently laugh at, I think as a way of lifting the ego-heaviness of the questioner's mind. Watching him relate in such unique ways to each person as spiritual guide taught me something about the potential of spiritual leadership to connect directly with where a person is and respond accordingly. I had a sense that the responses that Rinpoche gave emerged in the moment from his willingness to be present in/with a person behind their words, responses that were surprises I think even to him, not calculated in his conceptual mind but given from his direct in-touchness with the person's psyche. Sometimes in response to a question he might invite the questioner to question themselves by asking, "Where does that question come from?"

In Christian spiritual tradition, I think such spiritual leadership would be conditioned by a sense of deep, open givenness to the Holy Spirit alive in the moment, a givenness that transcends the conceptual mind's more mediated way of seeing—directly from the spiritual heart.

After an average ten-hour day of meditation practices (together and alone), lecture, and dialogue, including three silent, vegetarian meals, I saved just enough energy to open the gospels and read for a while at night in my room. Part of doing this was a defensive reaction: I didn't want to lose my spiritual lineage. A second motivation was open concern: I wanted to see what would happen in a daily dialogue between Jesus and

Gautama, between the Christ and the Buddha. Would they deeply clash or coincide? So many books have been written about their relationship, with many different conclusions.

I was amazed to find how many of the difficult sayings of Jesus began to appear freshly lucid—for example, what it means to "lose your life to find it" (Mt 16:25); for "a sound eye to lead the whole body to be full of light" (Mt 6:22); for the kingdom of heaven to be "in our midst, within us" (Lk 17:21), and on and on.

So much of my biblical education had been focused on analysis and interpretation of the text. Now the words were clicking intuitively in relation to my developing firsthand attentiveness and "letting go" of surface chatter and thoughts in meditation and daily living. An inkling of Jesus's intimate awareness of the deep Real behind his words began to trickle into my consciousness. I felt a new intimacy with him. Indeed, I began to feel a depth of trust in him that I had never known. In John's gospel I was moved by his inviting us to share his consciousness in the power of the Spirit given to us.

Seeing the intuitive awareness of Rinpoche at work brought me even closer to Jesus. I sensed a little of what it must have been like to be around Jesus, who had the capacity to see through you, show compassion, and provide prophetic insight. In the light of the many miracles of healing and other powers in Tibetan tradition, I also began to accept more readily Jesus's miraculous powers.

Jesus still was my foundational spiritual guide. I trusted that he incarnated the astounding sacrificial and guiding love of G-d, the heart of deepest Real. He encouraged us to recognize and live out our own incarnation of the Spirit's creative love, having been formed in the image of G-d. Rinpoche, on the other hand, contributed to my sense of the liberating layers of human awareness and compassion, assisted by many "skillful means."

I did not leave after two weeks. To go to bits and pieces of retreats and talks in other spiritual centers now would be like bobbing up to the spiritual surface for the rest of the summer. I felt myself being pulled down from a cluttered, unaware, driven surface consciousness to a place of calm clarity and unattached caring. The surface was still there with all its desires and fears, yet it was a bit lighter, less important, just "there." My usually hard surface of ego identity was becoming a permeable mesh through which a deeper, truer Self-in-G-d could be exposed.

At the end of the two months I had a long private interview with Rinpoche, my third of the summer. No two months of my life had ever been so mentally challenging, at a time when I was so ready to be vulnerable to deeper awareness. An immense horizon was opened to me that was much too vast and bright to more than glimpse in so short a time. No religious boundary lines made sense at this point—the fullness of truth felt too big for that. Yet Rinpoche had reinforced and respected my Christian particularity throughout the summer. He insisted that one needs to go down deeply through one lineage, one deep contemplative tradition, and it didn't need to be Buddhist.

He meant so much to me that in that last interview I asked if I could be his Christian *chela*, his student. He laughed and said our karma had brought us together, and this was a gift. He went on:

> I am your Tibetan priest-friend, Tilden. We are priest-brothers. You don't need to be a Buddhist student. You can learn everything I have to offer and use it within your own tradition. There is nothing to gain by crossing over. It is all there available as a Christian.

This nonproselytizing response increased my respect for him, though I felt a little cheated. There was so much more I needed to let go and to learn. He helped me realize, though, that this work can go on all the time, at any place. No master and no tradition can do your work for you. I needed to let go of endless obscuring attachments still in me and let the Spirit show me the kin-dom of heaven in the midst of daily life. I needed to pray for the grace that lets this surrendering and illumination happen. There is no place to go but here and now. Here and now is our teacher if we allow it to be so. Every here and now can be illuminating.

The interview ended with sitting on the floor together face to face, eye to eye. Rinpoche asked me to think of the people and places I was returning to. As I did this, his eyes seemed to disappear deep inside me, as though he was transmitting a spiritual presence into my future life. When he came back to everyday consciousness, he asked me, "What happened to your mind in that silence?" After my fumbling response, he casually left the whole episode, softly spoke of our families and future meeting again, wishing me well.

We indeed met again in the years ahead: he stayed with my family and came to Shalem three times to teach.

A Jesuit Retreat to Reconnect with My Christian Roots

After leaving the Nyingma Institute I felt the need to spend a transitional week in an intensive Christian setting. Before returning to my work I needed more time to see how I might better connect my experience with some classical Christian means of presence in the deep Real, in G-d. Earlier in the summer I had anticipated this and signed up for an eight-day Ignatian spiritual exercises retreat at the Jesuit Center for Spiritual Growth in Wernersville, Pennsylvania. These exercises in their original form were put together by St. Ignatius of Loyola in Spain, which in their fullness stretch over forty days (and still do for Jesuits themselves). It was a long-tested and serious retreat meant to press you deeper in its own way, and I felt it would be right for my transition. It offered a lot of silence and a daily rhythm of scriptural meditations on Jesus's life in relation to my own, personal reflection questions, spiritual direction, and Eucharist.

I recently discovered a daily journal that I kept during the retreat, and I was amazed at how much I had forgotten about what a powerful time of evolving graced spiritual awareness it had been.

When I arrived, I and other retreatants listened to Father George Schemel, a creative interpreter of Ignatius who helped connect the exercises with modern spiritual consciousness. The way he spoke of moving toward nonattachment, "indifference," and its freedom and availability for

G-d connected with Buddhist teaching in ways. I also felt the connection when he spoke of bringing your whole being into your practice and understanding—body, breath, mind, feelings, and transpersonal self.

Afterward I met with my assigned spiritual director for the time, Judith Roemer. She was a Franciscan sister who partnered with Father George in offering this retreat. She was the first woman ever to live in as a staff member in the Jesuit center. The two of them pioneered such male-female collaborative spiritual leadership in that era. Her warm, accepting, perceptive presence each day gave room for shared conversation in which I could see the threads of my experience beginning to weave a fabric of needed understanding, a stimulus for deeper listening, and a lightening of attachments that blocked my freedom to realize G-d's loving presence and my capacity for selfless compassion and awareness.

A sign of lightening attachment was my not being disturbed by the loss of my suitcase. Instead, I realized that I didn't really need it. Jesus's words to his disciples about not taking anything extra on their preaching and healing journeys came to life. I realized that the love of G-d finally is all that is needed. I didn't have to grasp for anything more.

Later in the week this was aided by a strong, sudden sense of radiant light within. I bathed in that light. Attachment to my little ego self-image and its striving were lessened. I felt I was an expression, a creation, of the light. I felt a belonging to the wholeness of life in G-d. I had a sense of strength and compassion within, yet not *my* strength or compassion, and a sense of fearlessness, for there was nothing to lose—my little "self" already was lost as a fully separate entity.

There were so many other graced qualities of awareness given to me during the week, as we moved through the Ignatian scriptural sequence of G-d in creation, my sinfulness, forgiving love, relationship to Christ, and the Passion and Resurrection. I came to see faith as a gift to be received.

Each day was divided into four blocks of time, with biblical passages for each, and a process of bodily relaxation. This was followed by an hour of prayer and meditation, and writing down the thoughts, feelings, and experiences that occurred.

On the seventh day I was elated by Jesus's resurrection story: the peace, gladness, and Spirit he gave the disciples, and the commission to feed his sheep, faithful to them despite their foolishness, trusting their potential as carriers of good news. Afterward I went on a long, deep walk. I found myself singing and dancing, very little bothered by the heat and flying insects. I simply walked unselfconsciously in the present moment, letting everything be just what it was, letting it all come and go, with no need for interpretation.

One of the most mentally fruitful times of that week I spent reading some of the great Christian contemplatives: John of Ruysbroeck, Johannes Tauler, John of the Cross, Teresa of Avila, Thomas Merton, and others. I nearly leaped from my chair when some passages seemed to describe the same awareness of the deep Real that Rinpoche had asserted. I began to sense the overlaps of perception between them. Their gifted preverbal awareness, though, once translated into the imaged and conceptual consciousness of their minds, breaks into a spectrum of interpretations conditioned by the symbols and experiences of their cultures. To me, the shared pristine awareness is the immensely spacious, compassionate, indestructible energy of the Gracious One, shining through us and all creation.

The eighth and last day of the retreat ended with my sense of quiet presence in Christ, in Spirit, in Creator. The Jesus Prayer spontaneously came in stray moments. I felt enormous gratitude for all that was given me in the retreat, grounded in the grace of an abiding faith in the Great Love, who is the depth of life. I was more aware of the narcissistic, controlling observer inside who was still around, but I was committed to "desiring" my way deeper than that, with the help of graced self-emptying prayer. I noticed how much more difficult it was to lose self-centered consciousness when I was interacting with other people than when I was alone. Thus I acknowledged the importance of time apart to recollect who I deeply am and am not, time to give more opportunity for the Divine Light to show itself more fully and not be so hidden under my narrow ego consciousness.

I drove home to my family after the longest absence I had ever had from them. It was wonderful to be with my children again, and Ann and I recommitted ourselves to each other with a promise to get counseling help for our marriage. I knew it would be impossible to convey to her what I had been through that summer, especially knowing how different her own life and concerns were from my experience, but we were able to pick up personal and family living together with hopefulness that our differences could be complementary and not conflicting.

Chapter 10

The Birth of a New Spiritual Center

When I returned from the spiritual watershed of that summer of 1973, I felt a bit like someone returning from another planet. Would the people with whom I worked at the Metropolitan Ecumenical Training Center, as well as those seekers who were with me on retreat last spring, connect with what I had experienced? If I taught some of the practices and understanding of spiritual consciousness I learned with Rinpoche, and in the Jesuit retreat found myself connecting with Christian contemplative tradition, would it make any sense to them, or would it be dismissed as alien and irrelevant to their lives?

Hoping that there would be some people ready and meant to come together for a serious amount of time, I sent out an invitation to those who were on the retreat the previous spring and to others to join a seekers group in late September, limited to twenty people. We would meet weekly from 7:30 to 9:15 a.m. on Fridays in the big basement room of St. Paul's College in DC (later moving to the College of Preachers on the grounds of the National Cathedral) and continue through the following May. In the spring we would have a weekend guided silent retreat at a nearby retreat center.

My hope was realized as exactly twenty people responded positively, plus one more who pleaded to be included (which I'm so glad I agreed to; it was Dolores Leckey, who I will say more about later). It was a wonderful ecumenical mix of laypeople, clergy, a Catholic sister, and a seminarian, all of whom showed up faithfully each week if they weren't sick. In hindsight, I'm aware that I was riding the still largely publicly invisible wave of strong desire that I think the Spirit was raising up in many people besides myself, the desire to fall deeper into our true nature and calling in G-d's image, with the help of new contemplative practices and a supportive community of fellow seekers.

I was gratified that all of those who responded were active in jobs and causes that showed their concern for the common good. They were not passive, self-centered people seeking private enhancement apart from the calling to care for the world. They were seeking an interior depth of awareness that would free them from restrictive inner attachments and closer to their true being and calling in G-d, an energized openness that would serve their ways of seeing and caring for the world. One special offering to the group was given by Allanah Cleary, a wonderful Catholic Sister who had spent most of her vocational life serving the poor in West Africa, contracting malaria in the process, which she still found flaring up at times. She taught us a simple chant that she learned in a New York Hindu-Christian gathering: "Om Jesu, Om Jesu Om," which still spontaneously rises up in me occasionally. ("Om" in Sanskrit, "Own" in Greek, "Being" in English; could be called the largest name for G-d.)

The design I put together included this sequence: gathering in a silent circle, bowing with our hands together as we chanted "Shalom," being led in some kind of body relaxation and energizing, a guided meditation leading into silence, journal keeping, sharing in pairs or small groups, and then sharing with the whole group, ending with a chanted "Shalom" as we had done at the beginning. I encouraged the group to spend twenty minutes or more daily practicing the contemplative prayer form that I had introduced that morning. Early on I asked them to outline on paper a personal spiritual autobiography, to give each person a sense of its highlights over time.

The structure above all was meant to draw us away from an ego- and mind-confined sense of self and world and toward an openness to what today I would call our intuitive spiritual heart, a place of direct, loving awareness. That awareness, as it is graced, reveals our true self and interwoven community in G-d. It can free spontaneous compassion and heart wisdom for seeing and doing what is called for. The price of that awareness is willingness to let go or at least lighten the attachments that obscure that awareness, as we are empowered to do so.

The design included many Tibetan Buddhist and Christian practices to assist such vulnerability to our true nature and mutual belonging, as well as scriptural verses, often in the form of koan—that is, paradoxical verses that needed to be intuitively realized, such as "You must lose your life to find it" and "Having nothing, yet possessing all things." Other questions requiring answers from a deeper place than the thinking mind were asked as well, such as "Who are you?" "What are three words for contemplative awareness?" "What does 'seeking first the kin-dom of G-d, and all else shall be given you' really mean in your life now?" Other Christian practices included such things as the ancient Jesus Prayer and many chants.

I asked everyone to consider meeting monthly with someone in the group, where they would have longer time to share with each other how the Spirit seemed to be leading them—a kind of spiritual companionship. Today we might call the thirst for such an ongoing relationship the desire for a spiritual director or spiritual companion, who would give another person space to discern what's happening and called for in their personal spiritual life. It assumes that the spiritual journey is an evolving lifetime affair; having someone walking with you along the way, then, can be a precious gift. I shared that thirst, eventually asking Jerry May, a group member, if he felt called to set up a monthly time where we could be spiritual companions for one another; he did.

At that time, such long-term, contemplatively grounded, one-on-one spiritual direction/companionship was almost unheard of outside of Roman Catholic, Orthodox, and Anglican religious communities and seminaries. There was only one small residential program in the country that I knew of offering any help for the development of such spiritual directors, staffed by two Jesuits in Boston. I began to wonder if we needed to develop an ecumenical program available to laity and clergy that could enrich the confidence and understanding of people to whom other people spontaneously come to help them attend to their spiritual life. Historically spiritual direction is a charism marked by others spontaneously seeking you out. I explored the need for this with others and found much support. I discovered a Catholic priest, Shaun McCarthy, a member of a Trinitarian religious community, who was a spiritual director and teacher of theology and spirituality in his community's seminary. He confirmed the need to go forward with the development of an ecumenical program and offered his seminary as a place to meet.

As this planning went forward, it became clear that the many members in the just-completed first long-term group wanted to continue, and there were other people wanting to be in a beginning group, so we planned for that also. My heart was really in this, even as I continued to lead METC's other work. I saw that we needed to establish a special institute within METC that would concentrate on contemplative spiritual formation as a vital grounding for personal daily living and discerning social action. It would be a new dimension that expanded METC's educational work related to societal and racial justice, as well as its more recent work in the resolution of conflicts in congregations, to now include the deeper spiritual grounding I believed was missing in such work. A few board members really saw the value of this expansion. Others were more puzzled by it but trusted me enough to go forward in setting up an exploratory institute as part of METC.

After careful discernment about a name that would both respect our Jewish-Christian constituency and our mission, a small group I brought together from the first long-term group settled on the Shalem Institute for Spiritual Formation (*Shalem* being the Hebrew word for "whole," interpreted in the sense of moving toward wholeness, the fullness of life in G-d). We agreed to a logo for the institute that was a rendition of the first Hebrew letter in *Shalem*, a rendition in which some people also see a risen figure with arms raised.

As the Shalem Institute grew over the next few years, I felt called to give myself to it full-time. I made an appointment with my bishop, John Walker, who was the Episcopal executive on the METC board, and told him that after eleven years at the helm of METC, I felt it was time to leave, and I asked for his support for letting Shalem become an independent organization. He agreed, as did the other denominational executives that made up the METC board. In their deliberations about the future, they decided to dissolve METC and replace it with a new interfaith organization that would concentrate more on interfaith relationships, naming it the Interfaith Conference of Metropolitan Washington, which exists to this day.

The rabbis that had been involved with Shalem decided that they would bow out of a formal relationship with Shalem, basically because they felt that their offering contemplative spirituality was a hard enough task at that early point in its rediscovery on a popular level in Jewish congregations without having to involve Christians as well. Thus Shalem lost any formal sponsorship from the Jewish community. A number of Jewish individuals, though, including a few rabbis, were active in Shalem over the years.

The advisory committee of Shalem agreed to become its board of directors, which was made up mostly of enthusiastic people who were in the first long-term group, a few of whom had become leaders of new Shalem contemplative groups. We held a formal dedication service in the Resurrection Chapel of the Washington National Cathedral in January 1979.

Our independence was a relief. I no longer felt that I had to justify what Shalem was doing to a partly uncomprehending METC board. I felt fresh energy to further explore what we were called to do that would respond to the rising worldwide wave of desire for discovering the long-marginalized treasure of Christian contemplative tradition and practice and its relation to other major contemplative traditions.

The Mysterious Appearance of Money

How were we going to survive financially after becoming independent? We had inherited a little money from our division from METC, and we had had a little income from our beginning groups and contributions, but that was far from adequate to cover our costs. I had agreed to be only half-time for the first two years, which both reduced Shalem's costs and gave me opportunity to pursue a PhD in spiritual theology to help me better ground myself in historical contemplative literature and practices. But we still fell short.

A month before we went independent, a Shalem newsletter went out to our small mailing list that spelled out our need for an additional

$25,000 by December 15, 1979. We had no idea if we could raise that much. We knew no potential major givers, but I remember feeling that if G-d intended Shalem to live, the money would come. Small amounts kept trickling in during the year. At the end of the last day of the campaign, the staff gathered in our new office in Hearst Hall on the grounds of the National Cathedral to see if the goal would be met. We were amazed to see that we were within fifty dollars of our goal. Then in the afternoon mail a final check came in, for exactly fifty dollars. Ask and you will receive! I was awed and a little scared. I sensed G-d's Spirit really was behind this and wanted us to live, and that meant we really were accountable for carefully, prayerfully delivering the spiritual goods that were called for.

A few months later, an older woman who none of us knew enrolled in a new long-term Shalem group. She was so strongly moved to be in it that she hired a driver to take her to the weekly meetings; she had recently had a serious operation and she couldn't drive. In the early weeks of the group she had to lie down on a couch. She benefited greatly from the group and became a serious part of Shalem from then on. The next year she anonymously donated an astounding $50,000 to Shalem, enough to cover our growing budget and give us a little reserve. It felt mysterious to me that she had shown up so insistently for her first group, knowing virtually nothing about us, and then giving us such a gift. It felt like G-d's Spirit again had moved, confirming our sense of call and wanting us to expand our vision.

About the same time, we drew up two ambitious proposals to the Rockefeller Brothers Foundation for two years of support. One proposal would help us launch a two-year pilot program for the development of spiritual directors, grounded in contemplative tradition. The other proposal would support a national conference plus five regional ones for seminary faculty members, focused on spiritual formation. I and Shaun McCarthy would staff the latter; he, I, Jerry May, and others would staff the former.

I really didn't have a lot of hope for receiving the grant. I sensed the foundation "decider" really didn't grasp what contemplative spiritual formation was about as we understood it, and I didn't think he thought it was important. The foundation had never supported anything like this. Virtually all their money over their history went to theological schools, and we weren't one.

He came down from New York and attended a one-day Shalem workshop focused on corporate worship as a form of spiritual formation. That was the foundation director's only in-person contact with Shalem. He was unresponsive the whole day, and when he left, my hope for a grant sank to near zero.

The next week I was shocked to receive a letter from him saying the foundation would support both proposals if we would funnel them through the Association of Theological Schools. It turned out to be the final grant of the foundation before closing down.

Why did that foundation granter fund something in an area they had never funded and seemed to have no interest in, and give it to a start-up small organization that wasn't a seminary? Once again, I felt there was a mysterious sacred Hand behind this that doubled my sense of responsibility and awe.

Thus, the first major Shalem program was launched, an ecumenical program for the enrichment of spiritual directors that attracted seminarians, clergy, and laypeople—and it continues to this day. At the end of the two-year project, I wrote a forty-six-page report on what happened in those two years that was published in the autumn 1980 issue of *Theological Education*, the quarterly periodical of the Association of Theological Schools.

Over the rest of Shalem's history, money has continued to come in amazing ways. Sometimes the money came not from our carefully calculated planning and solicitation but from "left field"; an unknown or little-known person would give us a needed contribution out of the blue. Sometimes it felt that G-d loved G-d's freedom to bring in money when and from whom G-d liked, rather than rewarding our carefully made financial plans. That freedom could stretch to not giving us the money we thought we needed at times, to the point of having to reduce staff and other expenses, humbling us to respect and live from what was given. There were no guarantees of material support, only our trust and hope that the Spirit was steadily alive in our midst, through want and plenty.

During the early years of Shalem, I enrolled in the Union Graduate Institute, an innovative doctoral program designed for older, more experienced people based in Cincinnati. It was designed for people already working in a particular field who wanted to learn more through a nonresidential PhD program, so they could keep their jobs. I already had five and a half years of full-time graduate-level theological education. I could build on that learning through an intensive reading program related to spiritual theology and a doctoral dissertation, overseen by a faculty member and committee. The only residential requirement was a three-week gathering with other PhD candidates in many fields, based on the school's belief that we could be stimulated by one another's knowledge in different fields that would enhance a fuller understanding and context for our own field. Behind this was the school's belief that graduate education had become too compartmentalized and we needed to connect the dots of different human fields of learning.

The program required that dissertations have social relevance so that they could bring something of value to the larger society. My dissertation, agreed to by my adviser, would be a book about the nature and ministry of spiritual direction, a subject that at that time had very few published writings. The fruit was my book *Spiritual Friend: Reclaiming the Gift of Spiritual Direction*.

That PhD program was perfect for me. Despite its departure from standard university PhD programs, it was granted full accreditation by the regional college/university accreditation committee; it still flourishes.

A Meeting of Contemplative Leaders

In November of 1977 I and others at Shalem were moved to bring together a group of contemplative leaders from across the country for three days, meeting at the College of Preachers on the grounds of

Washington National Cathedral. Fresh, broad concern for spiritual formation grounded in contemplative awareness and practice, especially among Christians, was in its early stages in this country, and to my knowledge no national gathering of well-known Christian and non-Christian contemplative leaders had met together yet. I hoped we all could learn from one another's experience.

Fifty people attended, including all of Shalem's leaders. I don't have a list of the non-Shalem leaders, and my memory is spotty, but here is a small sampling: Rabbi Zalman Schachter-Shalomi, Joshu Sasaki Roshi (a Japanese Zen master), Seung Soen Sansa Nim (a Korean Zen master), Douglas Steere (Quaker scholar at Haverford College), a Cistercian monk (I think Basil Pennington), Cenacle Sister Rita Ann Houlihan, Ewart Cousins (a well-known scholar of Christian mysticism at Fordham University), and IHM Sister Sandra Schneiders (who created the first doctoral program in Christian spirituality at the Graduate Theological Union in Berkeley).

I was humbled by the wisdom and experience that was shared together. It was illuminating to see how we overlapped in our understandings and concerns and where we didn't; we had some honest dialogue about our differences. We had a general agreement on two themes: the importance of dying to false self so that the true center could emerge with its clarity and compassion, and a rediscovery of Western contemplative history and practices stimulated and enriched by Asian contemplative traditions.

The most amazing session was led by Rabbi Zalman, who was a well-known modern Hasidic teacher. He placed bread and wine on a table. Then he led us in a celebration based on the biblical story of Melchizedek. The story was followed by a dance of shalom. It began with people dancing together in pairs, slowing including others, until finally everyone in the room was dancing. It felt like a physical, ecstatic celebration of our transcendent connectedness across all kinds of boundaries. It reminded me of the saying, "A mystic isn't a special kind of person; every person is a special kind of mystic." Contemplative awareness can belong to everyone, in one or another of its many forms.

Joining the Ecumenical Institute of Spirituality

A few years later, in 1980, I was invited to join the Ecumenical Institute of Spirituality (EIOS), a national group of about twenty spiritual leaders who had already been meeting together for about ten years. It had been organized after the Second Vatican Council by two people who had been at that council: Douglas Steere, who attended as the representative from the Religious Society of Friends (Quakers), and a liturgical scholar from St. John's Benedictine Community in Minnesota. The members felt a great desire for spirituality to be attended on an ecumenical basis.

It was a humbling privilege and inspiration to spend four days a year in residence at different monasteries and retreat centers with this amazing group of people.

The members included, besides Douglas Steere and his wife, Dorothy, a Benedictine scholar: Constance Fitzgerald, a Carmelite Sister and renowned scholar of John of the Cross and Teresa of Avila; Glenn Hinson, a church historian and the Southern Baptist representative to the Second Vatican Council; Edward Farrell, who left teaching at a Catholic seminary to be pastor of a very poor inner-city parish in Detroit (where he brought a community of Mother Teresa's sisters to live); Basil Pennington, a Cistercian monk and the author of fifty books on the spiritual life; Thomas Clarke, a Jesuit theologian and director of a retreat center; Dorothy Devers, a leader of the ecumenical Church of the Saviour in DC; Richard Luecke, a Lutheran theologian for the Chicago Urban Training Center; Morton Kelsey, an Episcopal priest and the author of many books on psychological healing and other spiritual themes; Dolores Leckey, previously introduced; John Mogabgab, the founder and editor of *Weavings* magazine and graduate assistant to Henri Nouwen at Yale earlier in life; and Cenacle Sister Rita Anne Houlihan. A book edited by Glenn Hinson was published at one point with chapters by many EIOS members, including one by me on the spiritual attraction of war.

Our days together usually had the same basic ingredients: on the first day always sharing our "bios"—that is, what we wanted to share with one another about our lives and concerns in the year since we last met; time for prayer together; the presentation of one or two papers by members on particular spiritual themes, followed by much dialogue; free solitude time; and at the end, a concluding Eucharist.

Over my twenty years of meetings with the members, the one thing often missing for me was a sense of our dialogue growing out of our receptive, mind-in-heart presence. Our dialogue time could become very heady, which was understandable with so many brilliant "heads" talking. I didn't feel we built in enough times to relinquish our mind talk and return for a few minutes to a shared, listening spiritual-heart presence, times that could help our mind talk to be more grounded in the spiritual heart. Nonetheless, I was inspired and sometimes intimidated by the depth and breadth of insights and experiences shared. Especially in the early years, I felt myself to be a young newcomer; I wanted to listen much more than talk.

Toward the end of the EIOS's life, we tried to become an interfaith group, inviting a few people from other traditions, but the group's aging and dying membership finally led to its end. I still maintain contact with several of them, and I remain enriched by what was given me in that unique little community of spiritual seekers, finders, and enablers of spiritual understanding.

A Few Early Leaders of Shalem

Some amazing people bonded together in Shalem's early groups, some of whom became the core of its future leadership. I already have talked about Dolores Leckey. She agreed to colead the second beginning long-term group in 1974 with Jerry May, and she was a staff member in the first years of the extension program for spiritual directors. Over time she became one of the most widely known Roman Catholic lay leaders in the country through her work with the National Catholic Conference of Bishops and through her many popular books about Christian spirituality. Marlene Maier was another early dedicated program staff member going back to before Shalem was independent from METC. Here I'll speak about two other program staff people who have been central figures in the program development and leadership of Shalem from the beginning. I'll introduce a third leader in the next chapter.

Jerry May: A Major Presence

Gerald (Jerry) May and I met through the mediation of a METC staff member, Roy Oswald, a Lutheran pastor and church consultant who also became a lifelong friend of mine. He knew Jerry from a clinical pastoral education program at a hospital where Jerry worked with drug addicts in Lancaster, Pennsylvania. Jerry's interest in the spiritual life was growing, which was rare for psychiatrists at that time. He was particularly moved by the spiritual experiences that some addicts described on the way to recovery. He noticed that these encounters were the most important elements in their becoming free of addiction. He was disappointed in the discomfort the clergy in the pastoral education program had with talking about experiences of prayer, which Jerry was finding to be very important. He wrote an article about this for the *Journal of Pastoral Care.*

Jerry was thinking of moving with his family to the Washington, DC, area and finding some place where he could learn more about spirituality and its relation to psychology. He decided to move to Columbia, Maryland, where he found a job at a Maryland state prison as a psychiatrist, along with seeing some private patients.

Roy felt that Shalem might be the place for him to explore contemplative spirituality. He gave me a copy of Jerry's article, and he gave Jerry a copy of the report on my sabbatical time in California, telling us both, "You've got to read this." We both did, and Jerry arranged to meet with me. After asking him a lot of questions and sensing he really was in the same ballpark of spiritual concern as I was, I invited him to join the Friday morning group. I saw what a humble, open, insightful, and dedicated mind he brought to the group and to our meetings together. It was clear he felt spiritual awareness was not just a potential means of fostering psychological health, as some therapists in that time believed, but of intrinsic value with a purpose of its own. When I asked him that first spring if he would colead a new long-term group with Dolores Leckey, I was happy to hear him readily agree.

Jerry's nine books and many articles written over the years were widely read and respected. He was a pioneer in the ways he related psychology and spirituality, and in the ways he upheld the vital importance of spiritual awareness and experience in human life that transcended psychological health. He believed that deep spiritual awareness did not require psychological health; G-d's liberating, loving Spirit was available to all sorts and conditions of people.

We were able to bring Jerry onto the full-time paid staff of Shalem after several years. Eventually he had a place in almost all of Shalem's major programs, along with leading an annual workshop on psychology and contemplative spirituality that drew large crowds to hear his ever-fresh insights.

Jerry and I came to have a lot of respect for each other and a sense that deep down we were on the same spiritual track. I can remember intuitively feeling the truthfulness of his many insights when I heard him speak, read his writings, and in our personal conversations. We shared a sense of the deep mystery of G-d and the spiritual journey that meant none of our insights and experiences could ever be sufficient to comprehend. At the same time, we shared a trust that an indestructible radiant Love flowed from that great living Mystery, a love that showed everything and everyone to be in intimate communion, mutually indwelling, however hidden and unresponded to in our consciousness. Our deepest desire was to realize and live in that loving communion and its flow in the world, as Jesus and contemplative tradition invites us to do. Jerry might have worded this a little differently, but I think he would nod his head if he were alive to read what I've said.

Once Jerry told me that in prayer he asked G-d to show him divine love more fully. Right after that, he suddenly had an overwhelming sense of that love, so great that he couldn't bear it. We both sensed that in G-d's mercy we could be shown only a limited amount of the fire of that love; too much would consume us.

Paradoxically, our intimate underlying shared spiritual reverberation existed between two people whose personalities, life experience, and ways of responding to our experience were radically different. Jerry loved being a prankster with the staff. I think in part because he disliked pretentiousness and wanted everyone to be leveled through the prank and through laughter. His youngest son, Greg, showed his father's genes when he joined the Barnum & Bailey Circus as a clown for a few years. When the circus came to Washington, DC, Jerry would encourage the whole staff to attend together. He also coaxed us to attend the high school plays that his creative wife, Betty, staged. I can remember at one of them that when something funny was said, he would be the first person in the audience to laugh—uproariously.

All of us on the staff caught the laughter bug with him over the years. It had a good spiritual side in the way it kept us from getting overly serious and pretentious about Shalem's work. Humor toppled our idols and freed us to be just limited human beings before the great mystery of G-d. But I could never have led in the raw ways that he did. His way of coping with behavior and societal norms he disagreed with included various forms of rebelliousness, which at one level his humor expressed. I was more circumspect. I took my role as executive director obsessively seriously, including assuring that all our planning meetings began with receptive silence, wanting to give the Spirit time to move us and transcend our ego drives; cultivating Shalem's programmatic opportunities and developing structural designs for them; finding and keeping good staff; raising sufficient funds; reaching out to more people to participate in Shalem offerings; and helping to legitimate contemplative tradition in the Christian and larger culture where it was little known. At times I wished Jerry were more concerned with some of these areas, but at the same time I was glad I and others could protect his time so that he could produce the great books and talks that he did, as well as be available as a spiritual director for many people.

Shalem had several open houses during the year and I remember smiling to myself when I had a sudden insight into why we were present at them in such a contrasting way. Jerry normally would be seated or standing somewhere, not coming forward to greet or talk to people who came. He would wait for someone to come to him. I, on the other hand, would go up to people, especially new people, and introduce myself and talk with them.

My insight? Jerry was a psychiatrist with a long history of sitting in his office and waiting for someone to come to him. I was a priest, with a long priestly habit of going up to people in church gatherings and talking with them. This is an oversimplification of our different vocational experience, but it struck me as one factor in our different behavior, and the insight lightened my feeling miffed sometimes that he didn't reach out to people.

Jerry was very independent in his thinking. He read much classic spiritual contemplative literature with sincere appreciation. He once developed a historical "time river" that listed the names of over a hundred significant contemplatives in Christian history along with some from other traditions that reflected contemplative spiritual values. Later I added to the list. We gave it out to participants in various Shalem programs (and still do). But when it came to the relation between psychology and spirituality, his thoughts came from an interior frontier of his own that advanced that subject to fresh ground internationally. My writings perhaps brought some fresh thinking to old subjects, but nothing so significant and pioneering as his.

We had an easy and vital relationship as spiritual companions for each other over a twenty-year period, meeting for two hours once a month—an hour for him and one for me. I once had a night dream where we were on retreat together in a desert. When Jerry was sitting in still meditation, that somehow freed me to move around, and vice versa. To me, that was a sign of how close we were. A few later years, outside of spiritual direction, our psychic differences caused a rift between us. In a sense I think our very different ways of coping with our psychic childhood scars were a factor in that, leading to misinterpretations and different views of what was needed. But we never stopped loving each other.

Eventually we were graced to grow closer again, and that continued to the end. When Jerry first developed cancer and the staff found out about it, I asked him to lie down. All the staff encircled him and laid hands on his body, and I gave a fervent prayer for healing. With the help of chemotherapy and surgery, he had a reprieve, but eventually new cancer cells returned. Years later, when I arrived home from a trip overseas, I learned he was close to death. I went to the hospital the next day. Betty, his wife, was sitting in his room and said to Jerry, "Tilden is here!" Jerry was thrashing around in bed with his eyes closed, semiconscious. He could not speak, but when Betty said my name, I think I saw a faint smile appear on his face, even as his eyes remained closed and the thrashing continued. I was devastated to see him in this condition, and at the same time I was so glad to see what I hoped was a smile of recognition and gladness that I was there. That was such a gift, in the face of my concern that he might still feel a bit distant from me, and my sense of guilt at feeling I was not with him enough in his years of struggling against his cancer, although I'm glad he did have a lot of good physically present supporters during that time.

Jerry died the next day. The next week a memorial service was held for him in the huge chapel of the Bon Secours Spiritual Center, where so many Shalem programs were held. The chapel was packed. So many people had been deeply inspired by him in his writings and speeches over the years, and through his spiritual guidance. For me, he was a vital mentor and friend, for whom I will be forever grateful.

Sister Rose Mary Dougherty: Another Major Presence

Rose Mary Dougherty, a member of the School Sisters of Notre Dame, eventually became the third full-time major Shalem program developer, leader, and author, wonderfully complementing me and Jerry.

I met her when she joined the first class of Shalem's long-term spiritual guidance program for the enrichment of spiritual directors in the fall of 1978. When it ended in 1980, recognizing her mature spiritual life and awareness, I asked her to become part of the staff for the second class beginning that year. She radiated a confident, intelligent, discerning, and caring presence that would continue to serve Shalem for the next thirty-five years, including as director of that program for about fifteen years. She also developed a major extension program that in effect stretched the intent of personal contemplative deepening in the original local long-term groups into a national program. Overall, she became an essential, greatly respected, and loved member of Shalem's core development team.

I really came to know Rose Mary while being in residence together for three weeks in South Africa in 1994. I had received an invitation from the Ecumenical Institute in Cape Town to lead a ten-day spiritual directors training program. I knew it would be too demanding for me to lead alone, and I asked Rose Mary if she would share the leadership with me. She agreed, and thus began a unique adventure together at a watershed moment in South Africa's history.

When the schedule was fully put together, our time there was expanded to include leading a workshop on contemplative spirituality in Johannesburg, followed by the ten-day spiritual directors program in Cape Town.

In Johannesburg we were met at the airport by a white Anglican priest who took us to his home in a northern suburb. We were surprised to find his home surrounded by a high fence of barbed wire, as was true of most of the houses in that enclave. Robberies were a major problem. His wife met us at the door and showed us to our rooms for our three-day stay.

After settling in, we came into the living room; through a window we saw a one-room concrete hut just a few feet from the back door of the house. A little later a black woman came into the main house from there. We found out that hut was her home. She was the housekeeper and cook (and I expect earlier a nanny) for the family. We guessed this was a typical arrangement at the time for many white families.

Maybe the living conditions were better than wherever the rest of her family lived, but it's hard to believe that compensated much for so little living time with her own family and community when she was able to do that. I was aware that, to use their terms, black and colored (i.e., mixed-race or South Indian) were never slaves, but they certainly were at the bottom of the heap in terms of political power and material and educational resources. Black South Africans were divided into large tribal groups. The Afrikaans-speaking early European settlers considered themselves a white tribe. Their dominance, reinforced by many British immigrants, created a hierarchical apartheid system, with whites clearly on top, followed by the coloreds, and then the blacks, who maintained their own tribal identities and customs. The blacks at least had the dignity of their own ancient tribal identity, language, and customs, all of which were suppressed in the terrible United States' enslavement version of apartheid.

Rose Mary and I shared leadership for our contemplative workshop in Johannesburg with an audience of English-speaking clergy and laypeople. We weren't sure if we communicated well with them, but the contemplative practices we led at least gave them opportunity to taste firsthand something of what we were talking about. In the rest of our time in Johannesburg (or simply "Jo-burg" as people called it), our host took us around to some famous sites, including the large, bustling Soweto black community packed with small houses and huts that was so important in the struggle against apartheid. We also visited a famous gold mine museum, showing us where so many blacks labored in the white-owned mines responsible for much of South Africa's wealth.

From there we flew to Cape Town. As the plane descended at sunset, we saw a beautiful scene looming below: the dominant tabletop mountain with a big city nestled below it, and the Atlantic Ocean to the west. We were met by someone from the Ecumenical Institute and taken to our "home" for the next two weeks in the Herschel Anglican Girls School, which was out of session at the time, in the suburb of Claremont.

We were housed in a very small apartment on the second floor, which had two tiny bedrooms, a shared space in between to sit together, and a bathroom. This was luxurious compared to the dormitories where most of the live-in participants would be housed. We were shocked to hear how large the group would be: ninety people. They were from various parts of South Africa: clergy and laypeople; Anglicans, Roman Catholics, and Protestants; black, colored, and white. This was the first-ever major program for spiritual directors in South Africa, and the broad racial and ecumenical mix of people coming together probably was a first for most of the participants. We were there at a historical moment. Nelson Mandela would be installed as the new president of South Africa in less than a year. Apartheid was coming to an end after many decades of battles. You could feel everyone sensing that a new day was at hand for the country, full of both hope and uncertainty about what was ahead. You also could feel that they were pioneers spiritually in their hope to bring spiritual direction as a ministry into their churches, deepening the spiritual life of members and ultimately the congregation as a whole.

Rose Mary and I had put together ten full days of seminars and contemplative prayer practices for the gathering, with many seminars selected from Shalem's own much longer spiritual direction program. Out of so much that I could say about those days, including so many wonderful conversations with participants, I'll mention just three special happenings.

Rose Mary had a marvelous memory and a quiet confidence from all the many years she had been practicing, teaching, reading, writing, and praying about contemplatively grounded spiritual direction. Although I had a lot of teaching experience, I never fully trusted my memory or the adequacy of what I would say. Every day I spent much time in our apartment going over my notes, sometimes revising them, and then making sure I had my notes in front of me when speaking, even if I strayed from them at times when some spontaneous insight came to me.

While I was doing all that careful preparatory work, what was Rose Mary doing? Casually reading a novel! I couldn't believe her seminars weren't going to suffer. She stood up before the group with a few handwritten notes outlining what she would say, and she just started talking. What she said was incredibly coherent and insightful and just enough to cover what needed to be said (including her responses to participants' questions). All of our seminars were recorded, and when we returned to the US, I listened to the tapes; her talks were so well put together that I could swear she was *reading* them word for word, but she hadn't read a word of it! Everything just spontaneously flowed out from her super-organized mind. Evaluations at the end reflected the group's great appreciation of what she offered (as indeed all Shalem spiritual guidance program groups felt before and after that summer).

The one place she lost confidence was when she locked herself in our bathroom, and the lock wouldn't unlock. I tried and tried from my side, but finally I had to find the school handyman to come up, unscrew the handle, and push open the door. She walked out of her unexpected little prison with a sheepish but relieved look on her face. Word got around about this, giving a light note to our serious day.

Offerings of Movement Meditation and Holy Eucharist

In the middle of the ten days, we set aside an evening for movement meditation, led by me. It was optional because it required the nonresident participants to come back in the evening. We had no idea how many would return, and amazingly almost everyone showed up in the school gym, which was large enough to give us room to move around freely.

Even though I had much experience leading this seminar in the Shalem program, I was anxious about whether this mix of people would trust what I asked them to do enough to really participate. Almost all of them were members of churches where prayerful presence through spontaneous movement to music was unknown. I had carefully chosen two different kinds of recorded instrumental music: an American modern pianist-composer, Michael Gettel, playing pieces from his San Juan Suite, including several that included sounds from nature, such as seagulls and a thunderstorm; and a recording of "Township" music, an indigenous music of the South African black culture.

I first asked everyone to gather into one huge circle. Then I explained that we were going to have the opportunity to heed G-d's Spirit in us and let ourselves be guided into spontaneous movements of our bodies, giving them a chance to silently express praise, thanksgiving, and joy. I asked them to let their bodies "pray" in this way—open, free, childlike, unselfconscious, in the living Presence, until the music stopped. I told them that when the music pauses a few seconds between pieces to let their body briefly freeze in the position it was in when the music stopped. I also told them that if they had trouble moving around, they were welcome to just sit and let their arms move with the music.

Then the music began, about twenty-five minutes with the piano music, then an equal amount of time with the Township music. People slowly began to move their arms, then some began to move their feet and slowly move around the room. Occasionally someone would move in rhythm with someone else, mirroring one another, or move in a circle with someone, then they might move on to do the same with someone else. I sensed especially the black participants really beginning to let go once the Township music began. When the music ended, I asked them to silently re-form the big circle and hold hands. I quoted from psalm 87:7: "The singers and dancers will say, all my fresh springs are in You." After a minute or so of silence, a black woman began to speak in tongues. We all silently absorbed her expression, and then I asked everyone to leave in silence and remain in silence until we gathered again the next morning.

When the silence was broken the next day, I asked if anyone wanted to share what happened to them in the movement meditation the night before. I will never forget the enthusiastic response of a Zulu Roman Catholic priest who had just been appointed the spiritual formation director in a Catholic seminary. He mentioned that moving the body in dance was integral to his Zulu culture, but he had never had opportunity to bring that part of his culture into his Catholic corporate worship time. He was so happy about this. I silently hoped that he would find a way to bring that freedom to the seminarians with whom he would be working in his new position. Everyone else who spoke also found it so good to be able to let their bodies pray together. I felt so grateful for this discovery of the body's place in prayer and hopeful that they would let this evolve and bring respect for their bodies as "temples of the Holy Spirit" in this way to their churches.

At the end of our ten days we sat next to one another in the school chapel for a closing ecumenical Holy Eucharist. I was the presiding celebrant, wearing a white alb and stole. I think everyone felt the poignancy of this final time together. We had crossed racial and denominational, clergy and lay and regional lines in an intimate way, developing new personal relationships. We had deepened our spiritual lives through the many spiritual practices we shared. We had gained more practical knowledge of a newly emerging ministry available to clergy and laity alike in South Africa: spiritual direction. Our shared, intense, and revelatory time together was a foretaste of what everyone hoped would grow in the emerging post-apartheid South Africa. Together we were feeling the birth pains and hopes of a new era.

After we finished praying the shared prayer of confession printed in the order of service and I was about to proclaim G-d's forgiveness, an amazing thing happened. A white man stood up and made a moving personal confession to all the non-whites present about his participation in the white privileges of apartheid, asking their forgiveness for the harm it had caused black and colored citizens. After a pause, several other whites stood and likewise asked the non-whites for forgiveness. When it became silent again, I raised my hand and made the sign of the cross over the congregation with words asking for G-d's forgiveness of all our sins and to strengthen us in all goodness. I felt those words were carrying the forgiveness offered by the non-white people present there also, who I sensed were too shocked by the personal confessions to say anything themselves. After that I proclaimed, "The peace of the Lord be always with you," which came at that point in the liturgy after which they exchanged those words with their neighbors, holding one another's hands as they did so. Never has that exchange of peace been more rightly placed in the service.

The chalice used in the Eucharist was made of wood. During the prayer of consecration, when I lifted the chalice and proclaimed the words, "The Body of Christ, the cup of salvation," a trickle of wine dripped from a leak in the cup down my raised right arm, streaking my white alb red. I could hardly continue. I had the immediate sense of the sacrificial, reconciling death of Christ visibly showing itself for this congregation, a reconciliation that was empowered by those spontaneous confessions and exchanges of peace. Never have I felt the "Real Presence" in the consecrated wine more vividly!

I think all of those present felt G-d's confirmation of our life together and our hope for the future in that truly blessed Eucharist. The Spirit was palpably alive among us.

A Memorable Gift of Exploration

The rest of our stay in South Africa was a cool-down time, more relaxed and with opportunities to see the earth's great beauty near Cape Town. A highlight for me was our visit to the magnificent, world-famous botanical gardens there. South Africa is a cornucopia of unusual and beautiful flowers, plants, and trees, many of which have been exported to other parts of the world. The gardens were a real feast of cultivated nature.

In appreciation of our work in South Africa, we were offered a participant's cottage in a small town on a bay overlooking the Atlantic Ocean shore for a few days. Rose Mary and I had our own bedrooms, plus a little living room and kitchen. No one there knew we were a priest and nun, so we didn't have to worry about wide-eyed gawkers. Besides, we were a wonderfully innocent pair together who just enjoyed each other's company. We had many conversations about our experience in that country and our hopes for its future. We went alone at times for long walks along the shore, and we were in solitude with our books, including novels by famous South African authors that helped us burrow into the mental climate of the country.

Toward the end of our stay, the owner of the cabin picked us up and drove us several hours to the Cape of Good Hope at the southern tip of Africa. As we came closer to it, the land narrowed to the point where we could see the Atlantic Ocean on the right side of the road and the Indian Ocean on the left side. We also began to see wild ostriches running around the flatlands around us. When we arrived at the tip of the Cape, we parked the car and walked to the lookout over the ocean, surrounded by a family of wild baboons. It felt awesome to be standing at the point where the huge Atlantic and Indian Oceans merge.

We drove back to our cottage and the next day were driven to the airport for our flight home. We shared how much we had learned on that trip about the unique cultures and churches of South Africa, and how much more there was to learn. Over the following years we both corresponded with a number of the people who were with us in Cape Town. Several of them enrolled in Shalem extension programs and brought back more contemplative and spiritual direction enrichment to groups in South Africa.

When we were in South Africa, we had visited a home for handicapped children, and Rose Mary was very moved by the experience. She mentioned to me her sense of possible call to return and work with them. When we returned home, though, she discerned that her call was to stay with her work at Shalem. In later years, she added another calling beyond Shalem. She became a Zen sensei (teacher), after being part of a small zendo in Baltimore founded by two other sisters and after receiving teaching and leadership authorization from the head of the White Plum Asanga Buddhist lineage, founded by Taizan Maezumi Roshi. Rose Mary was given permission to begin a weekly Zen meditation group grounded in that lineage in her living room. Years later, she was called to take a course with a Buddhist group in San Francisco that specialized in ways of companioning dying people, after feeling a call to have such a ministry from her work in a hospice for AIDS and other patients in DC. Eventually she started such a teaching program herself: Companioning the Dying: Open Fully to Living. She remained a Catholic sister loyal to her community throughout.

Rose Mary's Passing

A few years ago, Rose Mary sadly developed Parkinson's disease, as did one of her blood sisters, Mary Ellen, and one of her brothers. When she became so ill that she had to move to nursing care in her religious community's motherhouse in Baltimore, my wife, Mary, and I visited her there a number of times. On March 14, 2019, I received a call that she was rapidly dying. She died that evening. I was devastated. We had been friends and coworkers for forty years. I was mentored over those years by her very way of being herself: a person without contrivance, calculation, pretense, or false piety, but with a profound faith, honest humility, great integrity, determined passion for justice, and spontaneous compassion and wisdom.

Rose Mary's funeral took place in the huge chapel of her community's motherhouse, Villa Assumpta. The crowd was so large that her community's offer of lunch for everyone had to be limited. I was asked to be one of the people offering the eulogy. It was impossible to praise her enough. To me, she was a supreme and unique example of the pioneering, reformist spirit of a post–Second Vatican Council Roman Catholic sister. I will be forever grateful to have had her in my life.

Chapter 11

Carol Crumley and the New Call to Pilgrimage, Clergy Leadership, and the Shalem Society

Another person who became a long-term friend and early Shalem leader was Carole Crumley. Her distinctive Tennessee accent was a delight to hear, and her caring, reflective, discerning insights were a frequent gift. She was one of the few graduates of the Intermet interfaith seminary before it had to close. Eventually she became the canon educator and canon pastor at the Washington National Cathedral, where she established a Prayer and Pilgrimage Center, among other innovations.

Leading pilgrimages was her deepest sense of calling and delight. Together she and I led Shalem's first overseas pilgrimage to Assisi. She then led a two-week pilgrimage to the Holy Land and Egypt, which was an extraordinary experience for me. I will never forget the night we spent in sleeping bags in a remote section of the Sinai desert, my skin stroked by a gentle wind, my eyes drowned in brilliant starlight, my ears hearing the deep silence—the whole scene pervaded by a mysterious sense of larger Presence. When I woke up at dawn, there were four Bedouin children sitting on a sand hillock nearby and watching us, very still and silent like the desert sands that were their home. Their father eventually appeared and laid out some trinkets on a blanket to sell and then sat down next to them, just as still and silent as his children.

That day we climbed into our big jeeps after a campfire breakfast and drove for hours through the desert to the massively walled ancient Greek Orthodox monastery of St. Catherine at the foot of Mount Sinai. It was the home of some of the earliest classical icons. One was the sixth-century icon of the Sinai Christ, a copy of which has filled my eyes every morning for many years in my home prayer space. We spent the night in the monastery's dormitory-like guesthouse. The next morning, we climbed Mount Sinai in honor of Moses and the Ten Commandments that scripture says were revealed there. Though marred by the trash that pilgrims left along the way, the powerful silence of the mountain and of the barren mountains surrounding it as far as the eye could see was awesome.

When we drove farther into Egypt, besides spending some time in Cairo we visited two major desert Coptic monasteries, both founded by an early Desert Father: St. Anthony was one, the other St. Macarius. These monasteries are pilgrimage sites, especially for the large Coptic Christian population of Egypt. Many thousands of people visit them on special holy days. The monasteries gave me a sense of eternal time. In the St. Macarius monastery I remember seeing a family in front of the grave site of the founding Desert Father, praying to him with a faith that he was as much alive today as in the fourth century. That view inspired in me an intimate sense of his living, loving intercessory presence.

Carole also has led many Shalem pilgrimages to the holy island of Iona in Scotland and to Lindisfarne in England, as well as to Cuba, Paris, Newfoundland, and Chimayo and Navajo sites in New Mexico and Arizona. I have helped her lead a number of local interfaith pilgrimages, including to the Holocaust Museum, and the Vietnam and Martin Luther King Jr. memorials.

My image of her at the head of a group of pilgrims trekking somewhere is always the same. She walks slowly, steadily, unperturbably, with a radiant smile on her face that I think expresses her sense of calling to lead pilgrimages; she looks completely at home. Carole never seemed phased by whatever crises happened along the way; she just absorbed their reality and found a way to calmly respond. She is steadily confident that G-d's presence is available for people in the vulnerable, alert, yearning place of the heart that the pilgrimage cultivates. She organizes the pilgrims on major pilgrimages into a spiritual community with special self-chosen monastic-inspired leadership responsibilities, such as almoner and porter. Each day has a schedule of guided contemplative prayer and small-group reflection times, and visits to various sites. There's always one day of complete silence. She asks everyone to "bring home the blessing" of their experience on the pilgrimage to their families and communities. That blessing often includes some surprising and sometimes transformative spiritual deepening and sense of calling for the pilgrims.

When Carole was ready to leave her work at the cathedral, I asked her to join the Shalem staff full-time to head up (in additional to pilgrimages) two new extension programs that I had been led to feel were needed: one for spiritual/contemplative grounding of executive leaders in any kind of organization, such as government, health, and social service agencies; the second for the spiritual deepening of parish clergy. These would complement our major programs for spiritual directors, for personal spiritual deepening, and for forming leaders of contemplative groups and retreats. The last one had been developed in response to the need for such leaders in church and other settings everywhere, as the hunger for contemplative understanding and practices in the country (and beyond) grew steadily over the years.

We had many clergy in Shalem's existing programs, but none of those programs focused on contemplative leadership and life in the local church. No program in the country that I knew of focused on cultivating contemplative grounding for the leadership and daily life of clergy, and what could be done to cultivate contemplative grounding in the whole life of the church and its members. I felt such a program could set the stage for deeper spiritual discernment and life together.

I felt the same way about executives in different organizational settings. Their leadership also could benefit from an opportunity for greater contemplative grounding in their spiritual hearts rather than being dominated by fearful, controlling ego-level identity.

The first classes of both new programs were full and enthusiastic. I was a member of the staff of both programs and learned a lot about the pain and hopes of executives in very different kinds of organizational settings. Evaluations of the programs showed a lot of appreciation for the content and support they received. Both programs over time suffered from competition from other educational centers, although to my eyes none of them tried to offer the in-depth contemplative grounding that was our priority. The yearlong executive program lasted for three classes; it was sad to see its ending, then, for lack of enough applicants. Many years later, a longer, fresh form of it came into being through Shalem's current executive director, Margaret Benefiel. "Soul of the Leader" now has programs in Boston, DC, England, and Korea.

The yearlong clergy program continues to this day. In the last meeting of its sixth class many years ago, one of the participants passionately shouted out, "We can't stop now! We're just beginning!" That motivated Carole and me to do what we long thought was needed but had never been done. We launched the Shalem Contemplative Leadership Society for graduates of any of our extension programs. The contemplative journey is a lifetime affair, with layers of fresh awareness over time. Participants in our long-term programs—"associates," as we call them—often found themselves digesting transformative understandings and experiences of who they were and what they were called to do. We strongly encouraged ongoing one-to-one or group spiritual direction for them. But that left out the value of an ongoing community of graduates wanting to inspire one another's still deeper unfolding of what could be done to bring contemplative understanding and practice to their congregations, families, communities, and workplaces.

Membership in the society includes commitment to daily contemplatively grounded prayer, having a spiritual director, an annual private retreat, called-for forms of contemplative leadership, and prayerful mutual support. For those who were willing and able, we created an annual national five-day gathering for members. We also provided guidelines for regional "Shalem Circles" of graduates across the country and abroad that would meet every month or so for sharing.

Liz Ward, the director of the spiritual guidance program, and Ann Dean, the director of the leading contemplative groups and retreats program, along with Carole, have had decades of experience with Shalem leadership, and most of the Shalem Society members would be graduates of one or both of their programs. I trusted and respected them implicitly for their contemplative depth and desire to bring forward Shalem's mission as G-d's Spirit inspired us to see it. We met monthly together as the Guardian Circle to oversee the Shalem Society's development. Over time we found the Spirit drawing us deeper in our own contemplative awareness and understanding, which was a personal gift to each of us After many years we all have retired from the society's leadership, and it is now skillfully headed by Margaret Benefiel and four volunteer regional members, who have wonderfully bonded together. The four of us continue to meet monthly as a Shalem Circle. I always look forward to our mutual spiritual stimulation, prayer, and support for one another in those meetings.

Over the nearly half century of Shalem's life, many other people have been Shalem staff leaders, almost all of them first having participated in at least one Shalem extension program beforehand. Program and e-course graduates now number in the thousands. In the appendix I mention some of the longtime leaders beyond those already mentioned, out of so many gifted ones in Shalem's history that I have been blessed to know.

Chapter 12

Contemplative Outreach Beyond Shalem

Over my years at Shalem, I accepted many invitations to give talks, lead workshops and retreats, and participate in radio and TV interviews and several gatherings of leaders who were moved to create new contemplative organizational opportunities. I'll share with you a few of these happenings that were particularly memorable to me. After that I will share the outreach offered through my books, and finally I'll describe Shalem's concerted outreach to South Korea.

National Public Radio

At one point in my Shalem years I received a phone call from Lynn Neary, one of the regular voices on National Public Radio. She wanted to come to Shalem and interview me about its work. During the interview, I told her about a chant inspired by a poem of Elizabeth of the Trinity, a Carmelite nun, and set to music by Jerry May, which we often sang in Shalem programs. Then she asked if I would sing it. I didn't expect that. I don't have a good singing voice, and she was recording this interview; maybe she would include it in what she would take from the interview and publicly air it. I hesitated, but finally agreed. I swallowed hard, opened my mouth in prayerful hope that what came out of it wouldn't be a disaster, and sang: "Changeless and calm, deep Mystery, ever more deeply, rooted in Thee."

When the interview was aired nationally several days later, to my chagrin, it included the chant. When I came into the office the next day, the whole staff greeted me by singing the chant together, in great glee, as I cringed. They all had heard it on the air. That evening, my brother-in-law

Larry called Mary, my wife, from San Francisco, saying that he awoke in the morning to the sound of the chant, feeling the voice was vaguely familiar, and then heard that it was me. I was even more embarrassed because I knew how sophisticated his appreciation of music is, but he was polite enough not to be critical, just amazed.

I think G-d's Spirit has an impish sense of humor sometimes, and that it had something to do with this massive public exposure before millions of people, wanting to keep me humble. Indeed, it helped! Hopefully some people ignored my voice and were moved by the Carmelite sister's words.

Trinity Institute

On another occasion I received a phone call from the Trinity Institute in New York City, inviting me to moderate a panel with three well-known national spiritual leaders in the Episcopal Church. I can remember only one name: Martin Smith, who had written some fine books and previously was the superior of the Society of St. John the Divine, the Episcopal monastic community in Cambridge, Massachusetts, that I've previously mentioned. It was to be live-streamed to subscribing parishes across the country. I agreed, although I had never done anything like that before.

I took the train to New York and found my way to the institute. It was meant to be a spontaneous, free-flowing conversation about contemplative understanding and practice in the context of the needs of the church and society today. I envisioned that this conversation, at its best, would involve all of us leaning back into our spiritual hearts and listening openly for what the Spirit might inspire. After about a half hour of greeting one another and being briefed by the Trinity staff about the process, we took our seats around a table, facing the TV monitor in front of us. I was told that I would likely be fed some email questions from the viewing audience. I had an earpiece wired to a staff person who could talk to me privately whenever necessary.

We fell into silence for several minutes, watching the clock tick toward the 3:00 p.m. live-stream start time. I was prepared to look at a special TV monitor and read what was printed there: a five-minute welcome that I had written for the audience, and an introduction to the subject and the panelists. When the clock struck 3:00, I heard in my earpiece, "Tilden, begin." But the monitor remained blank. No words. I tried to signal this to the technician, who finally saw that the monitor wasn't attached to an outlet. But I couldn't wait for that. The audience was watching. Squelching a moment of panic, I began to ad-lib, hoping I could remember enough of what I was supposed to convey in a coherent enough way. It wasn't easy for me. Midway through, the monitor suddenly came on, but I had already blurted out some of what was there and couldn't quickly find the words I hadn't yet said, so I had to ad-lib to the end.

Still shaking a bit from that sputtering beginning, I gave a question to the panelists and they began to interact, with my trying to summarize points and suggest further questions as we went along. When email questions came in from the audience, I had to hold them in the back of my mind until they could fit into the flow of the often very sophisticated conversation. When the two hours were finally up, I was exhausted and greatly relieved. I don't think I've ever been so tested in a public-speaking event. The small audience in the studio itself felt okay about it, but I felt I had lost any semblance of a calm spiritual leader settled into G-d's presence. It felt like another lesson in humility.

A Crash That Could Have Been Mine

Another happening I'll share involves a time that I had agreed to give a lecture and a practice of contemplative presence at a national spirituality conference at Emory University in Atlanta. It began to snow early in the morning of the day I was to speak. Atlanta doesn't usually get much or any snow, and it's not prepared for anything major. By that afternoon when I was scheduled to speak, the snow was falling heavily. Just as I was beginning my talk, someone came into the room and announced that the conference was cancelled, because a huge ice and snowstorm was underway.

I made my way back to the motel where I was housed in blinding falling snow. When I walked through the front door, I saw water streaming down from a leak in the roof over the lobby's registration desk. I quickly went to my room, packed my bag, ran downstairs, and miraculously found a taxi willing to take me to the airport in the storm. As we drove along, many cars were ditched on both sides of the road. The courageous driver managed to get me to the airport. When I entered the terminal, I found myself in a refugee zone. What looked like thousands of people filled all the seats and a lot of the floor space of that huge Atlanta international airport. My flight and many other flights were cancelled. I was on a wait list for another plane, but I had no idea when it would be able to take off. After several hours I was relieved to hear a voice on the loudspeaker announce the readiness of my delayed flight to DC.

When the plane arrived in DC, I took a taxi home. As I opened the door to get out, I saw Ann running out of the house in a panic, having been worried that I was on the plane that had just crashed-landed in the Potomac River! I had been in the taxi driving along the river as it happened, but it wasn't visible from where we were. When I walked into the house, I felt much gratitude for my getting out of Atlanta and safely home, along with offering prayer for all those in the downed plane and for the people of Atlanta. The whole trip was a humbling reminder of how much we do not control the weather or the safety of our means of transportation, and how arbitrary it feels as to who is hurt, killed, and saved. Life finally is fragile and unpredictable and yet I try to trust that whatever happens is redeemable in the mystery of divine love and inspired human resilience.

Spiritual Directors International

In the gentle hills of Burlingame, California, on the San Francisco Peninsula, sits the Mercy Retreat Center of the Sisters of Mercy. Two spiritual events there over the years are branded in my memory.

The first was a small gathering of spiritual directors from across the country, mostly Roman Catholic clergy and religious community members, who wanted to pray and reflect together about national collaboration in the furthering of the ministry of spiritual direction. This was in the early years of the growing awareness of the value of spiritual direction for laypeople and clergy, and the need for the development of more spiritual directors to meet the need. Shalem's spiritual guidance program was only a few years old then, and there were a few Catholic centers beginning to offer small programs.

After several days of deliberation, one of the Catholic priests and I were talking together in the retreat center's elevator on the way down from our bedrooms to the meeting room. We shared how we both felt that it was time to begin a national organization for spiritual directors that would meet annually for sharing our learnings and for mutual support. We brought that conviction to the rest of those gathered, and we all together discerned that this indeed was a called-for major step for us to take.

Thus the seed was sown for what eventually became Spiritual Directors International (SDI). Today that organization has many thousands of members from different denominations in the United States and around the world. Among other offerings, it prints a major quarterly periodical, *Presence*. Jerry May sat on the first steering committee, and whoever was the director of Shalem's spiritual guidance program at the time attended the annual meeting, beginning with Sister Rose Mary.

We had some tension with SDI's original ethical guidelines statement for spiritual directors, feeling that it was too influenced by a psychological counseling model rather than a listening-to-the-Spirit model. The steering committee agreed to at least some modification of the original statement. At Shalem we were committed to the ministry of spiritual direction as it was seen historically: as a personal charism marked by other people spontaneously coming to you to help companion them on their spiritual journey by listening together for the Spirit's guidance. To this day, that is a primary qualification for entering the Shalem program: other people have sought you out for such companionship, along with signs of openness to a contemplatively grounded way of being present. Psychological counseling is not distained; it's just seen as a distinctly different ministry than spiritual direction.

Zen with Thomas Hand

Some years later I found myself again at the Mercy Center for a very different gathering: a Christian Zen retreat with Thomas Hand. Tom had been a Jesuit missionary in Japan for twenty-nine years, teaching in a Jesuit school. He was drawn to some practices of the ancient Zen Buddhist tradition there, beginning with the writing of haiku, brief three-line poems that in Zen tradition were meant to express the mutual indwelling of everything, often using imagery from nature. That practice has been diminished in modern secularized Japan to the extent that he found himself teaching it to high school students there for whom it was a new practice, especially with the intent of expressing mutual indwelling.

I have taught haiku in some classes I lead in Shalem programs, with guidelines I learned from Tom. I'm always amazed to find out how many people in those classes were used to reading or writing them, although in their often-secularized context in America they often lose their original Zen intent of expressing mutual indwelling, an intent that makes it a contemplative practice.

Another practice that attracted Tom in Japan was Zen meditation. He was hesitant to go to a Zen master, wondering if it would compromise his Christian commitment. He had been meditating in a zendo (meditation hall) for three months when he was granted an audience with Yamada Koun Roshi. After finding out that Tom was a Christian, Roshi told him, "There are two kinds of Zen: there's Buddhist Zen with all its teachings, images and chants; then there's just Zen, which can go with any religion. You just do Zen and you will become a better Christian." This freed Tom to become a student of Yamada Koun. He came to realize that his central problem as a Christian was that he was too much in his head rather than in his immediate intuitive awareness, which he saw as a transforming, liberating awareness of consciousness. He continued to practice in the zendo for a long time. Roshi eventually was convinced that Tom had both authentic enlightenment (intuitive realization of the true nature of reality) and the knowledge of Zen practices and teachings adequate for transmitting Zen to others. He was given *inka*, a teaching certificate.

When Tom retired, he convinced the sisters at Mercy Center to let him develop a Christian zendo in their basement. That's where I met him, as a retreatant in an eight-day retreat. He donned his Zen sensei (teacher) black apron and led us in meditation and chanting in the zendo, with about twenty of us sitting on small Japanese prayer benches carefully lined up in two rows facing one another, with an altar at one end. On the altar was a statue of Buddha and a uniquely sculptured Holy Mother and Child Jesus. Once daily Tom led a Eucharist in a chapel upstairs, with a homily that insightfully expressed selected Christian scriptural passages as contemplatively grounded in ways that connect with Buddhist awareness.

Each day we had a number of meditation sessions in the zendo as well as free time to walk the wooded trail outside the center, an old trail that Tom had personally enhanced with hard labor. The whole retreat was in silence until toward the end, when he had a private interview with each retreatant about what was being given to them in the retreat. When I met with him, I sensed he had retained the classic intellectual acumen cultivated in his twelve years of Jesuit training, now enlivened with what he felt was missing in that education, which (using my words) was particular contemplative practices and understandings that could open the spiritual heart and leave one more vulnerable to realizing the contemplative heart of Christ and the Christian tradition. I asked Tom how he connected the Holy Trinity to Zen Buddhist tradition. He said, "The Father is emptiness, the Son is form, and the Spirit is the breath that moves between." Now there is the makings of a special koan, a Christian Zen riddle, to ponder! The linear thinking mind needs to be suspended in order to do so. It can be "realized" only intuitively, inspired by grace.

When I returned to Shalem, I asked Tom if he would lead a weekend retreat for Shalem, which he did to a full house. He published two books, one on Zen and one on Taoist understanding and their relationship to Christian understanding, both available only from the Mercy Center bookstore.

When he was eighty years old, Tom developed terminal cancer. In his last public letter to his friends that I know of, right after he found out he had only a few months to live, he wrote,

> So my cancer adventure is coming to its climax. To be very honest, it's all quite exciting (I can't think of a better word). All I want is that it be a time of transformation.... What I really want is to become the flow of the Spirit. My desire is to fully enter the movement of Reality. No scenarios about what's to come. Just live the Now.

Tom was a gift to me and many others, one of a number of well-known Jesuits stationed in Japan in Tom's day who were positively influenced by Zen Buddhism and wrote about it in many influential books. Tom and the rest of these Jesuits were pioneers who gave fresh interpretations of Christian-Buddhist relationships in a time of new interfaith openness, culminating in the Second Vatican Council's amazing declaration that Roman Catholics are to "acknowledge, preserve, and promote the spiritual and moral goods of other religions, rejecting nothing that is true and holy in them."

A Unique Event for Young Contemplative Leaders with Richard Rohr, Thomas Keating, and Laurence Freeman

In the summer of 2016 I received an email from Thomas Keating, the well-known Cistercian author of many books and videos related to contemplative practice and understanding and the founder of Contemplative Outreach, which fosters a form of contemplative practice called Centering Prayer around the world. I first met him around 1980 when he came to dialogue with the staff at Shalem about contemplative awareness. I had been with him earlier when he was a speaker at a large, pioneering Christian-Buddhist gathering in Boulder, Colorado, with the Tibetan lama Chogyam Trungpa. A few years later I went to his monastery, St. Benedict's, in a beautiful small valley near Snowmass, Colorado, for an eight-day personal retreat, in which he had agreed to be my retreat leader. I met with him daily there. It was a bonding experience that lasted to the end of his life. I was grateful that he was willing to write a personal endorsement for one of my books, *Living in the Presence*, in which I include a description of Centering Prayer, among many other contemplatively oriented prayer forms.

I was surprised to suddenly receive a message from him, having been in direct contact so little over the decades, and doubly surprised by its content. It was an invitation to meet with him and two others: Richard Rohr, the well-known Franciscan author and founder of the Center for Action and Contemplation in Albuquerque, New Mexico; and Laurence Freeman, a Benedictine monk who founded the World Community for Christian Meditation, which promotes a mantric form of Christian meditation first taught by Laurence's mentor, John Main. Thomas invited us to come to his monastery in Snowmass, Colorado, for a three-day meeting. The purpose was to pray and talk about ways we could collaborate with one another in fostering contemplative awareness around the world.

We all agreed to come together in October 2016. It was my third visit to St. Benedict's: the first being for the retreat with Thomas that I've mentioned; the second for an exploratory conference for twelve people about how contemplative practice and understanding could enter seminary formation more fully (at which unfortunately we never saw Thomas, who was laid up with pneumonia). The monastery is at an elevation of eight thousand feet, which is problematic for me at my age—I have trouble slowing down my breathing, which sometimes kept me awake all night, but after the first two days it became easier.

Thomas led us in a series of meetings together that began with a period of silence, followed by an open discussion that ranged over many dimensions of contemplative practice, understanding, and outreach.

Toward the end of our time we agreed on one concrete thing we could do together in the year ahead: invite a group of twenty young—roughly between thirty and forty years old—contemplative thought and practice leaders to come to Snowmass for four days, where they could stimulate and support one another as a new generation of leaders taking the contemplative movement forward beyond our leadership.

Thomas was ninety-three years old when we gathered. He had been through many illnesses in recent years, but his mind was still very sharp. He realized the awakening and importance of contemplative awareness in the world was a huge task that needed as much collaboration as possible to carry forward. I felt great respect for his willingness to transcend our organizations' borders and help us complement one another's work in good ways. I think all four of us felt that bringing together a group of budding contemplative leaders from diverse backgrounds could well serve the contemplative awakening with fresh spiritual-heart grounded thinking, approaches, and collaboration.

We decided that each of us would invite five participants to gather with us the next August. When we returned home, the four of us had much back-and-forth correspondence about who we would invite and about the format of our time together. We decided to call the gathering "The Contemplative Exchange of Young Contemplative Thought and Practice Leaders." The four of us communicated on an egalitarian basis with no clearly designated leader. I felt the daily design of the summer gathering needed to be carefully laid out in a way that would maintain a contemplative grounding with an open listening to the Spirit as we shared insights and what we were doing and caring about in the contemplative movement. Shalem had extensive experience with designing such residential meetings in its long-term extension programs, more than I thought the three other organizational founders had, and I finally risked volunteering to write up a provisional daily schedule. Laurence and Thomas were worried about whether it provided enough freedom for the Spirit to show itself, and I tried to help them see that the design I proposed actually would cultivate that freedom and at the same time save it from falling into chaos or into a too-heady academic exchange.

I felt strongly that the facilitator of the plenary sessions should be someone familiar with this kind of format, yet who wouldn't be one of the four founders. They agreed to let Margaret Benefiel, Shalem's executive director, be that person. She had decades of experience in leading such groups.

Margaret was one of my five chosen people (even though her age made her no longer a "young" leader). She helped me choose two others who she knew but I did not: Bo Karen Kim, an associate professor of spiritual formation at Princeton Theological Seminary; and Jessica Smith, who was a researcher at the national United Methodist Church in Washington, DC. The other two invitees were Matthew Wright, a brilliant contemplative writer and Episcopal parish priest who is a Shalem graduate; and Stuart Higginbotham, also a Shalem graduate and a parish priest who has developed an inspired re-envisioning of the parish church as part of a contemplative reformation movement that affects all dimensions of life.

I think the Spirit was truly involved in the Contemplative Exchange gathering of young leaders that August. The first sign of that was that every single invitee agreed to come, and every single one of them actually came—seven of them from other countries in Europe and South America. I don't think I have ever seen such perfect attendance at a broad-based conference happen before. They really were meant to be there together! The four founders wanted them to be upfront as much as possible in the meetings. We stayed in the background. In plenary sessions, small groups, meal conversations, and beyond, they came to know one another, shared amazing things they were doing (including in contemplatively grounded social action), and inspired and supported one another's fresh contemplative thinking. We were glad to see them in effect take over the design on the last full day, when they decided not to share in small groups in the conference room that morning as the design called for but instead take a long hike together on a nearby mountain trail, spontaneously sharing things with one another along the way.

We wanted everything to evolve as organically as possible, as the Spirit moved people. We didn't want to suggest any ongoing organization or leadership. That would be up to them if they felt the calling to do that. As it turned out, one person volunteered to set up a website for the group to continue communication with one another. Some of them agreed to contribute articles to a book focused on fresh contemplative thinking and action: *Contemplation and Community: A Gathering of Fresh Voices for a Living Tradition*, edited by Stuart Higginbotham and Jessica Smith, with an introduction by myself. I think many of those who came felt it was a watershed experience that affirmed their often pioneering work and enlarged their circle of ongoing learning and support with other contemplatives of their generation.

As it turned out, there were many people who heard about the gathering and wished they could have been there, or at least were very glad that it was happening. One regional gathering for such people was held the year after, primarily for people living in the southeastern United States. It focused particularly on the possibilities for radically contemplatively grounded congregations. Stuart Higginbotham, inspired by his time with the Snowmass gathering, was the inspirer of that conference.

Outreach through My Books

I've already mentioned several of my eight published books. The first one arose from the visit of an editor of Paulist Press in 1976. Shalem was very young then, but the editor had gotten wind of what we were doing in relation to the budding contemplative awakening at that time. He asked me if I had anything relevant to that subject about which I would like to write a book. I had never thought of writing a book, but he encouraged me to think about it. A theme for one did come to me, the editor supported it, and the next summer I holed up in a Jesuit retreat house in Los Altos, California, to write it.

I came up with the title, *Living Simply through the Day: Spiritual Survival in a Complex Age*. It included ways to help keep daily life in contemplatively grounded simplicity, with chapters that brought the theme to six dimensions of life: relating, serving, eating, playing, aching, and sleeping. I gave a draft to Jerry May and Henry Atkins at Shalem to review. After a little revision I then sent a final draft to the editor, having no idea how he would respond to it. I was shocked to hear him say, "It's a minor classic."

The original version stayed in print from 1977 until a slightly revised version came out in 1998. It's now out of print.

My next book, published in 1982, was *All God's Children*, which Robert Raines, a well-known social activist and director of Kirkridge Retreat Center, asked me to write as one of a series of books for Abingdon Press on "Journeys in Faith" during the societally turbulent 1960s and '70s in the United States. It did not sell well, as I think was true for the series as a whole, partly because such a limited historical timeframe wasn't worth the hardback price charged for it.

In 1984 I edited *Living with Apocalypse: Spiritual Resources for Social Compassion* published by Harper and Row, which included chapters by many insightful Christian socially and spiritually concerned people at that time: Jerry May, Parker Palmer, James Forbes, Basil Pennington, Rosemary Haughton, Constance FitzGerald, Joanna Macy, John Haughey, Glenn Hinson, Dolores Leckey, and a conversation with Henri Nouwen. (Henri once spent the night with my family when I had invited him to meet with the Shalem staff for that conversation. I'll never forget his spontaneous generosity of giving the Dutch cap he was wearing to my twelve-year-old son Jeremy when he showed interest in it.)

Spiritual Friend: Reclaiming the Gift of Spiritual Direction was published in 1980 by Paulist Press. I wrote a complementary book on that theme in 2001 from Paulist Press: *Spiritual Director, Spiritual Companion: Guide to Tending the Soul.*

Living in the Presence: Spiritual Exercises to Open Our Lives to the Awareness of God was published in 1987 by HarperCollins, with a second edition in 1995. Beside the twenty-seven spiritual exercises described, it includes a long section on practical dimensions of leading contemplatively grounded groups.

In *Sabbath Time* (1992, Seabury Press, revised version in 2000, Upper Room Books) I give a history of the important rhythm of time in Jewish and Christian practice, and present practical ways of rediscovering that rhythm in a modern form—a rhythm ultimately between the rest and labor of love.

My last book was *Embracing the Call to Spiritual Depth: Gifts for Contemplative Living* (2010, Paulist Press). Among other themes, it includes looking at contemplative spiritual formation and leadership in congregations.

Besides these books, I wrote *Valuing and Nurturing a Mind-in-Heart Way: The Promise of a Contemplatively Oriented Seminary*, a forty-eight-page booklet (2010). I've long been concerned that seminary education has neglected the importance of the interior faculty of the spiritual heart as a means of direct, intuitive, firsthand "knowledge" that grounds and complements cognitive knowledge. (I still teach an annual six-week Shalem e-course on living from the spiritual heart.)

This book you're reading may well be my last, although I likely will continue to write occasional articles (as I have been doing between all of my books) as long as I'm blessed to have a decently functioning mind and heart and some inspiration of the Spirit.

Writing for me is a very demanding discipline. My own obsessive desire and capacity to stay with a subject and connect the dots into a coherent and hopefully insightful and helpful whole has helped me hang in there with a subject through months and months of attention (or a number of years, in the case of this book, which I've had no set timeline to finish). An ascetical dimension of this process is the need to let go and delete insights and stories that come to mind but which just don't fit in a particular book or article.

One major reason I'm able to bear all the frustrations, details, and alone time involved in writing is what I discover in the process. As fresh words suddenly come to me about a subject or experience, I'm taught what I didn't know before. That includes finding connections between fragments of knowledge that I never thought were closely connected, as well as being taken beneath the surface of a subject and finding deeper ground.

Where do such insights come from? That's a mystery to me. My job primarily is to pray for the Spirit's inspiration as I sit in front of a blank page on my computer, openly ready for my fingers to start spontaneously spelling out words that come to me. However, I never feel I can confidently claim just when the Spirit is moving versus the movement of my accumulated knowledge, desire for coherence, or other mental factors. I try to trust that the mélange of sources will find their rightful place and that something of value will be given the reader, especially the value of bringing to consciousness something that they recognize as true, affirming, or expanding of their own experience and desires.

Outreach in South Korea

Unexpected movements of the Spirit continued to happen at Shalem over the years. One outstanding example was the visit in 2005 of Francis Park, the Anglican bishop of Seoul, Korea, accompanied by a few priests from his diocese, including Ambrose Kim and Jonathan Kim. The bishop had read and heard about us from others. He was convinced that spiritual direction and contemplative practice and understanding were missing and badly needed dimensions of the churches in Korea. He asked us if we could come to Korea and lead a special program for his parish clergy and others.

When Carole Crumley and I heard this request, we were amazed at the depth of his concern for what in effect was the heart of Shalem's teaching, and his trust in our ability to lead such a program in Korea. We strongly felt, though, that a preliminary step was needed; we asked whether a few Korean priests could enroll in Shalem's eighteen-month extension spiritual guidance program and maybe other programs so that there would be a few people who had an in-depth time with us and be able to become long-term contemplative leaders and teachers in Korea. Carole and I then would go to Korea and lead a two-phase teaching retreat, spread a year apart, that would be open to clergy from any denomination. The bishop agreed to this. He sent the two priests with him to the next Shalem spiritual guidance program class, followed by a few other Korean clergy from different denominations.

In 2008, Carole and I went to Korea to lead the first year's week-long introductory course (along with my wife, Mary, who would remain in Seoul and explore it on her own). When the invitation was sent out to clergy by Bishop Lee, the maximum number of forty-seven people who could be housed in the retreat house we were to live in was quickly reached, with a waiting list. Most of them agreed to be in monthly meditation groups for a few months before the retreat began and to continue in such groups between the first-and second-year retreat. This was an astounding response to us. We were told that little was done ecumenically in Korea; denominational walls were high, and certainly nothing had ever been done ecumenically like this, related to contemplative grounding and spiritual direction.

The participants came from various parts of Korea and from all the major Protestant Korean denominations: Baptist, Presbyterian, Methodist, and Anglican. There obviously was a great hunger for such a program. One pastor I think spoke for many when he said, in effect, "We've gone as far as we can in our own spiritual lives and in the prayer practices of our churches; this program speaks to what is missing, one that promises to open us to the contemplative spiritual depth that we need. We know it transcends our denominational lines. We can do this together." Two Christian psychiatrists were allowed to enroll who were especially concerned about the unexplored potential of spiritual direction in Korea. Many of the clergy shared a strong concern for social service and action as well as for a deeper spiritual life.

When we arrived at the huge Seoul international airport, we were glad to see signs in English to help us find our way out. In preparation for our trip, I had spent a fair amount of time trying to learn the Korean alphabet and some basic phrases and grammatical formation, which wasn't easy. It's a radically different language than English, which led me to appreciate how hard it must be for Koreans to learn English, which I think is required as a second language in all Korean schools. One special phrase I made sure to memorize was *An-nyeong ha-se-yo*, which can mean "Good morning," "Good afternoon," "Good evening," and "How are you?" It literally means "Are you at peace?" I thought that was a wonderful sentiment to offer someone.

Ambrose Kim met us at the airport and took us to our hotel. He told us what we would be doing the next few days before the retreat began, including our leading several contemplative teaching sessions at the Cathedral of the Anglican Church of Korea.

The day before the retreat began, Ambrose drove us to the Sisters of the Sacred Heart retreat center an hour north of Seoul, on a hot, humid late summer day. A welcoming sister escorted us to our assigned rooms. When I entered mine, I felt like I had walked into a sauna bath. I swallowed hard and realized this would be an ascetical discipline for the retreat's duration, with the ample supply of hungry mosquitos' present allowing extra purgation. I realized, though, that most of the world apart from the developed West lives without air conditioning and I was just sharing their reality for a while.

The retreat house had a striking chapel, with a polished wooden floor covered with sitting cushions and mats, but only two chairs stationed in the back corners. In front was a simple altar, cross, tabernacle, vigil light, and several fine holy icons hanging on the wall. Every morning of the retreat, all participants would gather here at 7:00 for some form of body prayer and silence.

When Ambrose led the body prayer, it was one that he had not learned at Shalem: it was a Korean Zen influenced "bowing practice" (for Christians, bowing to G-d). It involved cycles of standing, kneeling, and bowing with head touching the floor that continued nonstop for fifteen minutes. If you try that, you'll discover how demanding that cycle is to do for that long! Carole and I gave up after the first few minutes, but all the participants kept going until Ambrose struck the gong. (The gong was used throughout the retreat, not only for beginning and ending sessions but also at other times to draw people to the Presence in the moment, as we do in Shalem programs.)

I later heard that some of the participants felt we should have continued longer with the body prayer bowing practice! Such a desire was an example of the tremendous dedication these clergy put into their prayer life. A few of them got up to pray as early as 5:00 each morning, praying in solitude until the rest of us joined them in the chapel. We learned of a special hill in Seoul where many Christians pray aloud simultaneously and continuously for up to several hours, including many charismatics, who have a major influence in many Korean churches.

When I saw the participants in perfect sitting posture and stillness on the cushions in the chapel, I felt as if I was meditating with a group of Zen monks. They could be like that because Koreans are raised to sit on the floor in their homes, so it's an easy posture for them.

Since Korean Christians on the whole seem to clearly separate themselves from the Buddhist side of their culture, Carole and I tried to respect that in our design for the retreat days. The only time we dealt with the contemplative dimension of Buddhist and other faith traditions in relation to Christian practice was late in the second-year retreat, by which time we felt they would have come to trust our Christian grounding and be more open to looking at the positive contemplative connections across faith lines. Zen Buddhism is a major influence in Korean history. In a recent survey (whose source is unknown to me), about 25 percent of the population identifies with that tradition, about 30 percent identify themselves as Christian; the rest identify with no particular organized religious tradition.

However, Korea's early Confucian heritage is still alive in terms of valuing an ordered, transcendent social harmony. Ancient Korean Shamanism also still lives, not as an institution but as an oral tradition handed down from one shaman to an apprentice shaman. Most of them are women. We were privileged to have a private meeting with a well-known seventy-nine-year-old shaman woman who has been declared (along with certain other national figures) a "national immaterial treasure." Shamanism has an ambivalent place in Korean society. Some people feel it is a superstitious tradition, yet others turn to shamans for healing, protection, and assuring the peaceful rest of those who have died. A Korean anthropologist has theorized that people turn to shamans in part because they find a deeper root to illness than the material symptoms that Western-derived medicine emphasizes.

During each session of the retreat, Carole and I would sit next to each other on a platform in a big room, with an interpreter near us (who often was Hyeran Yang, who later became a leading staff member of Shalem Korea). One of the clergy, who I think spoke for many there, told us on the side that we sent a gender message to everyone there by sitting side by side, visibly consulting with each other as to how to respond to certain questions, and generally showing an equality of leadership authority. This was a new experience for most clergy present, who came from a church culture that normally did not allow ordination of women and a Korean culture that often supported male authority.

One day I offered a practice called "Radical Presence" that I had led in American Shalem programs. However, using it in Korea worried me. It involved a number of guided steps toward realizing our "mutual indwelling," which requires letting go of our interpretive mind and over-separating ego identity, thus allowing a quality of direct presence. At one point it involves each person sitting for ten minutes in front of another person, silently looking into each other's eyes, encouraging intimate heart-to-heart connection.

I was worried because we knew that in Korean culture, direct eye contact tends to be avoided, and this practice involved a very direct, sustained, vulnerable presence eye to eye. Because of that, I changed the guidance to "let your eyes rest on the throat of the other person" (rather than on their eyes). In classical Christian icons, the throat is where mind and heart are said to meet. However, the typed English text in the hands of the interpreter inadvertently retained the original text: "Look into the eyes of your partner." We didn't know that until afterward. As it turned out, the participants reported very positive things from looking eye to eye. I should have trusted the Spirit would turn such a culturally threatening practice into a fresh opportunity for realizing what is so foundational in contemplative awareness: our mutual indwelling in G-d, in one another, and in all of creation.

Most daily sessions began with singing, which is highly regarded in Korean Christian spirituality. As people gathered, Ambrose would start strumming his guitar and begin to sing a song, usually a chant created by the Taizé community in France. We would just keep singing until all were gathered. Then the bell would ring, and we fell into a brief silence before beginning a scheduled seminar.

From what we saw and others told us, Koreans overall come to teachers, especially older ones, with a sense of great respect, to be listened to carefully, with the expectation that they had something valuable to say. I was amazed at the deep silence the participants kept as we spoke and the respectfulness shown in their questions. Rather than giving me the sense of the power to "lord it over them," I found their attitude a call to really try hard to humbly listen from my spiritual heart rather than ego and say something that might truly be valuable for them. I felt more responsible for what I said just because they expected and trusted me to have something worth hearing.

Both year-apart retreats ended with a party. We ate, drank, and participated in what I believe is a Korean party tradition: asking different people either to tell a story, recite a poem, or sing a song. At the end of the second-year retreat, I was asked to offer something. I knew I couldn't sing well, and I couldn't think of any memorized poem, so I told the story found earlier in this memoir about my funny and poignant experience as a young priest driving an ex-army bus that broke down.

This custom of such spontaneous sharing I felt had a wonderful leveling effect on the group: whether it was a bishop, an older pastor of a big congregation, a young pastor of a small church, or Carole and me, the stories exposed some personal experience, loved poem, or story that made us all feel equal and gifted by one another's personal sharing. The strong tradition of singing in Korea I think also allows for an egalitarian bonding and potential transcendence of ego and analytical mind presence.

After both retreats, we had a few days to get a feel of Seoul and places beyond. This included Ambrose taking us to the demilitarized zone dividing South and North Korea, where armed soldiers face one another on each side of a small bridge. It was a sad reminder of the potential catastrophic cloud that continues to hang over Korea. Seoul is only several hours driving distance south of the border, and I think the massive nuclear bomb–equipped North Korean arsenal close to the border could decimate Seoul, a city of ten million people, in a preemptive attack, despite South Korea's defenses. Thousands of American troops are stationed there to help discourage such an attack.

When we finally flew home from Korea after the second year's retreat, we felt that the groundwork had been laid for the formal creation of an independent Shalem Korea, which in fact came into being the next year, with Ambrose's special leadership. Its evolving work has led to, among other things, a variety of contemplative meditation and learning groups, as well as spiritual director and soul of the leader programs. Shalem America has continued to be involved by sending Ann Dean, Marshall Craver, Liz Ward, and Margaret Benefiel to lead programs there, and by inviting some of their leaders to attend Shalem Society gatherings in the US.

One of the psychiatrists on the retreat, Dr. Man Hong Lee, who founded a spiritually grounded healing institute in Seoul, was responsible for translating and publishing several of Jerry May's books into Korean and one of mine. Two other books of mine have been translated into Korean and published in 2021. Sister Rose Mary made a video on spiritual direction with Korean subtitles.

I feel grateful for so many signs of our long-term collaboration. I sense G-d's Spirit moving through what has sprouted up there. I'm humbled by the incredible dedication and desire to embrace the depth of contemplative grounding that I see in the Korean staff and their desire to spread it far and wide, including to other Asian countries.

Chapter 13

The Evolution of My Personal Family Life

St. Stephen's, the Metropolitan Ecumenical Training Center, Shalem, contemplative outreach, and writing books consumed a great deal of my time over these many years. I tried to save enough time for my family life. It centered especially around our children, Jeremy and Jennifer.

As I mentioned earlier, my daughter Jennifer Gabrielle was born fifteen months after Jeremy. This time I was allowed into the delivery room. What an awe-inspiring sight to see her appear out of her mother's womb! Ann's gynecologist had an intern with him, who announced that it was a boy. I can still remember the old doctor immediately saying, "Look again, son!" It was such a privilege to be present at Jen's emergence into the light of this world. When we left the hospital, we felt a lot more confident in how to take care of a new child than we did with Jeremy. I remember the photo we took of Jer standing by Jen's crib when we introduced him to her. He showed both fascination and hesitation, not being sure about what competition for his parents' attention she would be. We tried hard in those early months to help him feel the fascination and let go of the hesitation. As it turned out, they grew very close together over those early years (even though Jer as the older child had a way of manipulating her to do what he wanted her to do with him at times!).

Ann worked part-time for a plant-shop cooperative for a few years, then she decided to become a full-time mother. We enrolled Jeremy in preschool when he was three years old, and Jen when she was just two and half. I can still remember a sentence in Jenny's first-year evaluation by her teacher, Nancy Tepper: "She is a very sturdy little girl." She was right on. Growing up, she always showed a certain grit through the circumstances of her life.

One day I visited the preschool shortly before Jeremy "graduated" from it. Parents could go into a room with a one-way window into the classroom (where I could see him but he couldn't see me). The class was in a "nonteaching" mode when I looked around for him in the room. I spotted him sitting on top of a table with no shirt on, very confidently explaining something to a younger child (at least that's what it looked like). I was amazed, because he had seemed so unconfident when he started at the school. A quality of social confidence stuck with him from then on.

I set up shop for my work and prayer in the basement of our house. The prayer space included an icon of Our Lady of Vladimir with a candle in front of it. I sat on a prayer bench, next to which I kept a cushion shaped like a pig for my children to sit on whenever either one of them came down to the basement at times to sit in silence with me for a few minutes before toddling off.

During this period of my life I was moved to take up playing the piano again. I found an ad in the paper for a 1919 Steinway Grand that someone was selling just two blocks away. It badly needed repair and refinishing, but it was selling for only $900. I bought it and had a mover wheel it down the two blocks to our house on a trolley. I still had all my old sheet music from my teenage years. David Ruth, my good friend who I earlier introduced, gave Suzuki-method piano lessons weekly. That piano has been a great solace and inspirer over the years. Sometimes we gathered around it as a family and sang together.

When the children were in their younger years, we had a tradition of gathering in the living room together for an hour on Sunday afternoons. We had a kind of high tea while Ann read a children's book to us; our dogs and cats calmly sat nearby.

In those early years of parenthood, I would go bike riding with the children on weekends in nearby Rock Creek Park, a huge, mostly wooded park that ran the length of DC. The Smithsonian Zoo in the park was close enough to us that we could hear the haunting cries of hyenas and other animals from our house. I remember our biking fast down a hill near our house at the beginning of one of our trips to the park when Jeremy suddenly fell off his bike. Jen was about four years old then. She was sitting behind me and screamed with great concern, "Dad, Jeremy's fallen off and he's hurt." Fortunately nothing was broken. I was glad to see Jen showing such concern for her brother.

Every summer we traveled to California to be with my mother and grandparents in San Jose for a week, and for a brief visit with my father and stepmother Mary, who was a psychiatrist and Dad's fourth wife. We also had brief visits with my siblings: Pam, David, and Paul.

My grandparents were always very welcoming. I have this image of my grandmother one year opening the front door when we arrived and, with quiet, happy tears in her eyes, stooping her aging body down to her knees to embrace Jer and Jen when they were toddlers. Later in the day I would see Grandad holding Jen on his lap on the back patio with great contentment. She had her trademark second and third right-hand fingers in her mouth. That evening he took all of us out to dinner. I can remember him swelling with pride after we were seated and telling the waiter that "we were four generations of family."

Besides those annual trips, when the kids were growing up we often took them away somewhere during spring or summer vacation. They were times when I could give undivided attention to my little family and enjoy an adventure together.

We had a good summer family trip to Great Britain when Jeremy was about twelve and Jen was ten. We rented a car and visited places in Wales, England, and Scotland. I was especially interested in Wales, where my brother David had traced the Edwards' family tree over four hundred years, back to the son of a mistress of Henry the Eighth. Henry, as kings often did with such recognized offspring, gave the child to a family to be raised, in this case to one in Cardiff, Wales, with the name of Edwards.

That trip included a memorable day with a young Welsh Anglican vicar and his family in the eastern hill country of Wales. The priest took me on an outing to visit an ancient little Anglican church hidden behind a grove of trees, with no road to its door. We walked through the grove and a simple stone church appeared. We entered what was a still living early Christian Celtic church. Its remoteness allowed it to escape the Puritan attempts to destroy all the stone altars and crosses in churches, and it preserved the ancient Celtic tradition of a graveyard built in the round rather than a square.

The sense of stepping into the living past was reinforced when we were taken to an inconspicuous nearby little pool formed by a spring that was a "holy well" stretching back to early Celtic centuries, a place for prayer and healing. Next to the well I spotted a piece of paper with a prayer written on it, showing that this was still a sacred place.

On the drive back to the priest's home, he suddenly stopped the car at the bottom of a small hill and invited me to climb with him to the top, where I felt a fresh, gentle breeze blowing. He opened a book he was carrying and read a poem by the famous Welsh poet and Anglican priest R. S. Thomas, about the wind breaking like bread over the land. We walked in silence back to the car. My heart was branded by those words blending nature and Eucharistic bread, spoken in a spot that likely was similar to the one that inspired Thomas's words.

About two years later we took a family train trip across Canada. My first memory of that trip was the young porter who was aboard our train car the whole way. He was a friendly French-Canadian college student working on the train for the summer. When we were talking together about French and English languages, he said that even though French was his first language, when he visited France he soon began to speak only in English; he was infuriated by French people who tried to "correct" his French-Canadian pronunciation of French. I sympathized with him, sensing how English people might look down on American English accents, although I think there's a grain of truth in the critique due to the way Canadian French and American English can slur consonants in a way that makes them more difficult to understand.

Recently I looked through my files of lectures, workshops, and retreats that I had led across this and other countries over my twenty-seven years as head of Shalem. I was amazed to see how many times I had been away from home leading these, which were in addition to various conferences

I attended every year as well as the many things I led at Shalem. I felt a twinge of guilt about having been so consumed by my public vocation that kept me away from home so often. It helped a little to know that Ann felt a vocation to be a full-time parent and liked spending a great deal of time with our children at home, school, and on the sports field. Hopefully I was with my children just enough, and their lives were full enough with school, sports, and friends that I wasn't missed very much.

Growing Up: Jeremy

I have three special memories of my son Jeremy's years at St. Patrick's Episcopal School.

The first was his great relationship with the school chaplain, who really "grooved" with him and many other children. With the chaplain's prodding, Jeremy spent about two weeks with him one summer living on an Indian reservation in Idaho. Given my anthropology background, I was glad that he was getting a firsthand glimpse of a Native American reservation's life.

My second special memory is from his last year in the sixth grade at St. Patrick's, when he made his stage debut as the Tin Man in a production of *The Wizard of Oz*. I can still see his visible face and body painted glistening silver. That was his last costumed public appearance I remember until many years later when he dressed as a rabbit and other animals as he greeted students arriving by car, as well as on other occasions at the Episcopal school where he is a teacher and administrator.

My third special memory also was from his last year, when he started his long basketball career on St. Patrick's team. I can picture him grabbing the ball in one game, racing down the court ahead of everyone, sinking a layup basket, and then crashing to the floor.

After St. Patrick's, Jeremy enrolled in the seventh grade at St. Alban's, the Washington Cathedral boys' school. He spent the next six years there.

In a seventh-grade history class taught by an African American, he wrote a paper about Martin Luther King Jr., who became his hero, which made me very happy. His best friend at St. Alban's was Mark Williams, an African American, who much later became best man at Jeremy's wedding and after that a godparent of his first child.

St. Alban's was very demanding academically, which created a lot of pressure on Jeremy. Many students were very smart and highly motivated, which doubled the pressure. I remember once going into his room after dinner to see if he was doing his homework. I found him asleep at his desk with his head resting on top of a book. His tiredness was helped by the great deal of time given to the baseball and basketball teams of the school, which he continued in college. Jeremy once told me that he was indebted to his baseball coach for fostering a capacity to be fully dedicated and confidently courageous.

When Jer turned sixteen and got his driver's license, we had just bought a new car. When it was two weeks old, I made the mistake of letting him drive it alone to some event one evening. When he returned late that evening, he climbed up the stairs to our bedroom and came in terribly upset, saying that he had an accident with the car. I went downstairs to our parking apron and there the car sat, the hood up in the air, the front of the car smashed in. He had driven it back to our house like that. I came back into the house through the kitchen and laid my head against the refrigerator door, in shock and close to tears. I was happy he wasn't hurt and furious that he had smashed up the car. It happened as he was driving down a main DC street and saw someone walking on the sidewalk who he knew. He took his eyes off the road long enough to smash into a jeep full of teenagers stopped at a red light in front of him. No one was hurt in that car, thank G-d, and it had only very minor damage to their fender, which had overridden my car's bumper. The police were never called.

Jeremy was ready for any punishment. He was grounded for some weeks and never allowed to drive the car again. When he went to college, though, I searched around and bought an old Honda Civic that he could bring to college (as I did for Jen the next year). He never had another accident. Maybe the first one shaped him into a permanently careful driver.

Growing Up: Jennifer

Jen, my daughter, thrived at St. Patrick's after leaving an overcrowded Catholic parish school where she had begun her elementary years. She became a really good swimmer in a program at American University for kids, where Ann drove her to swimming classes very early in the morning.

Jenny spent her high school years at Georgetown Visitation, a Roman Catholic girls' school founded back in the 1700s. The Visitation Sisters were a contemplatively oriented order, unfortunately slowly dying along with so many other Catholic religious communities, but the school still was its thriving crown jewel. Students came from all over the metropolitan area. Most of the teachers at this time were laypeople.

Sports became her great love in those years as it did for Jeremy. She joined the volleyball and softball teams. Both children also learned to play tennis, something the three of us could play together.

Jen did well enough academically, but in her last year her grades really soared. Among other things she had discovered politics and social concerns. We didn't have much conversation about her studies in high school until that last year, but then she passionately began pouring out all kinds of views about the political-social scene. We had many animated conversations that year. The religious dimension of the school never took with her, so that's an area we didn't talk about. She had obediently been to Confirmation class and went to church with us at St. Stephen's, but it never sank in. I just had to trust that G-d was secretly at work in her life.

I was happy that she volunteered to be a candy striper volunteer in a hospital while in high school. I can still picture her in her uniform. As it turned out, that was the beginning of work in hospitals that would return years later in a new way.

Life with and without Ann

My marriage to Ann was not an easy one. We were so very different from each other. Ann was very quiet, as she had been from the beginning of our relationship; I had a hard time knowing what was going on in her mind. We seemed to have little to talk about or do together apart from our children. She loved having dogs and cats around, and I liked them also. She loved reading novels; in contrast, I loved reading spiritual books and writing them. She was a good first reader/copy editor of several of my early books, and I was grateful to her for that, but we really couldn't talk about spirituality or easily pray together (except at St. Stephen's, where we normally went on Sundays and where both children were baptized and confirmed).

We had counseling to deal with our relationship at times over the years that helped us keep going, but that took us only so far. In the month before Jeremy's senior year in high school, after a shared talk about her unhappiness and my loneliness in our relationship, Ann announced that she wanted to separate. I wasn't ready for that. I valued my marriage vows and the love I still felt for her despite the limitations of our relationship. She had developed beginning symptoms of multiple sclerosis, which made me want to stay in the relationship even more and help care for her as it developed. My resistance was to no avail though; Ann was adamant. She wanted out as soon as possible. I felt a pit-of-the-stomach helplessness. When I turned to prayer, I was numb—too much in shock at this unilateral decision to be able to deeply pray.

At one point in the following weeks I wrote Ann a long letter saying how much I wanted us to remain married and grow old together. She told me she cried when she read it and that she would wrap up our good times together in a metaphorical box with a ribbon around it and give it to me for safe keeping, but she remained firm about wanting to part. I had no choice then but to accept, with a vague, persistent hope that we would come back together in the year ahead.

Who would move out and who would stay in our home of over twenty years? What was best for the kids? I couldn't bear the thought of leaving the house, my children, and my wife, but it clearly was the best option for them that I be the one to leave. Jen had been aware of our troubles, but it was a brand-new revelation for Jeremy, since he had never seen us arguing together (because we rarely ever did, even in private); he thought all was well. I found a third-floor walk-up rental apartment about fifteen minutes away, and Ann and I agreed that we would have the kids sleep over with me every Wednesday and Saturday.

I can't forget the day the movers came to take the furniture we had agreed I could take, along with my other belongings, to my apartment. Ann and her sister stayed on the top floor alone as I directed the movers. The kids were at school. The stability and sanctuary of my life there for so long was being emptied with every box that passed out the door. When I closed the door of my new apartment after the movers had brought the last box into it, I felt lonelier and more helpless than I ever had felt in my life. At that moment of destitution, something suddenly flashed through the deepest layer of my being. I can only describe it as a wave of pure compassion that felt like it was coming from beyond myself—directly from G-d's love. I wasn't alone after all—I was never alone, just blinded by a sense of abandonment. My faith was strengthened enormously, even though a deep human loneliness remained.

Jer and Jen accepted the situation as well as they could. They never talked about it with me. We just tried to live a normal relationship when we were together. I needed psychological help from someone who respected my spiritual life. For the first few months I found needed support from one of Shalem's associate staff, John Becker, who was a clinical psychologist and friend. He then recommended that I seek serious therapy with Rudy Bauer, a psychologist friend of his who was a leading Gestalt therapist in the area, who agreed to see me. Thus began years of my first truly *effective* therapy, which was very interactive and demanding. Rudy was an ex- Catholic seminarian who now was a devotee of Guru Maya, an Indian guru, but neither of these realities directly entered into our therapeutic relationship. Over my years with him I found myself empowered to better understand my psyche, care for my soul, gain greater confidence in my capacity to develop a new intimate relationship with someone else, and accept the "givens," the enduring limitations and tendencies of my psychological makeup.

I went about my work at Shalem as normally as I could. A month after I moved out of my house, I began coleading, with Marlene Maier, an experimental major new extension program I had developed for leaders of contemplative groups. No one in the group (except Marlene) knew what I was going through personally, and I did my best to keep my disoriented inner life marginalized so I could concentrate on leading the class. I was humiliated that my ego-transcending contemplative prayer practices were so easily overwhelmed by my sadness, but I at least could lead the practices that were part of the program and give others a chance to open themselves to the Gracious One. My inner prayer became very basic in those early months, pleading for relief from the pall that sat beneath the surface every day. The pall sporadically lived in me for the next year and gradually lifted, as I slowly accepted that there was no getting back together with Ann, despite my ongoing expressed willingness to do so. After a year we worked out a legal separation. Little by little I began so see that I really didn't want to return, that we weren't meant to be together anymore.

At Rudy's suggestion, I began lightly asking a few other women out for dinner, but there was no one else who felt right. Ann and I kept a tentative friendship: having a meal together occasionally, talking about the kids, even spending one Christmas Eve together with the kids, but our relationship was clearly over in terms of marriage. Neither of us pressed for a legal divorce, though. We sold the house and Ann moved into an apartment in DC; later she moved to the eastern shore of Maryland near Easton. I bought a condominium townhouse in Bethesda, where the kids spent much of their summers when they were in college. At some point it came to me that I really could be contentedly single for the rest of my life. But then Mary came along.

New Life with Mary

Mary Jane Teresa Lyon was a clinical social worker and longtime spiritual questor. She enrolled in the Shalem spiritual guidance program, which included two ten-day residencies a year apart. In the first residency we had several conversations that I really appreciated as we went through the week. I was drawn to her in a special way, but I had no idea that she was drawn to me until the last day. As I was leaving on the last evening of the residency, she left a sealed letter with me, which she asked me to read after she left. She didn't know how I would respond and didn't feel right to hang around to find out. When I later read it, she spoke of how good it was to be there with me and she hoped we might see each other during the year at some point.

I was surprised and delighted. As it turned out I was driving up to New York for a week's program with a Sufi master from Iran that summer; I would be driving close to her house in New Jersey. I wrote her saying that I would be glad to stop by if she wanted me to do so. She replied positively. When we were together, something deeply clicked. When I brought this experience to Rudy, my therapist, he reminded me of my recent night dream that I had told him about, where I happily found myself with a nymph. He said, "I think she's your nymph!"

On that visit I met her grown son from her long-ago first marriage, Patrick. He was a tall, strong young man in his twenties whose work then and in the years ahead would range from the army (driving tanks) to large-truck driver, to police and ICE officer, to well-respected chef.

Mary came down to visit me during that year, including at Christmas. We became engaged, and we were married on July 3, 1993, at St. Alban's Church in DC by Carolyn Irish (a close friend from Shalem) and Carole Crumley. Mary had been an opera singer in her early years and we included a song sung by her in the service, which brought her usually staid older brother Larry to tears. Jerry May was my best man, and Sister Rose Mary was Mary's "best lady," as she wanted to be called. A photo of Mary and me from that day still sits in our dining room.

Mary agreed to my proposal to have our honeymoon in Santa Fe, New Mexico, where she had never been. That was the beginning of a love affair with the New Mexican (and sometimes Arizonan) high desert. There's no other place in the world that we would better like to go on vacation. The haunting silence and vast, largely uninhabited (by humans) spaces of the desert open me to the larger mysterious holy Presence more than any other environment. Many times I've marveled at how far away you could see in places, far enough to see a rainstorm with lightning happening in the distance, and at the same time seeing the sun shining overhead, with nothing but open desert spaces in between.

No wonder it was to such an environment that the early Christian Desert Fathers and Mothers sought out to spend their lives in Egypt and the Near East. No wonder that the only appealing healing pilgrimage site in this country that I know of is in a village on the edge of that vastness: Chimayo, an hour north of Santa Fe, where we never fail to visit and pray. In the center of the village is an old, small adobe church, built by legend on a spot where a crucifix was found buried that was identical to one found far away in Mexico. It was a site that also had once been an ancient Native American healing shrine. Now it was a Christian healing shrine, where people would pray and take home with them a little dirt from a hole in the earthen floor of a small room next to the small, unpretentious sanctuary. On Good Friday, hundreds of people— people from all three of New Mexico's dominant ethnic groups: Anglos, Hispanics and Native Americans—go there on pilgrimage, some carrying crosses.

The presence of many Native American reservations in New Mexico heightens the power of the desert for me. They historically blend with the desert's life and ways, including building houses of earth and water, the basic Pueblo building material that still is legally normative in Santa Fe itself. The Native American gifted capacity to shape the earth's silver and turquoise into beautiful jewelry and weave intricately designed carpets still flourishes.

Mary and I both love to travel, and over the past twenty-five years we've been on many educational Elderhostel (now Road Scholar) and other group trips to many countries, in addition to Shalem pilgrimages. I've always tried to retain something of a "pilgrim mind" in all our travels, as well as a learner's mind, preparing myself ahead of time with some knowledge of the country and its language. I'm afraid "tourist mind" took over too often, though, especially as we usually would be taken to so many places that it could become a surface skimming rather than a sinking into a given place with time to feel its fuller human and spiritual pulse.

Each of us had opportunity to touch into part of our ancestral lands on these trips. On a Shalem pilgrimage to Celtic Christian sites in Ireland, we borrowed a car and found the small, thatched-roofed cottage of Mary's great-grandmother. On a trip to Dalmatia, we found the town of Starigrad on the island of Hvar where my grandfather was born. I had seen an old photo of Starigrad countless times hanging over his office desk. In the town's old graveyard, we came across many names of his family members over generations of time. I felt as if I had come home to part of my ancestral family who I had never known. A strand of it stretches to Venice.

I'll add here a particularly moving happening in the middle of an Elderhostel trip to Morocco. We were brought into the Sahara desert at one point and spent a night in two huge Bedouin-like tents, one for men and one for women. We slept on the floor side by side in sleeping bags. It was springtime, when the desert temperature during our daytime camel ride was cool, but by sundown the temperature dropped precipitously. I was so cold that night in my sleeping bag that I began to tremble uncontrollably; I could fall asleep only erratically.

At sunrise I was awakened by a haunting sound breaking the deep desert silence: the voice of a distant call to prayer from a village mosque. A minute later, another call to prayer began from another distant village. A minute after that, a third call broke the silence. I was so moved by this communal way of waking up that I found myself shaping my own morning prayer, joining all those villagers awakening to the divine Presence.

That experience branded itself in my memory. Unfortunately there was a downside to it. The extreme cold affected me in a way that within an hour of getting up, I was coughing, developed a sore throat, and felt my temperature rising. By the time we left the desert in a bus and found our hotel for the next day, my temperature was raging. A doctor in our group came to our room and felt my rapid pulse and found my temperature was 103. We had nothing but aspirin, and the doctor just told me to trust that I would be okay. By the next morning I was better and was able to leave on our bus with Mary and everyone else, but it took several days to regain my strength. My fever, though, could not erase the power and memory of those early-dawn calls to prayer.

A Lasting Move

The year after we married, Mary and I moved out of my townhouse and into a house at the end of a dead-end street on Page Avenue in Bethesda. It was surrounded by trees: hemlocks, hickory, Japanese maple, dogwood, and oak. One white oak's roots were married to a tulip polar just two feet away; a massive red oak in the backyard must have been over a century old. We decided to roll up the front lawn and replace it with plants, bushes, and an ornamental cherry tree. A wooded area behind our back fence was home to squirrels, racoons, and an occasional possum, all using the flat top of our high wooden fence as a day and night runway. An occasional deer, fox, and rabbit have kept us company as well, along with a variety of birds singing in the trees. One delivery man called it "the forest house," since no other house on the block was so surrounded by nature.

There were also many field mice; over the years I have told them they are not welcome inside our house, but they have found a way to make themselves welcome many times anyway, along with ants, centipedes, flies, roaches, stink bugs, and mosquitos. I warned all of them that there would be consequences if they stayed in the house. I rationalized that if they didn't heed my warning, I would be entitled to sweep them out or to take their lives, even though I'm always ambivalent about killing them. Sometimes I raise my fist to G-d and complain that the way of divine creation has involved so much incompatibility and conflict among living species (alongside some good reciprocity). At the same time, I harbor a hope that maybe there's a mysterious evolutionary process going on. I show that hope by always trying to kill without anger and with a prayer for the creature's good form of reincarnation (if there is any such thing).

What would we have done without Hensi through the twenty-eight years since we now have lived in this house? Hensi Lopez was a

The Evolution of My Personal Family Life

twenty-five-year-old immigrant from Guatemala who I saw building an addition to a neighbor's house. I asked him if he could build a screen porch for us, which he agreed to do. Thus began a still living relationship with this wizard of home care. Over the years he and his dedicated Central American crew have been our one-stop help for most every house need. No matter what we ask him to do, however complicated, his steady answer is "I can take care of that." He had a fifth-grade education in Guatemala, but the equivalent gift of a PhD in his intuitive and skilled capacity to do everything a house needed, inside and out, and to do it well.

In the early years, his young son, Alexis, helped him at times. I can still remember seeing Alexis in our front yard at the age of seven, proudly wearing a worker's leather belt with a hammer and other tools in it. We watched him grow up and attended his graduation from high school, the first member of his family to do so. Now he's the first to go to college. He has three younger sisters and a dedicated mother, Andrea, who is a Spanish interpreter in a hospital.

With four children plus his parents in Guatemala to support, he feels obligated to make as much money as he can. That's a story that in one form or another expresses the demanding situation of so many Hispanic (and other) immigrants.

Hensi is a wonderful example of how enriching recent immigrants are to this country, in terms of the skills and hard work they contribute, as well as the personal relationships they can engender that expand our appreciation of other cultures. We've been very privileged to have him in our lives.

Life in Delaware

Every summer we rented an apartment for several weeks a mile from the beach in Rehoboth, Delaware. When I retired, we decided to buy a little condo there where we could spend the summer. When our three grandsons came along, we exchanged it for a larger townhouse in next-door Lewes. We now stay there much of the year beyond the summer.

I use one of the upstairs bedrooms as my office and prayer center. It overlooks a small lake. Whenever I look up from my computer, I'm blessed with a panoramic view of water that attracts resident ducks, fly-over geese, and an occasional great blue heron and white egret. In high winds the lake's waters come alive and swirl in huge sweeping movements. In windless times they calm me with their mirrorlike stillness.

When I raise my head higher, I'm gifted with an expansive view of the sky, with frequent views of a pair of resident hawks that I sense are not just looking for prey but are simply enjoying soaring in the boundaryless sky. Often during the day, low, sun-drenched cumulus clouds float by, endlessly changing shape. I've come to see them as G-d's ever-changing works of art given to us to enjoy. Sometimes I'll leap out of my chair and shout down to Mary to look out the window at some spectacular passing cloud or at a gathering of wildlife on the lake or at a glorious sunset. Nothing in our time there gives me a greater sense of wonder than looking out that window. What I see invites me to a more expansive consciousness that transcends all the littleness of my mind's thoughts. I've written much of this memoir facing that window.

Reflections on Marriage

In hindsight, I feel grateful to Ann for sticking with her sense of calling to leave our marriage, despite my early pleas for her to stay. She found the freedom and new life she wanted. It took me awhile to see that marriage vows should be eternal only if there is enough confirmation that the relationship remains capable of sustaining enough underlying love and compatibility to be truly life-giving for each other. Given inevitable differences and illnesses, a sacrificial love and mutual forgiveness for transgressions and attempts to better understand and accept each other's differences are important to the viability of a marriage. The larger community as well as children in the family can benefit from the stability of a loving marriage. However, if over time, despite these efforts, the stability becomes a sterile, stifling, destructive prison rather than the life-giving home of two human beings, I think a separation may well be called for.

I trust G-d will bless whatever state of relational life will most support G-d's image in us, marked by authentic freedom for love, justice, creativity, forgiveness, mutual support, and joy. I feel such a blessing in the gift of my relationship with Mary. We are very alike in many of our values and preferred ways of relating, much more so than was true for me with Ann. At the same time, we are very different in ways. Those differences inevitably strain our relationship at times, but much more often they complement and challenge one another in good ways, so that between us we flourish more than we would being with someone who is just like us.

Once a year we gorge ourselves with the weeklong international film festival in Rehoboth, Delaware. Its many foreign films can be an eye-opener of personal life and societal challenges in different cultures. At the end of that week I feel like I've been privileged to go around the world, not surface sightseeing but getting inside a bit of the heart of a culture and some of its personal struggles, hopes, and values.

About once a month we've had the delightful privilege of having a day or so hosting our three young grandchildren (except during the pandemic). We feed them, read to them, talk about their lives, play with them, and watch them play on their own indoors with LEGO and outdoors with soccer, baseball, field hockey, and basketball. When they leave it feels like a hurricane of energy has departed; we're left both exhausted and content.

Mary has a boldness befitting her New Jersey upbringing and self-confidence. That can show itself in her capacity to doggedly research for the best places to get certain services and products we need at the best price, complain about poor service, and publicly support people like Errica, an African American woman living with her children in the most violent section of Baltimore who created "Cease Fire Baltimore," through which she tirelessly fosters violence-free days. For twenty-five years Mary has committed herself to take on the management of a former nursing home resident's finances and advocacy of better attention by the staff to his nursing home and personal needs (he was both mentally and physically disadvantaged). He recently died, probably due to neglect of a serious illness in his nursing home. In her daily life, Mary also avidly keeps up with news of many political and social injustices and crises (a passion we both share) and we talk about what actions we can take.

I call her a bulldog when she's up against a malfunctioning computer or other device. She is determined to fix what's wrong, even if it takes hours or even days, and she usually succeeds. I'm so incompetent when my computer and related technical equipment fail that I need to turn to Mary again and again for help, which sometimes brings a sigh and eyeroll from her, and always a sense of humiliation in me, but that side of my brain is really disadvantaged.

In church Mary doesn't hesitate to bring her full-throated operatically trained lyric soprano voice into the hymns. My heart swells a little standing beside her as her voice draws out the beauty of the song. My lousy voice is inspired to come to life more loudly, knowing I will be drowned out by hers and not have to worry about others hearing me.

At the same time, alongside all this boldness, Mary has a certain shyness with many people and humility about things she doesn't know that show her soft, open side. I love both sides (except when her confident boldness takes the form of strongly criticizing me sometimes!). In her professional work as a conflict mediator, as I've heard her describe it, she shows a careful listening, neutral-yet-discerning presence, but her boldness is still available to her when it's needed to gently prod people to come to agreement.

One of Mary's special gifts is cooking. What she loves to do is cook creative meals that go so explosively far beyond that puny menu I cooked for Jeremy and Jennifer after my separation and continued to cook for myself while I was single. She once owned and was chef for an Italian restaurant in Van Nuys, California. Her cookbooks could fill a room, although she normally creates her own recipes or revises those she reads. I still plead with her to bring together many of her creative meals into a cookbook, but she's not interested. She likes to cook what comes to her, and then let it go. She may remember what she did and cook something similar, but there's no guarantee. Maybe she's led by the patron of cooks, St. Pasqual (whose image hangs in our kitchen), to invent ever-new meals! In any case, I'm tremendously blessed. My main contribution is setting the table and washing the heavy pots and pans that usually go along with a gourmet meal.

It's struck me that all the thought and time that goes into a special meal is not only an art but also an ascetical offering: a creative act that feeds and delights others but one that requires letting it all dissolve into our mouths and stomachs, letting it all disappear in a matter of minutes. Creative cooking involves a willingness to offer something that cannot be kept, a gift of the moment that can only be for the moment; nothing is left but a memory of the taste buds and eye.

I'm reminded of a Tibetan sand painting that after many laborious hours creating it, then is purposely dissolved and prayerfully offered back to nature in the end, showing that nothing can or need be held on to. In theological terms, we could say that the art of cooking emerges from the blending of the Spirit within with our spirit, creating a meal that can be appreciated as passing gift.

Leaving the Nest and Moving On: Jeremy and Jennifer

Jeremy stayed with me the summer after Ann and I separated, and the college summers beyond. That fall he left for Haverford College in Pennsylvania. His major was mine: anthropology, complemented by two informal majors: sports and human relationship! He became the basketball star and captain of the Haverford team throughout college (although, as he would certainly agree, it was a competitively pathetic if enthusiastic and closely knit team). In springtime he brought his high school baseball proficiency to the Haverford team. He spent a semester at the University of Barcelona, living with a Catalonian family.

His major vocational life since graduation has included the foundation of a national sports leadership academy for high school students and their coaches, teaching, administration, and coaching in elementary and high schools (after getting a master's in education from Stanford). There also is his vocation of raising three boys after marrying Amy Nakamoto (and later Bernadette Devine).

Jen also stayed with me during most of the summers while in college. One summer she volunteered to join a workcamp in Germany for a few weeks. She wrote me from the site that they were excavating the prison cell buried in a bombing raid of someone named Dietrich Bonhoeffer. I was astounded and brought close to tears. He was one of my heroes. Bonhoeffer was a Lutheran pastor and theologian who resisted Hitler's rule and the Lutheran Church's accommodation to his leadership. He created an underground church and seminary. The Nazis arrested and eventually hanged him. His writings became famous around the world, and still are.

After high school Jen went to Drew University in New Jersey, majoring in Spanish. She spent half of her last year of college at the University of Valladolid in Spain where she met her soon-to-be-husband, Juan Fernando Merino, who was from Cali, Colombia.

Jen spent two years in a master's degree program in Spanish literature at the University of Wisconsin in Madison. After a time of living with Juan in Colombia, they moved to New York City, where Jen began what would become her lifetime profession as a Spanish-English medical interpreter in hospitals. Alongside such work, she has translated Spanish-language books into English, including one of short stories by Colombian writers that she compiled, and the University of Wisconsin published.

These are just a few glimpses of my two children's grown-up lives. We've had wonderful celebrative moments over the years. We've also had our differences and misunderstandings. I've agonized about both at times (as I'm sure they have over me), but our love for one another I've never questioned.

Inheritance of a New Family from Mary: Patrick, Rose, and Kathy

I've earlier mentioned Mary's son, Patrick. Over the years of our marriage I've had a good relationship with Patrick. He's held several jobs, but his favorite now is cooking and feeding people from his food truck and catering service. Several New Jersey periodicals have given him awards for offering some of the best food in the state. He inherited his mother's gift for cooking. Patrick recently married Marisol Santos, a wonderful lady from a Puerto Rican family.

Kathy Malanga, Mary's sister with whom she is very close, has one child, Rose, who we've steadily watched grow up from her birth. The four of us have spent many holidays and vacation times together. We were proud to attend her high school graduation in New Jersey as she received special awards and played her clarinet in the school's award-winning Scottish marching band. She's near graduation now at Tufts University and applying to graduate schools with a special interest in glaciers and oceanology.

Kathy has been a very wise and attentive mentor and a deeply loving mother throughout Rose's life. They both have helped with our grandchildren as well. Kathy has a wonderfully intuitive capacity for understanding them, befitting her thirty plus years as a very gifted kindergarten teacher.

Three Flavors of Grandchildren

I'm sitting before a large photo in my office of our three grandchildren at the ages six, eight, and ten, smiling and hugging one another. They've survived well the painful divorce of their parents and the re-marriage of both. Both parents and their new partners are very loving and responsible as they continue to care for the boys, moving back and forth from one household in Delaware to the other in Maryland. Nothing gives me more pleasure (and exhaustion) than being with them in person. Here is a little more specific sense of each one as I've seen them.

The oldest is Marcus, who Mary and I helped care for in our house on average about three days a week for the first year and a half of his life. He was particularly fascinated with shovels, cranes, and fire trucks. The lot next to us was being excavated by a big shovel truck to build a new house. When I carried Marcus to the kitchen one morning, he looked out the window and saw it scooping dirt. He excitedly pointed to it, mesmerized, and yelled "Tuck, tuck!" I think it was his first word outside of family names! A year later he sat on a curb outside our house totally still and speechless for nearly an hour, watching a huge tree across the street being slowly brought down by a crane, limb by limb.

When he was spending the night with us and old enough to climb out of his crib, he sometimes would crawl into our bed when he felt scared or lonely. If he hadn't stayed in bed with us, he would always get up about 6:00 a.m. and run into our room yelling, "Time to get up!" (For us, it was two hours too early!) Those were very long days for us old folks. Marcus has stayed with us erratically at various times of the year since then. He's forever asking hard questions, such as "Is God the sun?" "Why can't we see him?" "What does God look like?" "Is Jesus stronger than a superhero?" "Where does the rain come from?" When confronted with anything new, such as new people or a new activity, he doesn't jump in fast. He observes for a long time first (for some things, like taking up a new sport, maybe for months). But with such things as his beloved LEGO, he goes into long periods of concentrated play. In his early years, before going to bed, he would often carefully line up his little cars and other objects on the floor in a very orderly way.

When his brother Austin came along twenty months after him, life changed. He had a permanent playmate. I kept some notes from their early years together about their relationship as I experienced it. Like many older brothers, Marcus could be dominating—for example, taking the toys he wanted away from Austin, leaving him angry and crying. He also could be tender and caring for his brother. I remember him holding Austin's hand to keep him safe and close when we looked for a cart to ride in the supermarket, and later telling Austin not to wander off in the alley behind his parents' house. Once when they were sleeping overnight at our house, I heard Marcus helping Austin to stop crying by telling him, "You're okay" and then singing him to sleep, and singing to him again when he woke up later.

My first strong memory of Austin was when he was two years old, spending the night with us for the first time in his crib. I decided to sleep in the bed near him in case he woke up and became frightened. From his crib he couldn't see that I was sleeping in the bed. About 6:00 a.m. I woke up to the angelic sound of Austin singing what sounded like an original happy song, which went on and on. I remained quiet for a while, nearly in tears at the tender beauty of his voice. Finally I sat up in bed where he could see me. Instead of being startled, he just gave me a relaxed big smile. That was a harbinger of Austin's personality: laid back, imaginatively artistic, easily engaging with others.

The next year I remember Austin and Marcus wildly screaming as they ran back and forth in the hall between the two second-story bedrooms, chasing me and me chasing them, as I played a "hungry monster" for a long time. I loved their delighted abandon. When Mary and I put them to bed, after reading them a story, we would sing the song "Bless This House," which includes arm gestures for each phrase.

Once Marcus asked, "Why do you and Grammy want to see us so much?" Austin answered for us: "Because they love us, and we love them." We couldn't have given a better answer.

When Owen came along about two years after Austin, Marcus blurted out once, "What are we going to do with all these babies?" When I asked, "What should we do, Marcus?" He replied, "Get an adult to help." Myrna became that adult; she was a wonderful nanny for them in their parents' house. Both Marcus and Austin adjusted amazingly well to Owen's appearance. They thought he was really cute and loved to come over and hug him. That continued for several years until Owen decided that was enough hugging and started pushing his brothers away, announcing in effect that he was ready to be more independent. His brothers could lord it over him at times, but he's proven to be a very strong little boy. Still, I think it's been hard on him that he can't do all that his brothers can do at this point, especially reading well. But he loves to be read to. I remember when he was about three years old, sitting next to him on a bench, reading him a story. When I finished, he looked up at me and matter-of-factly said, "You're old!" I replied, "Yes, I am—that's what grandads are—old." That beat Marcus asking me several years earlier, "Grandad, when will you be old?"

All three of the boys joined soccer teams. Marcus is also on a basketball team, Austin is on a baseball team and was in a karate class with Owen. Their parents' love of sports is helping to spawn a new generation of devoted athletes. Whenever we see the boys at our house, they almost invariably will go outside at some point and form themselves into a three-person soccer or basketball team (sometimes expanded to include me and Mary, whose sloppy play they graciously overlook). Fortunately for the boys, they're all well-coordinated and manage to enjoy all the sports their parents put on their plate.

A fourth grandson, with Bernadette as his mother, now has come along: "Griffin," who at this writing is just seven months old. His older brothers, and Mary and me also, love to hold and feed him.

My growing hearing loss has been very frustrating when I'm with the boys. Children's voices sometimes are hard for anyone to understand steadily, but I virtually always have to ask them to repeat what they've said, and even then, I still might not catch their words, even with hearing aids. But they're very patient with me, for which I'm grateful. Mary often helps me understand them (as she does for me with other people and television programs). Hearing loss is by far my greatest disability. It's greater silence, though, does have the advantage of allowing me better concentration when I'm reading or writing, and a sounder sleep.

Life at the Gym

Ever since Shalem began, I've seen the physical body and breath as a locus of spiritual awareness and practice. As St. Paul says, our bodies are temples of the Holy Spirit. In all spiritual traditions we see the body taken seriously as a dimension of spiritual awareness, as well as of distraction, temptation, sensual pleasure, and pain. I almost never lead any spiritual talk without first drawing the audience to slow breathing in silence or some other form of bodily attention, such as posture. The huge spread of hatha yoga and other body practices inspired by Asian spiritual traditions has greatly broadened attention to the body as a dimension not only of physical and mental health but also for many people as an avenue of spiritual presence. I devoted a chapter to embodiment in *Living in the Presence*, where I address six areas where the body can assist our presence in G-d: posture, breath, movement, gesture, clothing, and diet.

Alongside such spiritual attention to the body, we give massive secular attention to it in the world of sports and personal exercise regimens. I've taken such attention to my body seriously for over twenty-five years now at the Bethesda–Chevy Chase Young Men's Christian Association, now just called the Y. It's for men and women equally now, and the "Christian" part is vestigial, although certain broad social values such as development of character, leadership, social service, and valuation of racial, class, age, and nationality inclusiveness still distinguish it from secular gyms. Until the recent pandemic, you could usually find me and Mary at the Y (just four blocks from our house) six or seven days a week for at least a half hour of aerobic exercise. During the years since my semiretirement, I'm there more regularly than anywhere else in my daily life except my home.

My first visit to the Y was as a sixth grader in Portland, Oregon. I and a group of my classmates were in a boys' swimming class where we swam stark naked. At that time, it was considered a way to help keep the pool clean. The same "in the buff" requirement held true in my college swimming class later at Stanford. I think it was a little embarrassing to most males, but men and women were so segregated in sports classes in those days that there was never an issue of a woman seeing us. There was a certain male bravado in trying not to look embarrassed by fully exposing oneself. Today it's always a gender mix at our Y, and swimsuits (however skimpy) are required.

Until COVID-19 struck, I spent a half hour swimming in the "therapeutic" pool; on other days I went into the gym and spent a half hour split between an elliptical machine and a stationary bike.

There are a few men regulars I talk with briefly, but with one I have developed an ongoing friendship over the years. He's an amazingly gregarious Chinese American, Choi Tak Taam, a retired mathematics professor at George Washington University. Whenever we've seen each other over the years, both in the gym and in the pool, we fall into a spontaneous conversation about politics, social issues, China, and whatever else comes to mind. We agree on a lot of controversial political issues, and we share them loud enough for others around to overhear; no one's ever challenged us (though I'm sure some have wanted to).

When Choi Tak moved into his upper nineties, the pool became too cold for him, and even in the gym he would wear gloves and a jacket. Recently, after not seeing him for a long time, I found his home telephone number and called to see if he was all right. One of his daughters answered and told me that he now was 101 years old (older than I knew) and he can no longer drive. He was just waking up from a nap, and she let me talk with him a few minutes. His voice now is raspy and soft, and with my hearing loss I couldn't understand him well. I knew we would likely never again have a real conversation. One of the prices of old age is watching old friends fade away.

One day in the gym a few years ago, a man who I would say was in his early forties came up to me while I was peddling away on a stationary bike. He asked me if I was Tilden Edwards. He had noticed that I was reading a *Christian Century* magazine. He had seen me somewhere in the past. It turned out that he was David Gray, the senior pastor of the wonderfully inclusive Bradley Hills Presbyterian Church in Bethesda. He was looking for a spiritual director, and although I wasn't able to take him on, I found him a good Shalem director who has been just right for him. We became friends and meet together occasionally. Once he gave me a tour of his unique church, which was built for two sanctuaries, one Christian and one Jewish. Now he's looking for a Muslim congregation in need of space so that all three branches of the Abrahamic traditions can be housed together. His many visionary gifts and his congregation's responsiveness to them gave me a sense that the Spirit was very much alive in that place.

Dieu Donne (French for "gift of God") is an African Cameroonian college student who worked at the Y cleaning the gym and locker rooms to make enough money for his classes. He with his aunt lived a fair distance away. Over time I befriended him and heard his dream of becoming an engineer. I was so happy to hear at one point that he had been accepted to conditionally join the US Navy in a special program for noncitizens, which would qualify him to apply for American citizenship. He quit his job at the Y, but several months later he reappeared, saying that the navy ultimately didn't feel he was sufficiently qualified. I felt very sad for him; I suspected his temporary status in the US was threatened. He soon left his job at the Y. I can only hope and pray he's found another way to remain here and fulfill his dream.

The therapeutic pool where I swim hosts aerobic classes guided by an instructor and music. I'm not in a class but in an adjacent lane, letting the music give a little rhythm to my powerwalking and swimming. The pool also serves people who have had strokes or other body limitations but can swim or at least walk in the pool. For years I've watched an older, one-legged man come into the pool area, lay his full-length artificial leg on a bench, and hop into the pool, swimming much faster and longer than I can.

I think everyone in the pool is visibly moved by a completely physically disabled young teenage girl who comes weekly. Two young adult caregivers take her out of a wheelchair into the pool and carry her around on her back for about forty-five minutes. Her eyes are often open, and occasionally I see a slight smile shaped on her face. She obviously enjoys it, even as her legs, arms, and neck are completely limp and she is unable to speak. The two women carrying her ceaselessly talk back and forth with each other in an upbeat way, sometimes looking at the girl with caring smiles. I find myself holding her up to G-d's light.

Prayer is not the only spiritual connection I feel in that pool. I bring to it my awareness of the healing pool of Bethesda in chapter 5 of John's gospel. How appropriate that this Y pool's official name is the "therapeutic" pool, a place of healing, in the city of Bethesda, Maryland. I always feel my mind and body, cramped with many tensions built up during the week, are released in that pool, leaving me feeling more whole. Sometimes I'm reminded of baptismal waters that cleanse the sinful, off-target part of my life and draw me closer to my true being in G-d.

In the winter sometimes, I will also get into the hot tub next to the pool. It holds about ten people, most of whom usually don't know one another. Everyone sinks into the same delightful, bubbling hot water and quietly sits mesmerized by it. I have a sense of returning to the warm, watery womb in which we all spend the first months of life. Sitting there also brings to mind the larger watery womb of the ocean, from which we've all evolved over eons of time. It feels as if there was some vestigial instinct left in us to find our home in water again. I remember my high school physiology teacher, Ms. Vollmer, telling the class that our bodies are 90 percent liquid. So, we could say that in the hot tub we're soaking our already warm, water-saturated bodies in a larger warm, watery home for a few exhilarating minutes.

Recently I gave a gift to the Y for a brick with my grandsons' names inscribed on it that will be placed as part of a walkway in a new garden next to the gym. Someday they will see it and hopefully appreciate how much I have valued what the Y offers and represents.

Chapter 14

Aging in a Tumultuous Time

I've mentioned my serious hearing loss, which means that every day I miss words my wife or anyone else says or that I hear on radio, TV, or computer, even when wearing hearing aids. I'm grateful, though, that my body otherwise is still largely intact and my mind is still functioning fairly well, even if my recall of words and names slowly diminishes. I could list a dozen symptoms of physical decline, but none of them are yet incapacitating. I take comfort in the words of St. Paul: "We do not lose heart. Even though our outer nature is wasting away, our inner nature is being renewed day by day" (2 Cor. 4:16).

I also find comfort in Kathleen Dowling Singh's hopeful books *The Grace in Aging* and *The Grace in Dying*, based especially on her many years of hospice care. She's written the first work I know that provides a sense of the normal *spiritual* stages of dying, complementing Elisabeth Kübler-Ross's classic *psychological* stages. Singh's books are full of case studies that express a hopeful last stage for many people, when they experience the touch of a higher Source that's brought them an overwhelming, light-filled, peaceful awareness. She emphasizes the great value of people's practice of contemplative prayer during their lives, because it conditions us to let go of so much that we hold on to, for the sake of a freer, deeper communion in the Gracious One and a capacity to live in the ever-fresh Now. My experience confirms that.

Although I have let go of a variety of things externally that my age no longer easily supports, I continue to lead a few seminars in three of Shalem's extension programs, write occasional articles, lead an online e-course that I earlier mentioned on living from the spiritual heart, dialogue with people on many subjects via email, watch good films, read spiritual books, articles, novels, poetry, and often some of the daily comics. (Humor is one of G-d's greatest gifts!)

I also read the news in the *Washington Post* and hear it online and on NPR. The news speaks of ever "new" expressions of human goodness, creativity, coping, tragedy, awareness of beauty, willfulness, evil, and delusion, as well as awareness of our earthly home's destructive and wondrous physical happenings. I get a dose of such wide-ranging news for several hours every day, with the concomitant emotions and questions it raises in me, especially the question of where G-d's Spirit is moving through what's happening, and what other spirits are at work.

I try to keep up with nonprofit social organizations as well as political causes that I support, the latter involving conversations with Mary as we try to digest the ever-increasing and challenging political and environmental developments and discern our responses to them. One recent small response was our joining an every-other-Sunday evening candlelight vigil sponsored by our church in Lewes, where we stand on the sidewalk of a busy street holding candles and signs, silently witnessing to our support for the immigrant children forced by the Trump-era federal government to live apart from their parents who are trying to escape life-threatening conditions in their countries.

My relationship with Mary in my old age has become more precious than ever. I love to be with her, whether it's just knowing she's somewhere in the house apart from me, eating a meal or just talking together, going out somewhere—anywhere—together, holding hands as we drive or sit in a theater or when we're going to sleep. Even when she's out of town I still feel her presence, even as I feel her absence. She is my deepest human comforter, goader, critic, adviser, helper, and companion. We have our frustrating psychic differences and disagreements, but they are always in the context of an unbreakable love and underlying trust and mutual respect.

In terms of my spiritual vocation, I doubly support Shalem's mission in these troubling social-political-environmental times, where learning to live from the spiritual heart as our true center is so crucial for the world's well-being. Authentic contemplative prayer and living spills over into discerning action for the peace, justice, and flourishing of human life and community, and for the flourishing of other earthly life forms with whom we have a reciprocal relationship and responsibility.

The intention and grace needed to maintain that overflow is an ongoing challenge for me. I lose that free flow between heart and world again and again every day. I lose its flow through a lot of what my mind thinks, my ego worries about, and my willfulness does in the world. I'm left again and again with fervent prayer to reopen that flow and let it suffuse my active life. The daily conscious awareness of my seeming cut-offness from the flow and its needed restoration reveals to me both the brokenness of my human condition and, at the same time, my underlying trust that the Spirit's transformative, redemptive flow through human life is always happening, however hidden and slowed by my and others blindness and cut-offness from the Spirit's flow.

The Breakout of New Social Crises

It's that human condition and that hopeful trust I bring to the multiple social, political, and environmental shockwaves that have stamped themselves on my public consciousness recently. On the mind and ego level, these crises have shaped serious discord, fear, anger, delusion, and disorientation in the United States, threatening our social and political compact as a nation (i.e., a compact to be one nation, under G-d, with liberty and justice for all, *e pluribus unum*, "out of many, one"). We're a nation that needs to better cultivate a common ground of civility, respect, and compassion in our relationships and different visions of the common good.

On the mind in heart level, I'm brought back to the inclusive Great Love that grounds me in a broader awareness of our human condition and possibilities amid our personal, social, and political conflicts.

Here are two public crises among many that haunt me now:

1. At this time of writing, we are well over a year into the COVID-19 pandemic in this country and around the world. Both I and my wife,

Mary, have contracted COVID-19, albeit without serious consequences, thanks to our multiple vaccinations. That virus is seriously sickening and killing people and negatively affecting economies in this country and around the world.

How is G-d's Spirit involved? At its best, it feels like this relentless virus crisis involves a kind of purgation, where we lose some of our normal controls, habits, and sources of sustenance and are placed in necessary physical isolation from one another. Many people feel more vulnerable, dependent on others, and uncertain of the future. Yet all this has somehow led to an astounding ocean of fresh feelings and acts of compassionate mutual caring that transcend all lines of division. If G-d's Spirit is made of liberating love, isn't there the likelihood that this agonizing crisis is an opportunity for that love to be mysteriously empowered to grow and draw us together?

Such wonderings go through my mind and heart as I listen on public media and to the people we know sharing amazing stories of creative mutual kindness amid many tragic tales of sickness, destitution from joblessness, and death. I sense we're being offered fresh hope for our communal human flourishing, as well as space and time for listening to what is ours to do that can contribute to that hope, as we bear the pain of this time. That pain includes stories of those who hold a more selfish or unsubstantiated conspiracy belief that detracts us from communal flourishing, such as refusing to wear masks or get vaccinated. Successful vaccinations are another gift of this time, increasing our hopefulness for safely being with others again. Once Mary and I were vaccinated, we met with and hugged our young grandchildren for the first time in over a year.

2. The police killings of George Floyd and other African Americans, and stories of violence and discrimination suffered by Asian Americans and Hispanics immigrants, has birthed a fresh national movement to recognize and challenge systemic racism. The earlier civil rights movement toward integration, dignity, and justice in which

I was so involved in the 1960s led to significant new opportunities and relationships, but it left full equity and dignity far from accomplished. The new movement wants to expose and erase the systemic racism that negatively affects so many lives, including most people of color. It feels to me like the Spirit has opened the way for this to happen. A much better justice system is being conceived, as well as a more accountable policing system, among other positive initiatives. However, such Holy Spirit inspirations must confront another spirit, the malicious one of white racism and defense of its privileges, and of a "I don't really care" lethargy.

The accumulated travail and struggle in dealing with such recent, sustained social crises that I and so many others have known led me to introduce in a recent Shalem Society gathering the practice of "moaning." I discovered this to be an old contemplative practice in African American tradition in Barbara Holmes's book, *Joy Unspeakable: Contemplative Practices of the Black Church*.[5] The moan is the entry into the heart of contemplation through the crucible of crisis and oppression, expressing loneliness, pain, and inchoate hope.

I adapted the moan and added to it in a way that felt suitable for us, asking the group to listen inside for all the crises that weigh on them, then name one aloud. Everyone would wholeheartedly respond with a sustained moan after each person named what weighed upon them. After everyone had done that, I asked them to listen for their yearnings, the hopes inside them, again naming one, and this time everyone responding with a sustained "Shalom," a call for G-d's empowering, just peace to prevail.

Advocating G-d's peace means advocating a vision and actions for communal life that reflect what Jesus called the kin-dom of heaven that is in, among, and ahead of us. I felt that so strongly in those years I worked in the parish during the tumultuous years of integration, racial justice, anti-poverty efforts, and the Vietnam War. Today is a new time calling for fresh attention to carrying the inclusive kin-dom vision that shows itself in the heart of world scriptures, great mystics, and when you and I are living from our spiritual hearts.

How do I best witness to the vision of the kin-dom? How can I bear the tensions of dramatically different views from mine while still maintaining relationships with those who hold them? What is the Spirit showing me in what's happening and further calling me to do? I bring such difficult questions to prayer again and again. A short poem by my good friend Charles Gibbs expresses well what I feel:

> I want to weep at least once each day to remember I am human, and Earth's broken heart is my heart; then all disabling hate and fear and despair washed away in my weeping; I ask what acts of healing and compassion, of justice and peace-seeking, this brokenhearted world calls forth from me today.[6]

The writer and activist Parker J. Palmer—an old friend who I greatly respect—connects with this where he encourages bearing the tensions of our time in a way that opens broken- heartedness to become broken-openness. Parker offers much understanding and many practical ways to engage positively in our current societal situation in his *Healing the Heart of Democracy*.[7]

One calling for me is to remember that reconciliation and its healing are long-term, G-d-given concerns. That showed itself to me in a night dream in late 2016. I was in a small circle of people listening to a wisdom leader. He tells the group to coat one another generously with a special ointment he gave us. After waking up and falling back asleep, the dream repeated itself, except this time the leader said we didn't really do the coating seriously enough, and we need to do it again. When I awoke, it felt like we had been anointing one another for mutual support and strengthening, in preparation for a calling to go out and anoint others for healing. The dream felt connected with the then very recent 2016 national election, realizing that we needed to be bearers of a vision of ultimate reconciliation for the long haul of conflictual relationships ahead, even as we seriously challenge views and acts that harm the common good.

I've tried to remember this, and I also keep examining my own views and actions more carefully to sense how I have inadvertently contributed to our current social conflicts.

Daily Rhythm of Life

In these late years I've evolved a daily rhythm that provides a needed steady container, a framework, for my thinking, feelings, actions, bodily health, and spiritual-heart awareness. It's a rhythm that I know involves the luxury of being mostly retired and without children or dependent adults to care for. I expect we all evolve a daily rhythm as best we can that hopefully provides needed room for attention to both our inner and outer life. I don't always do all I say here, but I normally do most of it in some form.

I try to begin the day when I awake with a quick nod to G-d beyond and within me, putting my hand on my heart and giving thanks for another day of life, asking in varying words that it be marked by compassion, wonder, joy, and awareness of the ever-gracious larger Presence. That frees my mind from being totally dominated by all the little practical thoughts that appear, telling me what needs to be done today. After shaving, I show respect for my old, stiff body's need for loosening up and strengthening by spending close to an hour doing twenty stretching and strengthening exercises taught me by physical therapists over the years, especially exercises that help my long-ailing back and neck.

I usually listen to NPR talk radio during those exercises, tuning in to some of the world's happenings. Sometimes I'll switch to the NPR classical music station, needing to let go the staccato of words and join the flow and rhythm of music. Music feels like it's composed from a creative energy drawn from a deeper, freer place than the mind or self-centered ego; good music draws me into that deeper place. Also, given my hearing loss, I can hear the language of music better than spoken words. Recently

I had an awesome night dream of listening to a theme from Rachmaninoff's Second Piano Concerto that felt like it was merging fragments of life into transcendent beauty, expressing the radiant wholeness of life in the divine beauty that is.

After my exercises I normally move to my prayer space, acknowledge the large icon of the Sinai Christ on the table looking through me, and then read at least one passage of scripture from the Common Lectionary, which gives me a sense of reading and praying with the larger church around the world. I also read a spiritually tinged poem or essay excerpt from various Christian, interfaith, and literary sources in the marvelous daily reader of Marv and Nancy Hiles' *An Almanac for the Soul: Anthology of Hope* (which sadly is out of print now). Then I move to whisper (if anyone else is nearby), say aloud, or sing at least the first few lines of the Lord's Prayer, ending with "on earth as in heaven." That's followed by leaning further back into my spiritual heart for a period of intercessory prayer, holding up people and situations in G-d's loving Light. After that I sometimes will sing a verse of praise, such as *"Adoramus Te Domine."*

Finally I move to a period of contemplative prayer, moving yet more fully if I can to the selfless spiritual heart. I let go the random thoughts that come as I'm able to do so, in order to sink further into receptive and beholding Presence. Sometimes I just sit openly still and let myself be seen through by the eyes of the Sinai Christ icon in front of me. Often my contemplative open time is brief, just wanting to remind myself of the deeper presence that is always there. Sometimes it's more drawn out, when I'm more patient and yearning to live fully from the spiritual heart. Sometimes it's just being lost in wonder as my eyes merge with other creatures of G-d that I see outside my window: the trees, swaying bamboo, birds, scurrying squirrels, and sky.

Then I move to the kitchen for breakfast with Mary and for reading what the reporters of the *Washington Post* have to tell me about what's happening in the world. I used to look forward to that, when there seemed to be so much more hopeful news. Today, the good news feels rare, effaced by so much happening that feels like I'm witnessing the decline of a hopeful, truth-seeking, mutually caring culture. I keep trying to trust that G-d's Spirit of liberating truth lives through what's happening and that it's empowering creative love will prevail and show itself to be the most substantial, enduring reality that is.

The rest of the day, through whatever I am doing (including my half hour of aerobic exercise), I'm given brief moments of return to awareness of the real Presence ever alive in my midst. These moments keep in perspective what I am doing. They bring me back to trusting that, as Hafiz says in *The Gift: Poems by Hafiz*, "There are two of us housed in this body, doing the shopping together and tickling each other while fixing the evening food."[8] The last things I normally do in the evening is read a psalm, usually from Nan Merrill's *Psalms for Praying: An Invitation to Wholeness*, followed by a little *examen* of the times during the day when (and if) I was aware of the "two of us blended together as one" and offering thanks for the day. Then I briefly open more intentionally to a self-forgetful, receptive spiritual heart presence.

Sometimes I ask at the end that the Spirit guide my night dreams. Usually I don't see that guidance when I awaken, but it at least expresses a heart-felt desire and openness for my dreams to be a place of receptivity for the Spirit's continued shaping of awareness in me, as we see happening in the dreams of various biblical figures. A third of our life is spent sleeping; surely G-d's Spirit and angels are awake and can be at work in us during that time. I keep paper and pen next to my bed so that if I'm given something, I can bring it to waking memory and later put it in my journal if it feels significant.

Monthly Meetings

For decades I have been blessed with four important monthly informal meetings that are both personally intimate and spiritually enriching.

The oldest is with a spiritual director. I previously mentioned that Jerry May and I were directors for each other for twenty years. After his death, I asked Marlene Maier, who goes back to Shalem's beginning days, to be my director. When she moved to Pennsylvania, I was without a formal director for a few years. Then eight years ago G-d's Spirit blew Charles Gibbs into my life with whom I have met monthly in spiritual and personal friendship. He has been willing to hear and counsel me when I have had something spiritually important to talk about. Charles is an Episcopal priest and the retired executive director of United Religions Initiative, a worldwide body of nearly a thousand small cooperation circles of people from different faith traditions, bound together by a desire for harmony among different faiths and for shared projects focused on peace and justice. Since retiring, Charles has been involved with major reconciliation work in Sierra Leon and Kenya. I have great respect for him in every way, including for his published books of poetry and of experiences with spiritual leaders in different countries.

My second monthly meeting is with three people I have known most of my long vocational life at Shalem and deeply respect as contemplative leaders and spiritual seekers: Carole Crumley, Ann Dean, and Liz Ward. Together we form a Shalem Circle (of which there are many across the country made up of Shalem Society members), coming together to share one another's lives and learnings as friends and as contemplative seekers and leaders. Since all four of us have been part of the Shalem staff in different ways, we also sometimes reflect on Shalem's ministry. Our two- or three-hour meetings for me have been an invaluable opportunity for honest, vulnerable, imaginative reflection on life experiences, difficulties, and probing hopes for ourselves and for Shalem, the church, and the larger society.

My third and fourth monthly meetings are divided between two people for whom I have been spiritual director for over twenty-five years. Over time we have come to know one another intimately. I have great respect for them both. They have blessed me many times by the way their experience of life and G-d connects with my own experience and questions, to the extent that I feel each session involves the Spirit's guidance for me as well as for them.

More recently I have been invited to a fifth monthly meeting by Margaret Benefiel, Shalem's executive director for the past six years, who's relationship with Shalem began thirty years ago when she was a participant in one of the early spiritual guidance programs. She shares with me things that are happening at Shalem, and we informally exchange views and wonderings about various dimensions of contemplative formation and understanding. I feel very privileged in such meetings because few executive directors want to meet regularly with a longtime past director and founder like myself. Margaret is a wonderfully unthreatened and open person, with an incredible amount of energy, gifts, warmth, and dedication brought to Shalem's life.

Special Losses

One fact of aging is facing the deaths of other people close to you. Earlier I spoke of the deaths of Jerry May and Rose Mary Dougherty. The deaths of three other long-term Shalem staff members and of the husbands of three others over the years, and my long-term friend David Ruth, have saddened me. Two other deaths of special people unconnected with Shalem I would like to give particular attention to here.

Bill Wendt

Bill, you'll recall, was the rector of that Episcopal parish where I started my priestly ministry. He took me under his wing at a very demanding inner-city church and tutored me in how to be a caring and knowledgeable priest in so many ways, including how to preside at a Eucharist; be with a dying parishioner; stand up for social justice; relate to the homeless, addicts, and the poor at the church door; connect with a huge range of parishioners and neighborhood people; give challenging homilies; foster a creative ministry using everyone's gifts; chuckle in the midst of absurd, difficult situations; and so much more. Bill had his flaws, and we were very different from each other in many ways, but his kinds of strengths and pastoral experience, and his acceptance and support of me, warts and all, were just what I needed in those early years.

We didn't have much contact after my five years as part of his team ministry in the parish, and yet to this day I still put my hands behind my head and lean back in various situations, just as he did. After finding out about my divorce, even though I hadn't spoken with him for years, he called me up and took me to lunch to see how I was doing.

After he left St. Stephen's about a decade after I left, he created the St. Francis Center, where he and others counseled dying people. He also sold plain pine caskets available at a time when they were difficult to find. He suggested that people buy a casket and put it in their living room as a coffee table, to help them remember what's important to do while they're still alive. What was particularly amazing about this new ministry to me was that I remembered him once saying how afraid of death he was. Instead of fleeing, though, he courageously looked death in the eye and tamed it—indeed transformed it into an opportunity to face the end of life in a positive and trusting way.

When I heard he had developed terminal cancer, I visited him at his nursing home in his last days. We hadn't seen each other for years, but we immediately connected again. His funeral was at St. Stephen's. I remember standing in a circle of people on the church grounds as his ashes were buried there. I suddenly started to cry uncontrollably but silently. Mary Wendt noticed and crossed the circle to stand next to me. I was grateful.

My Mother

The only other time I "lost it" that way was when a nurse in the nursing home where my mother was living in Hollywood called me and said she had just died. Mary and I had visited her just a few weeks before at Thanksgiving. We noticed then that a caregiver had put on the door of her room the jacket of the book she had written back in 1974, *The Challenge of Being Single: For Divorced, Widowed, Separated and Never-Married Men and Women*, a pioneering book in its time that led to radio, TV, and newspaper interviews and workshops across the country. When we knocked on her door and had a long visit with her over several days, we didn't sense that she was soon to die, although we realized her fragility at the age of eighty-nine and her suffering from vascular dementia. We were grateful that she could still recognize us and carry on a conversation, although she quickly forgot what we had just said.

Her caregiver who called to deliver the news of her death told me that when she had been sent to the hospital the week before for a urinary tract infection, my mother exclaimed, "I hope this is it; I'm so tired." But she was sent back to the nursing home a few days later, supposedly cured. The next day, her caregiver went to her room to tell her goodnight at the end of her shift; my mother asked to remind her of her name. When she did, my mother exclaimed, "Oh, beautiful Alma Jay—I'm done." The next morning she woke up and asked for a glass of water and when the caregiver returned twenty minutes later, she had died. Life had become a steady, hard struggle for her, mentally and physically; she was ready to let go.

I sat on the living room couch after receiving that call, with Mary at my side, and I cried uncontrollably for about fifteen minutes. Through all my tumultuous childhood and the divorce, she was the one person in my life who I could rely on to really care for me. As a psychologist, she had raised me in a way that gave me confidence, love, and freedom to make my own choices. Throughout my life she was supportive (although not happy about my divorce), and she loved my children. We were very different from each other in a lot of ways, and I needed a certain distance from her psychologically once I grew up. In the end, though, weeping on that couch, I knew how deeply we were connected and how much I regretted not having a final opportunity to thank her for all she had been and done for me.

When I walked back into my office after that, I discovered that an unframed painting that had long laid flat on a library shelf had just mysteriously fallen onto the floor, which had never happened before. It was an unusual painting by a Shalem graduate, Monica Armstrong, titled *My Opening*. At its center was a huge head and shoulders of a human figure; instead of a normal solid human body, it was translucent, made of blue sky and clouds. Around the seemingly ascending body was a vast, black sky full of stars; below the figure were mountains and flowers, with a river flowing through the middle. The figure seemed to be realizing its fuller being as part of a larger creation. I had a sense of my mother's spirit somehow causing this painted scene to land at my feet, wanting me to know that she now was part of the earth and all creation in a new way. That may be a fantasy and yet it felt so real. I felt her presence there. My prayer then was pure gratitude.

I busied myself the next day with arranging for her cremation. Most of her ashes were sent to the historic Santa Clara Roman Catholic Cemetery in Northern California to be placed in a columbarium long ago reserved for her remains, next to those of her parents. I had a small amount of the ashes sent to me, which I placed beneath a rosebush planted in our backyard in her memory during a family prayer service. I'm facing that bush right now in my office; it's just a few yards away. The rosebush still blooms every year, despite many threats from the weather, fungi, and insects.

Embracing Nature

That rosebush, those ashes, and that painting of a person's participation in nature express my growing sense of how much my embodied life is an integral part of the natural world. I was born and I grew up, I'm aging and will die as all living things do. I am made of ancient stardust, earthly atoms that shape me into who I am, infused with a Creator Spirit that is mysteriously drawing me, the earth, and the cosmos toward an endlessly transfiguring future. With the theologian Pierre Teilhard de Chardin, I want to trust that I'm living in a distinctive moment of an evolution toward the fullness of radiant Love, the fullness of the cosmic Christ. That trust is challenged by my awareness of so many willful, blind, and evil forces that keep emerging on earth, but I choose to see these as distorted products of human freedom that finally are unable to sustain themselves in the face of the foundational substance of true life: creative holy Love.

Recently my awareness of the gifted interwovenness of my life with the rest of earthly creation has been greatly enhanced by Robin Wall Kimmerer, a Native American botanist college professor. I recently read her book *Braided Sweetgrass* a few slow pages at a time. Each reading was a breath of fresh air that brought me deeper into my sense of kinship, reciprocity, and mutual responsibility with the earth's living beings beyond the human.

At one point I felt myself walking with her as one of her college students on a field trip she was leading. As she put it, "The students had devoted several years to the study of a single species: themselves. I had a whole three days to be subversive, to distract them from *Homo sapiens* for a glimpse of the six million other species with whom we share the planet." To science those species are impersonal "its." To Native Americans, they are other living beings personally related to us. Most of their Indigenous languages use the same words to address the living world as we use for our family, because they are our family. In some Indigenous languages, the term for plants translates to "those who take care of us."

Over and over Robin shows the amazing reciprocity of nature. She does so in very concrete ways that taught me so much about my neglected or ignorant relationship with so much of the rest of G-d's created life on earth. She also showed me the price of human neglect and ignorance in what we do to exploit the earth and destroy its needed balance and mutual caring, something I was aware of but never to the personal degree that she taught me. That sad reality has led geologists to say that we have entered a new geological era: the Anthropocene era, where human beings have evolved such devastating exploitative power that we now have the capacity to create conditions that can destroy much of the earth's life, including our own.

I'm so much more aware now that other living species are my teachers and gift givers in many ways, who need to be cared for as they care for us in ongoing reciprocal relationship. This includes respecting and avoiding the survival defenses of each creature that can cause harm to humans, as well as respecting the survival needs of us humans yet without causing unnecessary harm to other creatures in the process. Whenever I walk outside now, I feel so much more companionship with the natural world, so much less "loneliness" that Robin says affects us as a result of making impersonal *objects* of nature rather than related *subjects* of the natural world we see every day. Certainly the term *mutually indwelling and belonging*, so basic to contemplative awareness, extends to every living creature.

Chapter 15

Radiant Love as the Heart of Life

Stretching and Yielding: Love Sought and Known

In my teaching I sometimes include a practice that I call stretching and yielding. As we slowly raise our arms over our head with our wrists relaxed and our minds steadily inside the movement, we stretch high for the more of our true selves in G-d's love from a sense of incompleteness, from a Spirit-given desire to move beyond where we are. Then we slowly relax the stretch and bend forward, letting our arms drop until we come to the point of tension in our legs. We restfully hang there a moment, with a sense of yielding to G-d's gracious presence alive in our midst right here and now; our sense of the *enoughness* of G-d's grace here in this moment—its sufficiency for right now. We relax the strain and yield to the Spirit-given richness of what is already present.

As I look back over what I have written in this memoir, I'm aware of how much stretching, yearning effort has come to me over the years: for more knowledge, intimate love, courage to act in the face of societal and environmental oppression, freedom from anxious fear and self-centeredness, and more surrendered presence to the larger Presence that birthed, sustains, and lives in and around me.

Along with this stretching I'm also aware of so much grace I've been able to recognize in the moment: the wonders known in nature, human and divine love, the smiling innocence of a baby, music and beauty of all kinds, witnessing others' lives of sacrificial and courageous loving actions in the face of oppression and misfortune, and so many other times when I've experienced the routine linear surface of my little self-absorbed life broken open by the overflowing grace at hand.

I believe the same Holy Spirit energy inspires both the forward-looking yearning for and the present awareness of grace. I'm left in awe and gratitude for both movements in my life. The Spirit's loving presence seems inextricably woven into every "happening" of my life, however hidden. Along with that presence a certain freedom is given, a choice, in how to respond, a choice I earlier mentioned as intrinsic to the nature of love itself. Opting against collaboration with the loving Spirit leaves me vulnerable to resistant forces to which we name as sin, confusion, and evil. I regret my own times of noncollaboration, my sins and missed opportunities born in times of willful or ignorant separation of my consciousness from the divine loving Consciousness. However, these times are transcended by my faith in the forgiving and persistent nature of grace.

In special moments, I sense that the Spirit's goading love shows itself as an intimate, benevolent flow through my life, evoking awe and gratitude. In those moments, the veil parts and I seem to be in a quality of eternal time; it feels like a peek of heaven. I sense then that my experience of linear chronos time is part of an evolutionary process toward the full awareness of this flowing, heavenly kin-dom time. I stretch toward heaven on earth in ways I'm given while, when I'm given graced eyes that see, I glimpse my ever-present communion in radiant Love, my deepest home.

This paradox of life: stretching forward for fullness and yet finding moments erupting where I realize eternal loving communion already present. I believe this is a core awareness woven through my spiritual journey, however erratically perceived.

That loving communion to me is the most substantial reality in life. It is a transformative, relational intimacy reflecting the very nature of the Gracious One, who shapes us into unique images of itself and lives through us. Loving communion is the realization of my mutual indwelling and belonging, with other people, nature, and the ever creating and Guiding One. Nothing substantially and enduringly exists apart from that radiant Love. It is the mysterious depth of all things.

Such theological views must finally become silent in the face of the deepest reaches of Love's mystery. There I'm left speechless before its bottomless depth and its power to transform the clay of life into shapings of Love's life and beauty. I'm left with a marveling trust in what is beyond my capacity to understand. That trust is fired by my yearning for the fullness of Love, a yearning that I think is ingrained in me and in us all. Given our broken human condition, that is a lifetime affair, as we find that so much we cling to hides that ever-present liberating Love. As William Blake said well, "We're set on earth awhile, to learn to bear the beams of love."

The Hoped-For Life of Love Beyond This Life

My sense of radiant Love at the heart of true life is a powerful, often obscured background awareness that I see slowly growing through the various stages of my life. As death to this life comes ever closer at my advanced age, I ask myself, how might that love show itself beyond this life? In the faith of Christian tradition, death is swallowed up in Christ's resurrection, foreshadowing our own mysterious transformed embodiment. In that faith, that which is so fearful in human life, death, can lose its sting. The substantive font of reality, radiant Love, cannot die. It forever is expressing itself in the mysterious birth, dynamic life, death, and reshaping of life energies and forms that we see in all creation.

When I embrace that belief, I come to see death to this life as a trustworthy passage to valuable new life in some form that only G-d knows. As St. Paul says, "Here we can only see the future through a glass darkly," yet I find myself trusting beyond my doubts that the undying loving Spirit incarnate in Jesus also is incarnate in my own and everyone's unique life. Jesus himself invites us to realize this in John's gospel where he in effect says that "I am in you, you are in me, I am in G-d."

Together I believe we are part of a mysterious evolution toward the fullness of that Love. Such trust can be difficult to maintain, as my confused friend, protective ego, wants to keep my current form of life going without end. My deeper friend, though, my spiritual heart, inherently trusts the mysterious eternal Love that shaped me into being, to reshape my soul-being into new life in Love, beyond my imagining. As I come closer to the end of this life, I find myself applying T.S. Eliot's words in *Little Gidding* beyond a late stage of this life to *after* this life: "We must be still, and still moving into another intensity, for a further union, a deeper communion."

We will die to this life, but I sense that the energy of G-d's Spirit in our unique souls will be born afresh in some way and continue to serve the evolution of sacred Love in creation. The insubstantial energies in us born of alienating sin, evil, and illusion will not survive.

I find an increasing number of my night dreams and prayer time reflections recorded in my journal connecting with my aging. Together these entries reveal to me a string of wonderings and flashes of existential awareness that offer me little glimmers of light (maybe sometimes a false light) amid our human darkness, where we find such mystery, fears, and hopes.

Here is one recent glimmer of light that came to me that I recorded in my journal, connected with love beyond this life: during my morning prayer time, I suddenly was given an image of bringing a basket full of the loving times in my life to G-d when I die, the loves given to me (beginning with divine love), and the loves I've been inspired and willing to give others. I hope this basket of loves will have contributed a little to the larger human story and creative evolution of communing love that feels so central to life's purpose.

Whatever survives of my human "I" feels like it will be a collage of those love-happenings that are glimmerings of the Great Love. After death I expect "I" will more fully become a "we," a shared oneness in Love. This may well involve a stage of purgation, of Spirit-empowered awareness and willingness to let go of the many unloving times in my life and of the ways I willfully resisted the Spirit's many calls. Such purgative contrition I hope would further liberate cleansing, forgiving sacred love, enabling my capacity to live more fully in a transformed, selfless communion in G-d, and in some new way with the ongoing earthly community.

One other contribution to my sense of the afterlife recorded in my journal came in a dream I had a few months ago. A personal and spiritual friend who died a few years ago, Jim Fenhagen, hovered over me. He said he had returned from the Beyond to tell me that a radiant, sacred white light pervades everything. I saw that radiant light sparkling all around me. It felt like a purging, illuminating and uniting light, a gifted awareness of pervasive Spirit energy. I yearned for that light to purge me of fear and little self-centeredness, to free me for "enlightened" love. The dream branded my consciousness with a sense of the Spirit's liberating light energy that enfolds life, death, and whatever transformed life and consciousness may follow.

Just this morning I awoke with a sense of a huge circular entrance to a place I had never been. I only saw a dim grayness with a hint of forms in it. It felt like an invitation to enter, and I felt ready, without fear. Whether that was the birth of a graced capacity to risk moving into the unknown more fully while still in this life, or into the unknown beyond this life, or both, I don't know, but I'm grateful for its transcendence of my ego fear of losing the security of the known.

As St. Paul says, G-d has in mind for us more than we can imagine. So finally, I'm left with a naked, unknowing trust of whatever will be after my death, arising from the loving radiant light of the Gracious One.

Excerpts from Nan Merrill's version of Psalm 90 in her *Psalms for Praying* give me an inspired perspective for my spiritual journey, both in and beyond this life:

> *When our days on Earth are ended,*
> *You welcome us home to your Heart,*
>   *To the City of Light, where time is eternal*
>   *And days are not numbered.*
>
> *You gather those who love You as friends returning from a long journey,*
>   *giving rest to their souls.*
> *You anoint them with the balm of understanding,*
>   *healing wounds of the past.*
>
> *For our days on Earth are a mystery,*
>   *A searching for You,*
>   *A yearning for the great Mystery to make itself known.*

The years pass and soon the Harvest is at hand,
  A time to reap the fruit of one's life.
Who has lived with integrity?
Who will reflect the Light?
Who can bear the radiant beams of Love?
Who have reverenced the Counselor,
  and opened their hearts to the Spirit of Truth?

Help us to wait in Silence listening for your Word,
  Strengthen us with courage to face the fears within.
O, that we might be converted in our hearts
  and walk together in peace and harmony!
Let the grace and gentleness of the Holy Spirit be upon us,
  Guiding our feet upon paths of Love;
  Increase the Light within us—
  O Beloved, hear our prayer![9]

Thank you for letting me share some of my life's experience and reflections with you. May your own journey's Spirit-inspired stretching and yielding times flourish and draw you ever further into realization of Enlightened Love. I believe that deep down we all live in and from that ever mysterious yet intimately present Love, mutually indwelling, mutually belonging, mutually sharing our gifts with one another and the Earth as we are called.

Appendix

The Leadership of the Shalem Institute for Spiritual Formation

Nearly fifty years of my life have been marked by time spent with the leaders and thousands of participants in Shalem. I've always felt very blessed by the many people who have found their way to Shalem and vulnerably shared their spiritual yearnings, learnings, struggles, and joys with me and one another. Our shared commitment to the path of contemplative tradition and practice, and realization of its importance in serving the personal and societal well-being and spiritual depth of the world, has bound both participants and leaders together in a sense of spiritual community and calling.

Many people have been Shalem staff members over the years. I have named some of them in these memoirs. I would like to list here the names of all the long-term leaders that I remember, who have helped carry and enrich Shalem's life and ministry over the years. Each of them has brought special gifts and dedication to Shalem's mission.

Early Long-Term Program and Administrative Staff (Full- and Part-Timers)

Monica Maxon
Cecilia Braveboy
Marlene Maier
Bill Moremen
Jerry May
Rose Mary Dougherty
Dolores Leckey

Carole Crumley
Richard Byrne
Isabella Bates
Barbara Osborne
Lin Ludy
Joan Hickey
Rhoda Nary

Patience Robbins	Katy Gaughan
Ann Kulp	Phil Cover
Patricia Kirbey-Gibler	Marshall Craver
Sheila Noyes	Shaun McCarthy
Doris Froelich	Ann Dean
Clare Openshaw	Elizabeth Ward

More Recent Long-Term Staff Additions

Bill Dietrich	Bryan Berghoef
Trish Stefanik	Jackson Droney
Leah Rampy	Lorrie Conway
Ruth Taylor	Margaret Benefiel (current executive director)
Winston Charles	

As I write this, there are many more adjunct program staff members related to particular programs.

I also want to acknowledge the many dedicated board of directors' members over the years who have listened to the Spirit with the staff and helped to shape Shalem's life and mission. Then there are the many people who have financially kept Shalem afloat, including some major givers who have been vital to the flourishing of its ministry. Finally, there are the many volunteers who have come forward to help with many needed tasks beyond the staff's capacity to handle, including the regional leaders for the Shalem Society. Together, all the Shalem people and groups I've mentioned here have shown that it truly takes a village to raise and sustain a spiritual center like Shalem.

Notes

1. Rainer Maria Rilke, "God Speaks to Us," in *Book of Hours*, trans. Anita Barrows and Joanna Macy (New York: Riverhead Books, 2005).
2. Annie Dillard, *An American Childhood* (New York: Harper Perennial, 1987).
3. Thomas Kelly, *Reality of the Spiritual World*, Pendle Hill pamphlet no. 21 (Wallingford, PA: Pendle Hill, 1942).
4. *Harvard Crimson*, date unknown.
5. Barbara Holmes, *Joy Unspeakable: Contemplative Practices of the Black Church* (Minneapolis, MI: Augsburg Fortress, 2004).
6. Charles Gibbs, unpublished. Used with permission of the author
7. Parker J. Palmer, *Healing the Heart of Democracy* (Hoboken, NJ: Jossey-Bass, 2011).
8. Hafiz, *The Gift: Poems by Hafiz*, trans. Daniel Ladinsky (New York: Penguin, 1999).
9. Nan C. Merrill, *Psalms for Praying: An Invitation to Wholeness* (New York: Continuum, 1996).

Suggestions for Further Reading

A few of the many books (besides the Bible) that have influenced my understanding of the spiritual journey.

Bourgeault, Cynthia. *The Wisdom Jesus: Transforming Heart and Mind—New Perspective on Christ and His Message.* Boston: Shambhala Publications, 2008.

De Witt, Han F. *The Great Within: The Transformative Power and Psychology of the Spiritual Path.* Boulder, CO: Shambhala Publication, 2019.

Dowling, Kathleen Singh. *The Grace in Aging: Awaken as You Grow Older.* Somerville, MA: Wisdom Publications, 2014.

Gawande, Atul. *Being Mortal: Medicine and What Matters in the End.* New York: Metropolitan Books, 2014.

Higginbotham, Stuart, and Jessica M. Smith, eds. *Contemplation and Community: Gathering of Fresh Voices for Living Traditions.* New York: Crossroad, 2019.

Holmes, Barbara. *Joy Unspeakable: Contemplative Practices of the Black Church.* 2nd ed. Minneapolis: Fortress Press, 2017.

Keating, Thomas. *Open Mind, Open Heart: The Contemplative Dimension of the Gospel.* 20th ann. ed. London: Bloomsbury, 2019.

Kimerer, Robin Wall. *Braided Sweetgrass: Indigenous Wisdom, Scientific Knowledge and the Teachings of Plants.* Minneapolis: Milkweed Editions, 2015.

Laird, Martin. *An Ocean of Light: Contemplation, Transformation and Liberation.* New York: Oxford University Press, 2019.

May, Gerald. *Will and Spirit: The Contemplative Psychology.* San Francisco: Harper and Row, 1982.

Panikkar, Raimon. *The Experience of God: Icons of the Mystery.* Minneapolis: Augsburg Fortress, 2006.

Rohr, Richard. *The Naked Now: Learning to See as the Mystics See.* New York: Crossroad, 2009.

Sophrony, Archimandrite Sakharov. *We Shall See Him as He Is.* Essex, UK: Stavropegic Monastery of St. John the Baptist, 2004.

Tillich, Paul. *The Courage to Be.* New Haven, CT: Yale University Press, 1952.

Wiman, Christian. *Bright Abyss: Meditation of a Modern Believer.* New York: Farrar, Straus, and Giroux, 2013.

About the Author

Tilden Edwards is a leader in the rebirth of contemplative spirituality in an ecumenical context. An Episcopalian priest, he is the founder and former executive director of the Shalem Institute for Spiritual Formation, a respected ecumenical Christian community dedicated to fostering contemplative living and leadership. Since 1979, Edwards has designed and led many ecumenical contemplative leadership programs, ecumenical and denominational workshops, retreats, and lectures related to the spiritual life for ordained and laypeople throughout the United States as well as in Korea, Canada, and South America. His many books on contemplative spirituality include *Living Simply Through the Day*, *Sabbath Time*, and *Spiritual Director, Spiritual Companion*.

www.ingramcontent.com/pod-product-compliance
Lightning Source LLC
Chambersburg PA
CBHW020121240426
43673CB00038B/554